The Essence of Reality

A Clear Awareness of HOW LIFE WORKS

First published by O Books, 2008
O Books is an imprint of John Hunt Publishing Ltd., The Bothy, Deershot Lodge, Park Lane, Ropley, Hants, SO24 0BE, UK
office1@o-books.net
www.o-books.net

Distribution in:

UK and Europe
Orca Book Services
orders@orcabookservices.co.uk
Tel: 01202 665432 Fax: 01202 666219 Int. code (44)

USA and Canada
NBN
custserv@nbnbooks.com
Tel: 1 800 462 6420 Fax: 1 800 338 4550

Australia and New Zealand
Brumby Books
sales@brumbybooks.com.au
Tel: 61 3 9761 5535 Fax: 61 3 9761 7095

Far East (offices in Singapore, Thailand, Hong Kong, Taiwan)
Pansing Distribution Pte Ltd
kemal@pansing.com
Tel: 65 6319 9939 Fax: 65 6462 5761

South Africa
Alternative Books
altbook@peterhyde.co.za
Tel: 021 555 4027 Fax: 021 447 1430

Design: Stuart Davies

ISBN: 978 1 84694 083 5

A CIP catalogue record for this book is available from the British Library.

Printed in the US by Maple Vail

O Books operates a distinctive and ethical publishing philosophy in all areas of its business, from its global network of authors to production and worldwide distribution.

No trees were cut down to print this particular book. The paper is 100% recycled, with 50% of that being post-consumer. It's processed chlorine-free, and has no fibre from ancient or endangered forests. This production method on this print run saved approximately thirteen trees, 4,000 gallons of water, 600 pounds of solid waste, 990 pounds of greenhouse gases and 8 million BTU of energy. On its publication a tree was planted in a new forest that O Books is sponsoring at The Village www.thefourgates.com

The Essence of Reality

A Clear Awareness of HOW LIFE WORKS

Thomas Daniel Nehrer

Cover Image and Original Artwork By

Abraham Mathias Nehrer

Winchester, UK

Washington, USA

A Note to the Reader:

Most books convey information, carrying facts and description from the author's store of learned expertise to the doorstep of your rational mind. You read to consider, accepting and absorbing such knowledge as fits comfortably on shelves in your pantry of accepted understanding. Whatever seems out of place, though, to rational regard, inconsistent with what those shelves currently stock, is prone to be rejected.

In The Essence of Reality, I speak to your total Self.

Images I present here are meant to bypass the pantry of stored mind-stuffs, of shelves stocked with actions to be taken, truths to be refreshed, powers to be assuaged. Each short perspective on some aspect of life, each image of the workings of mind and reality offers not a single, isolated packet of fact to be pondered for storage, but part of a large, integrated package meant to be used.

To communicate to you qualities of Consciousness, aspects of your own being which you may not currently recognize, I must necessarily conjure up descriptions that don't fit neatly into your current, tidy, stored notion as to what you are and how the world works. To make best use of them in improving your life, you do well to temporarily disengage the rational filter and bypass the pantry. EoR goes to the living room, kitchen and bedroom of the house that is your life.

Perceiving The Essence of Reality does not make you a greater being. Indeed, it needn't – for greatness is already there. You need only become intimately aware of the quality, the innate power, creativity and esteem that you have always had, but failing to perceive, neglected to realize.

With Awareness comes a confidence and assuredness soon to be stocked on those pantry shelves. Understanding what you are and How Life Works, you attain the quality of life, success, health and personal freedom that are indeed innately yours.

EoR Table of Contents

1

Begin…

Imagine yourself as a young member of an extended family group 20,000 years ago, living – as all of our ancestors did in those times – off the land, migrating with the seasons, hunting game, gathering seeds and roots, avoiding all the while nature's risks.

Your group traverses a high, semi-desert region, bounded by snow capped peaks and high ridges where the sun would go to rest for the night and an arid expanse well off towards where the sun would always awaken. Your parents had taught you all things: building portable shelters, identifying the movement of game, tracking the seasons of blossoming and seeding, acting within cultural norms – and obeying the Great God of the White Mountain.

Always curious, always questioning, you had asked what was beyond the White Mountain. You wondered where the animals went, what the stars are, where the birds come from and why the streams sometimes dried up. Even now, having come of age to forage and hunt with the elders, you can't really accept the invariable answer: that the White Mountain God provides, that He made the animals, the birds, to give of their spirit, that He yields the waters and all things needed if beseeched with time-honored rituals, that He put the stars in the sky and moves some of them around to remind man of His splendor. And that He punishes, if angered, with the shaking of the ground, the dropping of freezing waters, the great flashes of light, gusts of wind and surging rivers.

But, even though you repeat their phrases and mimic the ancient rituals – having long since learned the dire consequences of not doing so – you silently question such rote acts to appease the Great Mountain God. And you dream still as to what might be out there, beyond…

But now, mature, strong and confident, you have become one of the leaders in the outings. You know the land and its bounty, its features and its dangers. And on this occasion, with late spring rains sparking active migrations among the herds, all of your guile would come into play.

You had caught sight of some horses up along the rim of a higher plateau and have just crossed the stream ahead of your hunting group to climb to a better position. Before the others can follow, suddenly your great competitors appear on the same chase – a pair of cave lions comes into sight, bounding down the small valley.

Your hunting group scatters rapidly, fleeing back up towards the camp, hollering and beating the trail as they go. Separated from them, you climb to the ridge and run across to the scrub forest beyond the level clearing – trying to spook the horses in hopes of distracting the lions. But when the massive felines appear over the rise, they continue to lope in your direction. You keep going, up and up as quietly and quickly as possible.

Returning home is out of the question for now. You travel for hours before finding shelter for the night high above the plateau. Alone, truly alone for the first time, you nibble at your supplies as you gaze at the great display of glistening stars that shine as twilight fades. Slowly you ponder that, with a pack of great cats prowling for horses, you cannot return to camp for days and only then by a circuitous route. And then you realize in a flash: you have the only chance of your life to explore beyond the Great White Mountain.

* * *

The climb has been arduous, but you could scavenge for the days it took to continue upwards. With the air cool now, as you had known only in the low-sun season, you've had to weave some long-grass sheaths for warmth. But where the trees no longer grow, you could move rapidly, unhindered, over the now flattening landscape. You choose the gentler slope, through the gap well off the great peak, to whatever lay beyond. Finally weary and breathing deeply, wary of all around you, so exposed as you had never been, you clamber over the crest…

The land below shimmers green beyond anything you had ever seen. You look over a broad, rugged terrain, dropping off into lower valleys, with tree-covered outcrops in a view that takes your breath. You venture down, soon following animal trails that wind through rich meadows and forested slopes. Plants, many of which you recognize, are plentiful, while others hold bounties of seeds, and still others grow pods that you can only wonder about. Signs of animals are everywhere.

We could live here, you think. This land has a great abundance, and you see no sign of others. We could live here! And with that wonderment you turn and head home.

* * *

A moon cycle and more had passed, they say, as they welcome you back with open arms. They had all thought the lions had gotten you, punishment – so the healer had said – from the Great Mountain God. They had tendered their burnt offerings and chanted entreaties to the White Mountain God, but feared the worst. Now you are back and it is a great miracle that the Provider has proffered to the people.

And then you speak.

You were on the White Mountain, you explain, and saw no god! It is simply snow, as in low-sun season, and stays there all day, even in the sun, above where the trees grow. And beyond that lays a green land, lush and full of bearing plants and incredibly plentiful game to hunt. You go on to tell of this wonderful place…

So, how might the people respond to your story? Would they praise your courage and follow you to the other side? Would they question their Great Mountain God?

Snow in the warm sunlight? Are you crazy? No Mountain God? Such blasphemy! Most would cower at your strange accounts. The leader would grouse at your impudence to explore without his authority. The shaman – highly offended at your usurping his role and questioning his status as communicator with the most Holy Source – would accuse you of bringing wrath down on the group by angering the great God. Others would simply not believe your venture or your account, presuming you had been dreaming or been taken by evil spirits.

But some, a select few with open minds, would listen and ultimately follow you to that better place...

THE ESSENCE OF REALITY

A Clear Awareness of How Life Works

I have been on such a journey, and I'm here to report to you a fertile region of abundance, of freedom and creativity, of peace and ease that lie on the other side of the mountain.

My journey, though, has not been over a terrain of granite and shale, but into the realm of streaming thought, over ridges of myth and conceptualization, through a mindscape littered with the brambles of beliefs and definitions that severely hamper progress. As you will see here, in encountering The Essence of Reality, that inner realm, previously pictured with a flora of archaic notions and traditional pseudo-truths, rife with a fauna of fears and imagined forces, is indeed far less intimidating than it is inviting.

The question will be: can you hear my account with an open mind? Can you follow my indicators to journey to a better place? Or will your current beliefs and notions inhibit your even hearing my accounts…

I have created The Essence of Reality, quite simply, to communicate to you an awareness of the nature of Consciousness and Reality, to nudge you towards a vantage point where you can see clearly, for yourself, How Life Works.

The difficulty to that end is that you, like members of the hunter-gatherer group, have a pre-conceived set of notions as to how this Reality functions. From the time you were born, you absorbed ideas, beliefs and definitions – primarily from your parents explicitly through their teaching and subtly through their actions and behavior. And via your immersion in a shared cultural outlook, you absorbed even more profoundly an impression of How Life Works. Every story, every explanation, every movie, novel and news report has subtly woven common cultural norms into your mindset, camouflaged more so by the very language used to communicate those stories. At this point, the features of your belief structure, whether incorporating gods or randomness, luck, fate or external forces and sources, seem very real to you.

At the outset, I present to you a first, key realization: **Whatever beliefs and definitions you hold will seem to be valid.**

The conscious mind – specifically, ***yours*** – dogmatized since toddlerhood to see life in the traditional way, invariably functions such that it filters sensory input and cognitive experience through its already-accepted belief system. Unwittingly, you discard information that conflicts with your preset basis of "truth" and interpret all else to fit into favored, base precepts. And it doesn't matter if that basis features a belief in a causal god, notions of luck and chance, formulae for momentum, expectations of astral planes or fealty to forest nymphs. However you have come to understand life, your world-view and the self-image within it will seem to function consistent with your beliefs and be validated by effects you encounter.

Ah, but the great hazard is this: **beliefs and definitions never clarify how Reality works** – ***they only distort perception of it!*** In short, that veil of time-tempered beliefs and definitions you gleaned from Mom, Pop and/or the rest of your environment is not valid; it only ***seems*** to be to the mind that is judging all input through its preset filter.

If you can accept that – not easy, as those vivid childhood impressions and cultural standards shared with those around you seem very real – you must begin to see the artificiality of whatever "facts" you inherited from a long, myth-based heritage of belief. Only then can you begin to break through fallacy and illusion to see what is happening here, for there is a sense, a flow and a meaning to the life process that is hidden by ***any*** belief structure.

The pathway to seeing clearly, then, to perceiving the flow that is, at every juncture of your life, leading to specific events and relationships, is not one of absorbing yet another paradigm, a more polished, sophisticated, esoteric set of beliefs and definitions. Rather the path toward understanding life is one of identifying awareness-inhibiting mind elements and ***discarding them*** – disassembling your belief structure, not building a new one. At each step along that path, you become more clearly aware of how Reality functions.

* * *

I will often refer to a "Clear Awareness" of How Life Works. That isn't a cryptic phrase of mystical, occult specialization or complex, esoteric secrets. It isn't a trance-induced, alternative consciousness. Nor is it an exclusive stage of advancement to be bestowed by a master or induced via guarded, ancient rituals. It is, as it says, a clear, simple, direct perception of the flow that life engenders…

So, understand this from the outset: I'm not here to philosophize great, vaunted truths. Philosophy – with religion and science being nothing more than specialized philosophies – attempts to explain the function of reality. But each philosophy, each and every religion and the scientific endeavor as well, fall prey to that innate limitation of the mind in perceiving beyond its own precepts: they each create a paradigm that describes reality, then go on to enhance that paradigm, in every case blind to the limitations – the invariable, apparent self-fulfillment – of the initial model. Thus, their "truths" are definitions valid only within the artificial confines of their presupposed paradigm.

My perspectives offered here in EoR, then, do not pass along to you another set of yet fancier definitions to replace the notions you currently hold – or worse, add to their conceptual jumble. Having, over the course of many years, cleared away all the synthetic notions, beliefs and definitions absorbed during childhood, I only depict for you How Life Works when seen clearly. My singular purpose is to ***help you see through*** invalid explanations that now form your mindset, so that you can directly, immediately perceive your essential nature in the life forum.

I will point out along the way, many a fallacious concept to common notions, some of which you may currently consider valid. While it is easy to see the falsity in somebody else's beliefs – ones you don't share – it is much more difficult to question your own as invalid. Indeed, to even ponder that your cherished truths are just artificial mental constructs is often difficult. Make note that if you find yourself annoyed at my comments, offended or uncomfortable with my perspectives in areas you hold dear, that is a prime indication that I've touched on a synthetic truth. If you really understood How Life Works, there is absolutely nothing I can write that would offend you!

But, given your inherent orientation towards your current set of beliefs, I will have to prod, nudge and occasionally blast you along the way by offering perspectives of how life looks when you see it, not through a veil of beliefs, but clearly. And I'll give you the means to delve inward to confirm what I say and to find the rest of the way for yourself, for that is the **only way** to come to see clearly.

If you aren't comfortable with that, if you think with great assuredness that your theology, your particle theory, occult specialization, medical training, enhanced enlightenment, advanced degree or esoteric accomplishment as bestowed or imparted by any institution, preacher, rabbi, master, psychologist, guru, academic or philosophical society, yogi, spirit guide, expert or channeled source is valid, true and likely superior to anything you might find here, you should close this book and go read something else in line with your accepted truths. I won't be able to do much for you.

But if you approach my perspectives here with an open mind, there is no real boundary to inhibit your path and no limit to the realization of abundance, personal authority, peace, ease and freedom you can incorporate into your life as a consequence to clearer awareness.

Oh, and while I've got your attention…

It is worth noting that all the sources of knowledge and supposed wisdom I mentioned above will want your money in exchange for their "truths." I won't. I have never accepted donations or payment for my writing or speaking, nor will I ever. The cost of this book supports its creation and printing; my royalty will be channeled into a family trust that will assure the availability of these perspectives during and long after my time here.

When you really understand How Life Works, you will live in abundance, as I do. If you clearly perceive your nature and have jettisoned the self-limiting elements of your mindset, you don't need to take money from people who are ostensibly less enlightened, in order to pass to them your wisdom.

My neither wanting, needing, nor accepting anything from you has another distinct advantage: freedom. I am free; since I'm not selling you something nor seeking you as a follower, I don't need to distort my message in order to talk you into it. And you are free as well – free to take my offerings and benefit by them, or walk away. Unlike the preacher, guru, scientist, priest, monk, philosopher and others, I have no vested interest, financially or emotionally, in your acceptance. Unlike them, I don't need your buy-in to validate my perspectives or to support my lifestyle. (Also unlike many of them, I don't dress up in silly outfits to look more spiritual or more official.)

Use of EoR

A Bit Beyond Casual Perusal

When my son was young and taking piano lessons – all the while masterly avoiding practice with excuses even better than those I had come up with – I used to explain to him that you don't learn to play the piano from the lessons but from the practice. That same effect is in operation here.

As you proceed through EoR, looking at life from four "Angles," you'll find, in the First Angle, many pieces that illustrate some aspect of Reality. In the Fourth Angle, I discuss the teachings of others who have come before and various philosophical roots to our cultural notions. There, I indicate the perceptiveness of individual messages and movements or where they miss the mark – because that teacher, theology or philosophy fell short of clearly understanding life, or because the message was distorted through time and translation. These pieces, each in its own way, help to break down some of the illusory aspects of cultural notions, particularly with a view of the core notions of cultural roots that permeate your mindset.

But the major strides you will take in coming to see life more clearly – and in the process, improving your life significantly – will be by personally delving inward. Techniques for that venture will be reviewed and illustrated in the Second Angle: Your Journey. Items in the Third Angle, Your Path, will be helpful as well to point out dead ends and obstacles along the way, just like lessons are for learning to play piano. But without your venture inward, EoR becomes, from ***your*** angle, the lessons without practice: you'll have heard what I said, but done nothing to implement it. Without your personal inner endeavor, EoR becomes little more than a new philosophy overlaid on your old ones rather than a personal, clear, unbridled Awareness, experienced directly by your having eliminated your old belief structure.

That almost covers an introduction to EoR. But not quite…

About this Source

Where I'm Coming From

Before you jump into a river for a swim, it's a good idea to know some things about the water: the temperature, the currents, the cleanliness and such. If you delve into EoR to any depth, it is just as critical to understand a bit about me, for I am the water here, the source of this flow of words that constitute the Essence of Reality.

* * *

Growing up in small-town Western Pennsylvania in the 1950s and 60s, I was handed the Presbyterian flavor of Christian pie and expected to eat it. I didn't like the taste.

Already as a 6, 7, 8-year-old, I was explaining, much to the consternation of my rather devout mother, that things I was told in church just couldn't be right. It didn't take too much sense to see through the miracles attributed to Jesus. You just couldn't change water to wine, since, to my mind, there was stuff in wine that just wasn't in water.

Oh, but you had to have faith…

How can you have faith in something that's obviously wrong? If part of an explanation presented as true clearly isn't, how can you trust the rest of the information?

Still, I had to go to church. But as everybody was nodding in unison, somber and dressed up, I was wondering how people, otherwise intelligent, could buy into ideas just because some guy in a black robe stood up there and said it (rather boringly to boot). And he didn't even take questions.

So I rejected religion early on. To my mind, even at that early age, an explanation had to conform to reality as I experienced it. I couldn't simply accept an explanation because some authority said it was right.

Added to that, I was always curious about how things worked – machines (which may or may not have gone back together when I was done figuring them out), nature, my body, puzzles, everything. So, dropping religion – and I distinctly recall the night, lying in bed saying my prayers, that I realized there wasn't anybody on the other end listening – I latched onto science, the latter-day belief system that came to share the stage with religion. That world-view of objectivity served me into my early twenties, the phase of unbending, post-teenage self-assuredness, and accompanied me through a bachelor's degree in chemical engineering.

Science is a handy tool; it leads to many useful developments. But the realm of rational explanations, of objective exclusivity, of consequential causality, I ultimately came to see, doesn't explain How Life Works any better than irrational belief in a mythological, event-causing deity. At that point, though, yet to realize the illusory effect of any belief system, my immersion in science carried a thorough understanding of the scientific method. Through the years my education and interests have covered most fields of science, from chemistry to archeology, through physics, astronomy, evolution and so forth.

Thus (worthy to note), my understanding of science is thorough. In fact, I understand science, including its politics, fudge factors and limited vision, much better than the typical scientific specialist who, caught up in the paradigm and dependent on derived income, doesn't see the limitations.

Well, that engineering degree served to keep me out of the army draft during the Vietnam War, one of the classically stupid ventures of western

Man. And that led to my early travels abroad and some eye-opening experience.

At age 24, tired (already) of working for a large corporation and newly freed from a brief marriage, having learned lessons in both ventures, I took off traveling. 'Twas quite an adventure, indeed.

From Ireland, where I picked apples for a week, through England where I looked up relatives, I made my way mostly by hitch-hiking to Germany. I worked awhile in Munich, scooting over to Vienna for a bit, and later traveled down to the Costa del Sol of Spain and into Morocco …

I could rattle on indefinitely about that great adventure! Each city, each ancient site, each Gasthaus, pub or Ristorante, each unique encounter with other young people – Europeans, Africans, Asians, Aussies – carried a new experience. But two main lessons, cornerstone in effect to my personal journey, came out of that great, year-long adventure: first, I could see that the gist of impressions I had absorbed via my American upbringing as to how things worked was not valid. Here were significantly different cultures, each with its own basis of understanding – and each one ***worked just fine***. Thus, what I had absorbed as an understanding of life was really only one version, one impression, not an absolute.

And second was…

Well, let's tune in on the young adventurer version of TDN, just about 9000 days into this incarnation, as I had calculated it on a ferry from Barcelona to Ibiza.

Here I was, months later, having made my way from Spain to Italy and taken a ferry towards Greece. I had made a stop on Corfu, a scenic Greek island just off the NW coast, where I spent a few days in the sunny spring season, enjoying yogurt, a lamb roast or two and lots of international company at the local youth hostel/campground. Life was good, but I was ready to travel on to Athens, so I headed to town to check out the ferry schedule.

Carefree, fresh of mind, I walked along in the clear, crisp air. Filling the scene were cedars and many shades of spring green not yet parched by the Mediterranean sun, white houses scattered about. Off, across the Adriatic channel rose the steep, high hills of Greece and Albania. Just shy of town,

I paused to take it all in.

As I peered down into the crystalline water, with the rocky bottom seeming but an arm-length deep through the clear blue, I had a "mystic experience." As if entering a new room, I felt the immediate, intense perception that I was not one thing looking at a collection of remote objects, but that ***I was*** all those things, a singular entity, a Oneness, looking at the whole of my Self from within.

(Bear in mind that most individuals who have experienced such an epiphany – and I will consider some in Angle Four – have carried into the experience a belief in some form of external, conceptualized god, who invariably got rolled into their understanding of that "Oneness." I didn't, which is a critical aspect to the whole picture.)

Words fail to relate the clarity of vision and realization of that perceptive moment or the sense of timelessness, the feeling of wholeness and well being that accompanied it. In the following days, that euphoric feeling and immediate perception would fade. But what remained was a lasting impression of a place, a status, a level of awareness that I knew possible, and that I knew in some fashion that I needed to return to. At that point, of course, and for a long time, I had no clue as to **how**. But in the ensuing years, that journey took place.

Leaving the scene of Corfu and fast-forwarding, these key points slowly shaped an open perspective into the point of view expressed here:

At 26, during the terminal illness of my mother, I encountered her near-death experience. Suffering from an enlarged heart, she had passed out during a meal and stopped breathing; I resuscitated her. After some time of unconsciousness her eyes popped open. I expected her to be groggy, disoriented, but she said clearly, immediately, that if that was dying, she would never again be afraid to die. She said she was floating off into a darkness, but was at peace and ease as never before. Only later did I read about such accounts of dying, and only as I came to understand life did I fully grasp that glimpse into the conscious focus leaving the body at death.

Shortly thereafter, back to Europe it was! Further travels brought me back to Munich and a hookup with a Fräulein who later became the Frau.

Through that time, including some competitive basketball, my share of quality beer, learning German, trips to my Great-Grandfather's hometown to find the family's roots, a lot of fun and many a hike in the mountains of Bavaria, I came to see that life, experienced in depth in another culture, through the lens of another language, was just plain different!

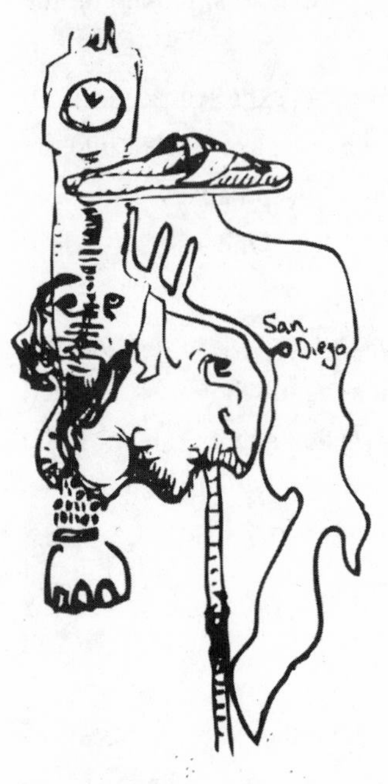

Later, at 32, I (with Frau) headed off to California. My third cross-country venture, this one in VW van #2, covered many national parks and sites. We settled in San Diego, where an anticipated year turned into six and a half.

For a guy who was always looking to ingest an understanding of life, Southern California presented quite a fast-mind-food conceptual menu. Every street corner featured an alternative healing practitioner, psychic, new age church, guru or pre-packaged path (please pay at the door).

Well, I've always looked at things with an open mind – always. And I took in what was there, always open to the message, but never bowing to the messenger. Inside those years, I…

- Joined Mensa (high-intelligence society), where, among many other experiences, I encountered a hypnotherapist, from whom I learned valuable technique in self-hypnosis.
- Attended (and later became involved with) a major holistic health conference, where I encountered numerous key, internationally known authors and practitioners in that movement.
- Began in earnest an Inner Journey, making use of self-hypnosis and meditation techniques.
- Expanded my reading to include the accounts of old and modern

mystics, seers, teachers and other meaningful writings, such as the Seth works (channeled by Jane Roberts) and *Cosmic Consciousness* by Richard M. Bucke.

- Attended talks by noted psychologists, psychics, teachers, authors, table-tippers, etc.
- Gained direct exposure to many non-main-line religions and spiritual offerings, such as Mormonism, the Baha'i Faith, Siddha Yoga, Jehovah's Witnesses, etc.
- Had a deeply perceptive psychic reading, then joined the psychic's informal "development" group and began to give psychic readings myself.
- Came to see ever more clearly, as a consequence of all the above, the Oneness that exists in the flow of life.

The psychic reading part is worth elaborating on. In a simple setting, I could relate things to people about themselves, their nature, their lives. The readings I gave were not fluffy, vague generalities, but reflected specific information concerning a subject, info that I could simply pull into my conscious mind. But the subject had to be open to it – which people invariably were who came to me.

Consciousness, I came to see, has no real boundary on information it is privy to.

Through that time, step-by-step, I cleared away the cultural, conceptual debris that inhibited my ongoing awareness. In the process – the basics of which are woven EoR's Angle Two – over the course of many years, I returned to the thorough, immediate perception of how life flows that I had experienced in a flash on Corfu. And I emphasize the word ***how*** in that flow – not only perceiving the Oneness clearly, but discerning the mechanisms for how that flow works.

During that entire process, that inner venture with its occasionally outer elements, my life has worked always invariably better in all ways.

* * *

Whether you read these words with the ink freshly dried from the first print or in a yellowed and dusty tome hundreds of years hence from my tapping a half million characters into an occasionally misfiring computer, I wish you all my best on your venture. The Inner Journey will be the most fascinating one you can ever make…

EoR – The First Angle: How Life Works

Intro: Hop Aboard

The essence of an automobile is not to be found in the pieces of plastic, metal, glass and rubber that constitute its physical form. The real car is found in its useful nature, primarily that of transporting the owner and others from place to place, but also in how it does that and why.

Transport may be accomplished with style and luxury, with sportiness or with economy and efficiency. The car may be rare and old so that it is seldom driven at all or could have a rough, rugged utilitarian nature and be driven a lot. It may be troublesome, breaking down often, or run forever without problem. It can engender anger or pleasure, feelings of freedom or entrapment. However it functions, however it performs, it does so immediately in the experience of its owner, the effect of which forms its essence.

Of course, the parts are included in the car's overall nature, but they are only one aspect along with many intangibles forming the essence of the car as experienced by the owner. An individual at peace in his life, enjoying the abundance that is his, for example, does not own an unreliable junk heap, doesn't drive a hot rod. The poor man, knowing only struggle as a way of life, will not be found in a luxury sedan. The qualities of the automobile reflect the nature, the essence, of the owner.

Commonly, though, a car is regarded as an object, a physical quantity consisting of countable, measurable parts of a certain monetary value, while its ***qualities*** are separated out as external, detached, inconsequential descriptors of the "real" car. In overall effect, though, the car's essence is the ***total experience*** of its use by the owner and absolutely reflects aspects of that person's nature.

Reality – the real world one encounters daily – in the minds of most individuals in this time and this culture, is thought of the same way as the car: a collection of objects. Very much like the analogy of the car, though, it just isn't that way.

* * *

Reality, in its essence, consists not of particles interacting pointlessly in an independent physical plane, but rather of values, psychological elements of mind, made real. The particles are there, perceivable, real in a fashion, but they combine in effect to formulate real events and relationships that function in specific, predictable ways.

Reality works in this fashion: what you hold in your mind – the self-image, the hopes and expectations, the world view, the beliefs, the fears, the feelings and all else – becomes realized in your life, continuously. What you experience, in all the events and relationships you encounter, is a reflection of this total set of collective values you hold within your mind. All that you perceive and encounter, including the Self, are aspects of a Singularity, an inter-related, cohesive Oneness.

This is to say that you are not just a remote observer, a driver somehow detached from the automobile that is your life, but you are intimately integrated into that life **as *the sum of all that it is you encounter*,** the very essence of the effect of your life's content. Those events and relationships reflect in absolute exactitude, in ever recurring patterns, what you are.

The overall point of this First Angle of EoR is to illustrate, through various short sketches, that cohesive, inter-woven nature of this existence.

I must emphasize that, ***whether or not you recognize it*,** this is **The Essence of Reality**! Regardless of what you believe in or conceive of as the functionality of Reality, the Oneness of you with all you experience in your life is an absolute. You can believe in a god or no god, can follow the Tao or chant mantras in caves, can calculate wave fluxes and postulate unified field theories all you want, celebrate cows as long lost ancestors or fight never-ending revolutions – and life will appear to conform to your notions. But behind the scene of any such endeavor will be the singular mechanism of the totality of your mindset becoming real in your experience.

There is no other rule in all of this Reality. In fact, this isn't even a "rule" so much as a nature, an inherent functionality. If you wish to live a life that goes well for you, you need to begin to see an automobile for the values it entails and your life as a reflection of your nature.

On Struggle and Conflict

A Long Tradition

Our culture has a long and deeply embedded fascination with struggle and conflict – we idolize those qualities; we honor them; we virtually worship them. Eliminate stories based on conflict and struggle, and your newspaper contains only ads. Preen struggle and conflict from history's typical treatment – wars, migration of peoples, religious struggle, power grabbing – and there would be nothing to record. Filter the two elements from literature and the protagonist becomes unemployed.

Conflict permeates our past, with tales of strong men fighting evil, decorated heroes of war, gallant knights struggling against enemies. The seeming addiction to struggle wends its way back through a Middle Age scarcely surviving famine, plague and invasion, through Roman battles to dominate the Celts, Germanic tribes and Middle East cultures. With roots in the very Indo-European way of life from which our culture grew, for six thousand years, and likely many millennia before that, the western culture has only known struggle and conflict. And it has destroyed or absorbed any other culture less prone to divisive, aggressive behavior.

Why is this? Why is our whole outlook formulated on conflict and struggle with the apparent need to do so? Why do our basic ideas inevitably picture a duality, a dichotomy of conflicting interests or forces in which struggle is necessary? We picture god as a force of good against the unavoidable evil. We seem to stand as a group pitted against nature, against other peoples or as individuals against our neighbors, against our bodies, our spouses, our children – without respite.

Is reality wrought from conflictual forces? Whether Darwin's natural selection or the church's good vs. evil, whether science or religion, some form of conflict or struggle seems to be the only mode of the function of this reality.

But all such default cultural views are based on the core assumption of our long tradition of observing reality ***out there*** and trying to understand how it works. That assumption holds that the observer confronts a reality consisting of elements separate from himself – soil and rocks, plants and animals, water and air, other people – all of which are isolated entities interacting with each other physically.

If one could only come to understand that interaction, so goes the reasoning – learn the rules for interaction and make use of them – then reality could be manipulated to make it work as desired. If there is a controlling god, for example, how should you offer entreaties to, make covenants with or pray to that god to attain favorable situations? If there is no god, how do you most effectively manipulate objects and people to control the outcome of things? In either instance, reality seems to be happening according to something other than your will. The key must be – according to longstanding traditional notion – how to manipulate things so that events and relationships, the real ones you encounter, ***confirm to your desire*** to be healthy, have abundance, have some authority and such.

If indeed, as per that paradigm, reality consists of isolated things, and you are one of those things, then for certain you will need to contend with whatever forces, natural or divine, control the resultant outcome of events – because those external elements will be unlikely to share your agenda!

But is that the functional paradigm here?

* * *

Let's look at nature again. For, if you come to see through the most basic traditional models that indicate isolation among reality's elements, if you come to observe nature clearly, without theories, theologies and western attitudes to pre-distort your interpretation, you see a different picture.

In nature, you don't see wolves attacking helpless deer that are struggling to survive; you see an interwoven relationship. You see carnivores culling the weak and old, thus keeping the herd healthy, and the herd producing sufficient numbers to supply the wolves. You don't see trees and plants producing a thousand times more seeds than they need in order to survive by chance, but rather you see insects, birds and squirrels dependent on those seeds and fruits, reciprocating to return the favor by distributing the seeds and fertilizing the soil. And you perceive trees, not as isolated objects, but as part of an interdependent system that supplies to animals sustenance even as they contribute to the forest's health. And when this interwoven, interrelated function of Reality comes into view, the idea of struggle begins to fade.

Seen clearly, individual elements of nature are not in conflict. Quite the contrary: they cooperate absolutely.

But somewhere along the way, somewhere sometime so remote that the notion is foreign to our "modern" way of thinking, mankind lost a sense of its own integrated role here, its fit into the scheme of things. Our long distant ancestors celebrated the abundance of nature, honoring the spirituality of the animals they lived from; they flourished within the wealth of nature that supplied their sustenance. But our historic ancestors were content to slaughter vast herds of buffalo, to denude broad stretches of forest or decimate entire fishing areas with no regard to nature. Ancestors? Our contemporaries routinely hold cows, pigs and chickens that feed our population under grossly tortuous, inhumane conditions. Indeed, our contemporaries kill, torture, maim each other…

How did man's mindset change?

Doubtless the hardy and challenging life of our hunter-gatherer ancestors evolved as man came to rely more on rational tools and complex language and less on instinctual emersion in the natural flow. I suspect that struggle, experienced as the challenge of bringing down large prey, and bravery in conflict with neighboring groups over prime territory grew to be honored prowess as storytelling evolved in early language. The cave paintings of 30,000 to 17,000 years ago show keen interaction with the rich animal life of the time. Coming ever more to see animals as things, separate and apart from the tribe that hunted them, humans began to build a gap between the self and things encountered, for which strength in conflict and determination in struggle were the requisite quality to bridge.

So the gradual first step was our ancestors starting to see themselves as removed from nature, as isolated from the animals and weather. Relying ever more on the intellect, they became the virtual Adam and Eve. No longer immersed in a providing nature, they began to control it and then **to *need*** to control it; with the rational mind overriding the intuitive, they left Eden. Strength and cleverness in overcoming nature's obstacles and dangers would have been of great desire, the stuff of lore and heroism.

Step number two came later with the discovery that the many grains and seeds that were available in the Middle East could be planted and relied upon for sustenance, along with domesticated sheep and chickens. The twist to the knot in man's destiny was as powerful as it was subtle: man's stories, myths, heroic tales of long ago bravery had become addictive, interwoven as cultural values to strive for. But while there had been glory in bringing down a mammoth or fending off a saber-toothed cat, there is little heroism in harvesting emmer wheat and cooking it with mutton. So, with the ongoing need to excel in conflict and struggle, at the demise of the great beasts of an earlier age and settlement into agriculture, man had to turn his addiction toward his neighbors, his body, his relationships…

And your predilection to struggle and conflict is the long-term result. In a very real way, you still fight the cave bear 10,000 years after it became extinct. Only that threatening presence is now your boss, your spouse (or mother-in-law), your sinuses, a big corporation, the government or your plumber.

You learned conflict most recently from generations who gave you the Second World War, Vietnam, Iraq and ________ (fill in the blank with the latest war). They had learned those same lessons from earlier generations who had fought WWI, the Crusades, barbarians on the edge of the Roman

Empire, the hill tribes that came to raid Sumerian grain supplies. Earlier lessons, now deeply rooted, had come from the dire wolves that stole the rendered aurochs meat.

The lesson was that the heroes were the toughest, the survivors the fittest, the best – strength and domination the ideal to be strived for. Is it any wonder you create struggle in every aspect of your life when you have learned from every story, every tradition, from every philosophical explanation that struggle is the fundament of reality? Is it surprising that you fight with your body using medications and manipulation, with your neighbors using laws and police, with your car, your children and/or your spouse when your goal in living, your ultimate self-image, is to fight successfully?

Take a look at the world and its problems, whether on a personal level or collective cultural scale: drugs, crime, prostitution, slavery, war, starvation, inequity, prejudice. You will find those problems rooted in human attitudes. And you will find those attitudes laced with conflict and struggle.

So how can you ever hope to come to some semblance of peace and ease in your life when surrounded by a culture addicted to struggle? The answer is easy, though the implementation may not be.

The flow of your life is not dependent on the apparent condition of the environment, only on your inner state. The elimination of struggle is not accomplished by struggling extra hard until you succeed; that only fulfills your inner turmoil. You end struggle and conflict by dumping the mental aspects that lead you to create it – primary of which is the very image that events you encounter are somehow separate from you. You attain real peace when you come to see clearly that your body function reflects your mind state, your career success reflects your mindset, your relationships invariably reflect your inner nature, your house reflects...

Perhaps you get my point. When you come to realize with clarity that everything you encounter is a coordinated display of real events that purely reflect your own nature, then you are, at the very least, on the path toward ending the need to struggle and fight.

In its essence, Reality inherently contains no element of struggle or conflict. But you will surely create both if you prize them as necessary, highly desirable attributes.

On Time

Never Was, Never Will Be

Many aspects of Reality are so routinely regarded, so widely interpreted in the same, virtually universal fashion that they are rarely even considered. ***Time***, around which so much of modern life is organized, would be such a standard. Yet, seen clearly, time must be the most subtly, but most glaringly, misconceived aspect of Reality.

Time has been a core concept in our culture's history literally for ages. The most ancient of remains, from the old-world Stonehenge to new world solar observatories show a notion of time. Science holds time as a cornerstone, building fundamental physical relationships and core definitions on time and its reactive bearing on particles, location, inertia, etc. History rests upon time for its index of events, Geology for its index of earth's development, the cake in your oven for its fate.

Yet for all that, for our appointments, our entertainment schedules, our calendar, our ever-present timepieces for all the vital importance time plays in the intricate coordination of modern events, time does not really exist. Time is an illusion. However secure in our minds as a convention, it is really only an invention, not a discovery.

In the Reality that you engage daily unfolding in your experience, it is always **NOW**. Memory that carries images of a "past," imagination that pictures a potential "future," each exists in the mind, right ***NOW***. In fact, the irrevocable essence of you exists only ever in this ongoing, ever-changing Now moment.

So what? Supposing that's true, what difference does it make to picture things differently when Time is such a convenience and so universally acknowledged?

The difference is enormous and vital.

A tombstone in a nearby cemetery records one Thomas Reed as having lived from 1783 to 1872. His birth is recorded, his death registered, his story finished as all necessary statistics have been marked. That is the picture Time serves up, a finite period, then you all hit that critical, terminal statistic, and the final gong of time has struck again, just like it did for ol' man Reed. The implicit picture is one of an end spot, a real boundary in existence.

And yet, regardless of what that table of Aprils and Augusts on the wall says, regardless of the marching, programmed numbers on that digital display indicate, here you are in the ever-present present. You exist in this ongoing ***Now***, conscious of an environment, perceiving and responding to a Reality that unfolds in changing, but consistently similar patterns. Awake, you find yourself facing a flow of life events, ebbing one into the other, without cessation. Asleep, you still find yourself embedded in a flow of Reality – though the symbolic dream events evince a different character.

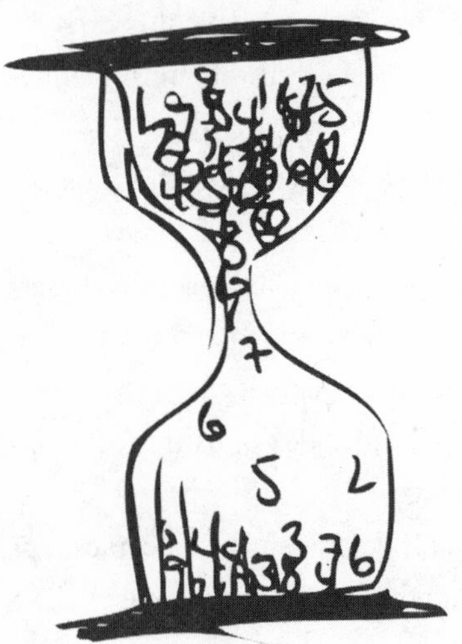

Faced with what appears to be a finite, bounded period of existence, an inescapable consequence of a world-view incorporating Time as a dimension, you must fear for your very existence. If indeed simply a biological creature, physical in your essence, resting on a preciously short candlestick supporting the flame of your life, you face obliteration regardless of any other thing.

And that inevitable consequence has lead to many a religious quest for eternal life, for the avoidance of an apparently inherent demise. But, in a Reality which really only exists in the present moment, one in which you are an extant, conscious entity, what is there of eternal life to seek after?

Eternity, as an infinite time span, is a non sequitur in a state of existence that does not feature Time! You don't need to attain eternal life, rather only to clearly see the nature of life in this unfolding Now moment. If you exist

Now, such that you are reading these words, you have no alternative but to continue – non-existence is not an option. You may pass into different states of being, just as the waking state and sleeping state differ, so do the currently-incarnated and not-so. But you will continue to exist if you do Now.

As you come to see that, you free yourself of the ongoing threat of an end to your existence. That is the real hazard of the illusion of Time – the desperation it impinges on each mind that has built a temporal concept into its foundation of understanding life. The ticking clock, the sands of time running out...

Indeed, time runs out for good when you see it as the illusion it is.

On Space

This and That about Here and There

Fresh off the concept of Time, while I'm at it, let me take a gander at the concept of Space. It is just about as illusory and in a similar way.

In regarding the real world out there, the volume surrounding the surface of this Earth through which humans scurry about, mostly right on the surface, but perhaps a tad above it or below it, you tend to think in quite objective terms. You regard the map of countries and cities as real, pondering roads that connect places and picturing yourself silently as being somewhere with a name attached to it. By default, movement through this volume is seen as transferring the body via some mechanism to another named place, with the base reality emphasizing the ***place*** as the real thing, solid and significant, and the body as a lesser significant, transient pseudo-essence.

In actuality, in the most fundamental essence of what is, you are **always** at a place denoted as ***Here***, looking out on an extended realm – not unlike the Now moment. You can see or otherwise sense out into that realm and experience it. You will perceive and interact with a flow of events and relationships within that experiential field. But if you go someplace else, you take your "Here" with you.

I don't propose dropping cognizance back to a state where the official notion of accepted cultural understanding regarded Earth and Mankind as the center of the universe. But, in fact and in essence, you **are** the center of ***your universe***. The events and relationships you encounter do indeed revolve around your being, and your existence has an effect on all that is out there as well. You are every bit as valid and significant as every other sentient being currently riding this train.

The value to this is in seeing Reality from the personal angle, including your essential immersion in it, and not simply accepting a self-image of insignificance in comparison to what is typically regarded as the external and detached world around you.

On the Flow

It Does, but Not Like That

The standard mindset of modern man considers that reality flows in a fashion. It regards the real world apparent to the senses and perceives as its function a flow of objects through time from the past into the future, passing through the present. The common cultural notion, whether based on a religious or scientific sort of interpretation, sees any of a number of "causes" to impel objects into events that take place.

Christian and Moslem views feature an independent, creative god (currently assigned names "God" and "Allah" respectively, though each is based on other earlier gods of other names) who **causes** things to happen – although there is no obvious or even implied mechanism as to ***how*** that ethereal entity can drive real substance beyond simply divinely willing it to be so. The scientific view depicts various forces that impel movement so that events result from a complex, driven interaction I call **Overt Sequential Causality** – in which a ***real*** action, either natural or intentional by virtue of conscious effort, is seen to ***cause*** a subsequent effect. (Although, likewise, science provides no specified mechanism as to how separate, truly isolated bodies can exert a force like gravity or magnetism on each other!) Also, though, subtly hidden in the back stitches of the fabric of standard western outlook, are notions of fate, luck, chance, a negative mythological character (named Satan or Devil) and other mechanisms that imply other causality even outside the creator god's power and any rationally controlled force.

Basically, then, the common mindset of 21st Century man features a muddled complex of causality, holding that events take place with some combination of the above – and relegating the individual to trying to control reality (re: Overt Sequential Causality), by making those events conform to the desired by manipulating objects and people in some way. And that manipulation needs to be rationally planned and executed based on a personal understanding for just how to effectively make things happen.

That interpretation of the flow of Reality and your default acceptance of most elements of it are based on a cultural indoctrination pattern that has passed notions along from generation to generation for millennia. You have been taught, indoctrinated and often basically forced to see life that way through a myriad of childhood lessons and cultural influences. At best you try to make some sense of traditional beliefs and definitions and use the ways you were taught to try to control things.

* * *

There ***is*** a Flow to life, a predictable, patterned Flow to the events and relationships that occur and recur in your experience daily and continuously. But it isn't a flow through time in the temporal cause-and-effect fashion that is commonly regarded. The essential Flow, the ***real way*** life works, can easily be perceived and affected – but it will be masked by conventional notions.

Many people, as they begin to break away from traditional thinking, substitute other mechanisms, other forces or sources, for the divine creation model or the manipulated reality and the blend of fate and such. Sensing that old explanations don't work, they will look to crystals or pyramids as causes or catalysts, somehow magnifying a mystic force. Others might reinterpret their God, substituting some other god notion as causal. Or they might try new ways to elicit favorable events from their current conceptualized god by intensifying other esoteric means of influencing that deity.

But the real Flow to life is hidden behind the fabric woven by those culturally transmitted beliefs and definitions. You will see it vividly as you lift that veil of fallacy and expose your perception to an unhindered view. For now, though, let me offer you a glimpse behind that fabric.

* * *

I often mention here a functional "Oneness" to Reality.

Before I illustrate the Flow to that Oneness, I need to connect for your regard something that is likely to appear split in your recognition by your world-view, but which really isn't: Consciousness and Reality.

I've already alluded to the traditional, scarcely questioned regard for objective reality as the basis of the universe. Indeed, both the scientific paradigm and typical religious notions regard reality – the real world out there – as innately existing prior to your appearance at birth. That concept consequently renders consciousness to be a limited characteristic of some localized portion of that universe, e.g., you (or anybody or anything else deemed to be aware of its existence).

In essence, though, however real and independently extant this universe seems, ***there is no such Reality without Consciousness*** to perceive it. By the same token, Consciousness will invariably create a Reality. The two, seemingly separated into different qualities of **substance** vs. **awareness of that substance**, are indeed, one and the same – like two poles of a magnet or two sides of a coin: you can't have one without the other. There is no Reality without Consciousness to perceive it; Consciousness innately engenders a Reality.

In the specific picture of your life, you perceive yourself to be a conscious entity encountering a reality and are used to interpreting that as two separate things: self and other stuff. But, because the two are not split, separate elements, but rather a Oneness, a Singularity, both your

Consciousness and the Reality you encounter, **are two integral aspects of the same essence**, thus sharing the same characteristics in terms of meaning.

This is not mystical sleight-of-hand or wide-eyed New Age conjecture. It is How Life Works: you are, at once, the Consciousness in the form of an entity who experiences a Reality and the Reality, in terms of value and meaning played out in your experience.

In the functional scope of this innate Oneness, you are the inherently aware Self that encounters a Reality purely reflective of your nature. Your "inner" nature is to be found in the totality of your mindset – your beliefs, self-image, world-view, expectations, accepted definitions, indeed the whole of the intangible inner realm that encompasses your individual character. Your "outer" nature consists of those same values built into real events and relationships, for your life, your health, your success and creativity, your attractiveness – or the lack in whatever degree of all those things – is a pure reflective statement of your inner self.

The Oneness of Consciousness/Reality, though, is effectively severed in your perception – first by the nature of language that draws a boundary around something by naming it and second, by the longstanding cultural view to which I've referred, that separates the Self from the events and relationships it encounters.

Recognizing that this interrelated Oneness exists and overrides all parts of your life is the first phase of effective enlightenment. Understanding how that works is the second.

But, all in all, portraying just how that Oneness functions is the most vital aspect, the most overwhelmingly ***important realization I will relate to***

you via EoR. Mystics and seers for millennia have been trying to convey a grasp of that Oneness – and Angle Four will look at some of their accounts. But I have indicated the inner-outer Flow of value effects and will, in Angles Two and Three, ***specify the Flow*** and how it works in detail.

But for now, begin to grasp that Flow: what you encounter in the real world, the events and relationships that constitute your life experience, is a ***result***, a product of your inner nature. The Flow in life is not a temporal displacement of moving objects, from a past into a future via a present. **The essential, ongoing Flow to this Reality is an emergence from the value set of your inner nature into the outer realm of events and relationships, *where it is then experienced by you in a Now moment*** and thus recycled back into Consciousness as evaluated experience. By virtue of that experience, your mindset may change, thus affecting the subsequent qualities embedded in the Flow.

The consequence of this innate inner-outer Flow is that the "outer" realm, Reality, contains **no element of causality**; it is purely a realm of effect. (Though it surely contains numerous "triggers" – activating agents that are typically interpreted as causes.) Causality rests entirely in the essence of your own nature as specified in your explicit mindset, for the inner engenders the outer. Thus, the only real leverage you have over the world is in ***changing your own inner mindset***.

In this regard, the key is shedding the default cultural notion that the objective world out there is innately real and that you are merely a temporary, incidental observer of the interaction of a realm of isolated things. This Reality is a purely subjective experience – the realm of people and things is a cohesive mesh that interacts in fulfillment of values. The values woven into events and relationships are not coincidental to the Real, but ***drive it.***

Thus, what you "**are**" in your core nature flows into the real world you encounter as events and relationships. What you "do" to try to manipulate the world is only ever functional within the scope of the nature of what you ***are***. Your efforts to manipulate things will be fruitless in end effect because the troubles you attempt to change by planned action are only really symptoms of inner problems. Indeed, since your rationally conceived effort is also tied in with inner characteristics, any seeming consequences will at best reflect your inner struggle and conflict. No such rationally impelled action is ***ever*** really causal, however it may appear in conventional interpretation.

So life does flow, but not from left to right on a time scale, rather from **inside** ***out***.

On Purpose

Wherefore These Words

I write these pieces, not to convince you of anything, nor to argue points for the purpose of proposing a new standard or a new philosophy – and certainly not to create yet another religious movement. Rather, my purpose is simple: to communicate a new and clean perspective of life that I often refer to as ***Clear Awareness***.

I have always had an unwavering drive to understand life – its purpose, if it had one, its function, its point. As I encountered explanations, though, I heard many a conflicting idea. Invariably, if a tenet of a religion or philosophy differed from how life obviously worked, I chose to trust my own senses, my own judgment. If it wasn't clear in earlier phases of life just exactly how life did work, uncertainty was in any case better than accepting some explanation that was obviously wrong.

Along the way of youth and early adulthood, as I mentioned, I explored many philosophies, various religions and the seemingly neutral science. (I'm amazed how people, before they buy an appliance, shop around exhaustively, then examine it thoroughly, measure it, read about it, test it, compare its features – yet they buy the first religion they were given without so much as a question!)

But the key point was realizing how thoroughly the mind was deceived by illusions created by its own beliefs, by definitions and conceptualizations implanted along the way to adulthood. Of the many religions man has concocted, each purports to be the only true one while all others are deemed false – indeed, each seems **exclusively real and valid** to its adherents. It became clear that accepting any religion, indeed, any defined conceptual structure meant to explain reality, would only lead to new illusions.

So my personal purpose became shedding beliefs rather than accumulating them, to see life clearly without somebody else's explanation. That, I slowly realized, could only be done by understanding not only the world out there, but also the first-person mind that was perceiving it, the mind within, ***my*** mind, from my perspective. So, over time, step by step, element by element, I did that.

Now I communicate that perspective to individuals whose minds are open to understanding – but not by handing out a new set of definitions or philosophical arguments. In the ultimate gesture, it is you who must come to see clearly How Life Works. If, rather than delving inward to perceive the Oneness and the Flow, you simply accept my explanations – none of which, distorted by the limitations of language (my ability to write it and your ability to understand it) can fully represent exactly what I mean – then I become yet the latest prophet, philosopher or guru to attract followers.

And that, as I said, is not my purpose. Life can only be fully perceived by a mind clear of definitions, free of external authorities: ***the essence of life must be seen clearly, directly, by you***.

Thus, my purpose here becomes not to teach, to indoctrinate, to convince, but simply to illustrate how things look from my perspective, from a standpoint of Clear Awareness. To that end, I will provide some handy techniques for looking inward and point out illusions and fallacies laced throughout our culture's most widely accepted ideas – those same notions I had to trudge through and clarify in order to dispel them. For sure, I will examine the most cherished of beliefs, showing that, behind the glossy trappings of great spiritual facades, of powerful, beautifully worded philosophies, lies only empty fallacy.

But it is never my purpose to seek and disperse "truth" – for truth, like a flag, ripples proudly in the wind of the beliefs in which it blows, the direction being irrelevant. My purpose is **only ever** to promote clarity of perception. When you see life clearly, the Essence and Flow of things is self-evident, not needing an explanation, certainly transcending the need to believe in something that is not apparent. Until you reach that point, any explanation consistent with your current views will seem true.

My sole purpose is to help you get there.

On Clear Awareness

Let's be Clear on This

In the phrase "**Clear Awareness**," I refer to a direct, immediate perception of the Oneness of Reality. A more traditional, more mystical term would be "Cosmic Consciousness," as reported and described during a mystic experience or epiphany. Other phrases have been concocted by various sources, but a simple, direct Awareness of life's function is best pictured without esoteric, occult terms, whose very nature tends to create implicit distortions and thus cloud perception in their own way.

The phrase here covers not so much a passing, fleeting glimpse of clarity into life's interrelated Flow, as I experienced on Corfu, but an ongoing perception of it, as I have now.

Clear Awareness is not a magical state to be attained by secret rituals, chants, pleading to some external source or emergence into astral planes, nor a status bestowed by a certified master. Nor is it a capability of yours that needs to be developed, strengthened or discovered. **Awareness is the *core attribute of your existence***; it only needs to be freed from all the synthetic definitions, beliefs, misconceptions, fears and other hindering fallacies your mind has absorbed through the course of your life.

The practical benefits to clarifying awareness are enormous. Because your health, your peace of mind, your success and your relationships – in short, your whole life – are a reflection of your inner state, coming to deal with the causal inner realm is the only path toward significant, definite and substantial improvement in your life.

It must be clear that, to benefit from use of precepts presented here, you must accept full, personal responsibility for the course of your life. Blaming external sources – luck, god, government, parents, conditions or even me (!) – for aspects of your life not only indicates a lack of awareness of your inherent creative power, but also hinders your journey towards that awareness by projecting creative power out to illusory, non-causal sources.

If you have trouble with the concepts offered here, either understanding them or applying them to your life, then stop reading it for now.

If you find that you "disagree" with something I've written, ***then you missed the point!!*** I'm not offering these perspectives as opinion, definition or greater philosophical adjunct, but only ever as illustrations of How Life Works when you come to see it clearly. Agreement is not relevant – you will only "agree" with conjecture consistent with your current, invalid notions. The point is to get rid of those notions.

On the New Age

Ready or Not

A New Age is emerging – don't doubt that in the least – but the nature of that Age and process of its emergence must be examined, since a lot of distortion abounds as to both what this New Age entails and how it will come about.

The emergence of self-awareness occurred in this forum for our species probably 5 million years ago – that's a good 250,000 generations ago. At some point, on a clear day not ostensibly unlike any other, one pre-australopithecine ancestor of yours and mine attained that level...

Picture the open, rolling high plain of east Africa – teeming with wildlife. Some dust blowing in the seasonal wind, a family group of a dozen small, but strong and agile, proto-humans, with their young, move somewhat warily along a familiar trail. Following a seasonal movement of the herds, these clever, alert individuals begin, as they have for so long, for so many generations, to settle for the day – a couple males head toward a rocky outcrop to check a sheltered area they have occupied previously. Meanwhile the core group awaits their return, some resting, a couple standing watch on a knoll, two young ones playing with broken bone implements in the dust.

Always close enough to water, one primary member, seeing no danger at the slow bend of a large stream, walks with an ambling gait over to the edge. Bending with the anticipation of a cooling sip, with a fresh breeze hardly rippling the surface, this creature peers into a clear reflection and suddenly stops. Startled by the vivid reflection, it pulls back, splashing as it withdraws in stunned awareness.

Slowly, as the surface settles, our long distant ancestor looks again, touches the surface and stays this time, watching as the image clarifies. Then it moves its hand and watches the reflection, touches its face and moves its lips, then waves and cries out. As others come hurriedly in anticipation of danger, the one can only cry out and try to pull the others to look into the stream, to see the reflection as it has. But the others only look blankly at each other, wondering what was meant by the unfamiliar gestures. They pull away, drink some, then wander back towards the outcrop to prepare the night's shelter.

But the one remains for a time by the water, transfixed by the image, the face, the realization. For, looking at his arms, the reflection of his eyes, the movement he could control, he realizes as never before ***that he exists***.

* * *

That scenario likely played out a thousand times before the immediate realization eventually became commonplace. But ultimately it did, and the age of self-awareness began. It continues today for the vast majority of humanity and even chimpanzees and other apes. (Monti, my Golden Retriever dog, with better hearing and vision than mine and much better sense of smell, as well as considerably quicker responses, is far more aware of what's going on in the forest than I am during a hike. But he does not recognize in the mirror that he sees his own body. Nor does a monkey, who is more likely to think he's seeing another monkey. Chimps and gorillas, though, recognize their own faces and hands.)

Self-awareness, then, represents **a status of *cognitive awareness*** for encountered reality. But, in not recognizing the complete picture, it is far from the end station on man's journey. Indeed, symptoms of the inadequacy of self-awareness – disease, famine, depletion of resources, eradication of entire species, brutality, war and turmoil in an environment bulging with abundance – are living evidence that something must be wrong here.

And wrong it is – or perhaps more accurately: incomplete. Self-awareness is a step beyond simple awareness, a mental cognition of a self interacting with an environment. But self-awareness is itself limited. It is true recognition in the imagery of mind that I, a self, exist in a real environment – but the ***relationship*** between that self and the perceived reality is not clearly recognized. And the limit creates the illusion of separateness and distance, an apparent division between Self and Reality: the impression that I am one thing and the world perceived out there is something else apart from me.

This self-awareness is the mindset of the Old Age – a 5-million-year long severed self-image shared through untold generations. It has seen manipulated rocks and bone evolve to knapped stone tools, to formed metals, to highly complex mechanisms. But, despite an enormous growth in the ability of complex, creative thinking, the fundamental self-image has remained remarkably static, for the self-aware mind recognizes the self in a real environment, but ***does not perceive the intimate interrelationship*** between these aspects.

For some time now, self-awareness has begun to give way to a new level altogether. On rare occasions during the last few millennia, an individual has glimpsed to some degree a realization a quantum step beyond that of self-recognition. And again, not unlike the long distant ancestor gazing at his likeness in the water, that occasional individual has had great difficulty communicating the new awareness to contemporary individuals.

The New Age is not one of bells and whistles and mystical special effects. It is not a fantasy state driven by the alignments of planets or the power of crystals, nor a metaphysical rising to higher plains of consciousness by virtue of chanting esoteric mantras. It will not feature the arrival of a thunderbolt-wielding god, ready to set up a final judgment by reviving hordes of old, decayed corpses. The ***real*** New Age is a simple, but stunningly profound, awareness that one's Self and all that one encounters are two aspects of the **same, singular Essence**.

Those who have not progressed beyond self-awareness imagine a New Age replete with a host of glittery occult effects, gods establishing kingdoms on Earth, idealistic huggy-feely banalities or far-distant better places. But those who exceed that level to perceive the Oneness, by whatever path, understand the New Age as existing here and now, featuring peace, health, creativity and a lot of fun.

A major gulf spans the two mentalities – a gap this tome endeavors to bridge. When you have traversed that gulf, the New Age is no longer conjecture on future idealistic states, but ***has already arrived***.

On Being Human

Come on, Man

There are no innate rules on human conduct in terms of your behavior towards others within society. All the rules you encounter, as stated in laws, moral codes and traditional behavioral standards are conventional, man-made. To the mind mired in the standard illusions of cultural definitions, rules are necessary, and a society based on such a mentality can scarcely function without them.

The Old Age mind sees itself as apart from the world, separate and distant, as an entity that must manipulate and control its environment in order to affect it, in order to carry out its desires and fulfill its wishes – often in the face of rejection and resistance. In the Old Age, rules are vital, for without defined limits on action, any individual, feeling isolated and powerless, blaming negative events on other people and other sources, might carry out acts of harm towards those perceived as enemies or opposing forces.

So rules abound, with blame and punishment accorded to those who break the rules. And the rules cover morals and ethics, not to mention traditional social behavior.

But, with the onset of Clear Awareness, one comes to see the world differently. The events and relationships, all effects that one encounters, become clearly perceived as part of the greater Self – and the Aware individual ceases to need regulation. Only ***after*** you stop blaming your problems on external conditions or other individuals do they cease to be any sort of threat to you.

Realize that events in your life are within your – ***only*** your – authority to create. When you see that clearly, you lose any motive of unethical action for the purpose (or with the coincidental consequence) of doing harm to anyone else. When you live in abundance – which is the standard state of a conscious entity in this Reality – you have no need to adversely manipulate your environment or other people to attain things. When peace is ingrained in your nature, conflict with peers does not manifest. When truly free of external, illusory forces and sources, you need never rebel against any authority, for you ***are*** the authority.

There is nothing wrong, negative or inherently evil about sex, yet cultural conventions and their moral codes dictate limitations to natural urges. To the female Clearly Aware of her essential nature, however, sex is only a positive expression of humanity; it will never result in pregnancy unless desired – because that person's body function reflects the will, the intent. To the male fully Aware of his essence in life, control and intimidation are not elements in any relationship. Being at peace, the individual will encounter and relate to a partner who is reflective of his/her own intent. There is no jealousy, no fear of losing that partner, since there is confidence in the Self and a full perception that all events reflect that Self and its qualities. And complex dictates governing behavior and relationships are not needed.

Clear Awareness presents much more than unfettered perception. It leads to a total immersion in Reality, a state of mind and being in which events fulfill the will, in which inner peace is always encountered in the outer experience such that creativity leads to accomplishment, not frustration. The individual who has grown to Clear Awareness needs no artificial rules to guide his or her life, because in that state, natural impulses don't portend the behavior such rules are assigned to avoid.

On Miracles

Exceptions to What Really Isn't

Life functions in a fashion. There is a mechanism to the Flow of life such that no event can take place that functions in a way outside that Flow. When you have grown to see that function, there is no action, no event, not the slightest occurrence that takes place outside the scope of potentiality.

The concept of a ***Miracle***, that is, an event that takes place somehow beyond the scope of functional Reality, is absurd. A miracle, in the eyes of one who interprets it as such, can only be an event that occurs outside the scope of what that person ***conceives or anticipates as possible***, based on their belief structure. It is never something happening outside the realm of potential events.

Visions are sometimes considered miracles. But visions are intense subjective experiences by individuals whose understanding of life is founded on preset ideas as to the nature of mind and reality. Any such vision will ***always*** coincide with the belief structure of the experiencer! Never did a Buddhist have visions of the "Virgin Mary." Not ever did a devout Jew have a vision of Zoroaster handing down truths, nor an Aborigine conjure up Dream-Time visions of Krishna. Visions always follow the mindset. They aren't miracles, just welled up emotional energy reflected back into the perception of the preconditioned mind.

People narrowly escaping death often refer to the emotional event as a miracle. Someone misses a plane due to an odd series of events, then the plane crashes. The person then thanks a god for the miracle. What about the hundred others who were on the plane? Some miracle! ***Some god!!***

Churches have collapsed and killed many people in them, whereupon the survivors go off and pray to their god, giving thanks for the miracle of saving them. Why would a supposedly all-knowing god destroy the poor slobs who were in there worshipping him? The lowest idiot looking for worshippers would know better than to do that. The only miracle here is that anybody with the slightest sense can believe such an image of life that a great and powerful god could (or if he could, actually would!) create such an absurd scenario.

You cannot picture life as a functional system, with whatever format of event realization, yet allow for relatively common events to occur ***outside*** the system. If there were a god conjuring up events, miracles would have to be a legitimate type of event! Clearly a mechanism of reality incorporating a supposedly "miraculous" event is self-contradictory!

All the events of your life are reflective of your inner state. All that happens to you – from the mundane to the spectacular, in terms of life or death, pleasure or pain, success or failure – is a consequence of the complex of mind-elements, values, images and such held in your Consciousness. No event occurs outside this picture. The person deeply at peace does not experience conflict and struggle. The person whose mind is steeped in struggle and conflict, though, will experience little else.

In order to understand life, your view of how things happen must expand to include what you perceive over and above what you hold as definitions. The events you encounter form the experience from which you can draw understanding, such that, if something happens it ***must be*** within the scope of the Real! There cannot be a true miracle. There can only be events that appear miraculous when you don't really understand How Life Works.

On Infrastructure

It's a Wrap – Kill the Set

Traditionally, man's rational mind seems to be enamored with superimposing an infrastructure on Reality. Since we all come into focus on a lifetime as a gradual clarification of alertness and accompanying amelioration of capability during the mandatory baby/toddler period, we assume – with significant help from everybody in our lives through that formative period – that the real world was there to begin with.

So the standard gesture of even the most brilliant of minds has been to take the explanations it has gotten as to the origins of the world and elaborate on them. That goes for the earliest of notions of a sky god, the various pantheons of mythical gods and their coming to being, the evolution of idol worship into the worship of a conceptualized god, various philosophical paths and the emergence of science and its Big Bang beginning. Each depicted notion for how things are and how they got that way lays its base validity on the presupposed infrastructure of the current picture.

Christianity imagines a creator god whose unlimited power created all things some time in the distant past. It doesn't bother to postulate where ***he*** came from or what he was doing prior to that. At least its more primitive precursors had colorful myths to cover the origins of their lineups of gods, with each religion conceptualizing a beginning – usually depicted as though somebody was there taking notes.

Science postulates a beginning with all matter currently in existence being compacted in a single, super-massive wad. Understand, according to the Big Bang theory, it isn't that all matter existed in a single point in a vast universe of empty space, but that **all space itself** with everything in it was compressed into this singularity. When, WHAMMO, it let loose, space as well as matter expanded and continues to expand today.

While Big Bang entails notable conceptual flaws, like other explanations, it appears valid to those who accept it: people oriented to scientific thinking created a paradigm and continue to enhance that paradigm, building on notions that have become ingrained in their mindset. Science, in this regard, echoes the evolution of the Il-El-Yahweh-Heavenly Father concept of Judaism/Christianity – changing as each succeeding age, replete with its current-generation prophets, adds its own flavor to the original paradigm.

In each case, the human minds that conjure up and pass along these paradigms as truths, sincerely accept them as true and valid. That acceptance itself creates an appearance to Reality that then ***becomes*** reality to the believer. It morphs in the process into an ever more satisfying, base infrastructure that ***itself*** becomes cemented into the world-view of its holders, evolving slowly as cultures mature and generations pass.

This Reality has no inherent infrastructure. Matter and energy are the props set on the stage wherein we work out human values. There is no creative god making things happen, but only a conversion mechanism wherein mind image becomes played out as real. As for the Big Bang, this Now moment unfolding in the scope of an engaged Reality always provides a valid-seeming past to extrapolate any paradigm from – BB is a highly polished belief set, seeming valid only within the confines of scientific tenets.

But this Reality, in the scope of the Conscious entity engaging and perceiving it, is much more like a dream than anything resembling an objective, independent universe that would be there regardless of whether anybody happened to be watching. Basically, this life forum is like a malleable stage we erect where we come to perform improv comedy (or more often, perhaps, tragedy) then take our bows and leave – or an empty lot we convert into a playground, where we come to play our favorite games, then head home to rest up.

While the mind finds security and intellectual completeness in assigning and often fitfully grasping at a defined infrastructure, the model it latches onto is an illusion. There exists only a ***mechanism*** by which meaning flows from intangible mind element into real event – and when you see that, all the postulated structures and cosmologies, built only of concepts, dissipate like yesterday's weather.

On The Self

You Don't Need a Mirror

What are you? What is the nature of your being? That most simple of inquisitive gestures ought to be the most driven motivator in all your curiosity. Yet most people never even think about it. They accept, without much thought or question, a conglomerate, default self-picture with theological aspects, evolutionary roots and physical flesh and blood aspects – an image which often has many inherently contradicting elements.

When you ponder the nature of what you are, you tend to get caught up in a very sticky illusion. Part of this illusion has to do with language and part with a traditional misunderstanding for the nature of being human. But the most fundamental part goes much deeper. Let's wade into the shallow end first.

When you speak about **your** arm or **your** leg, the gist of that statement is that you are one thing and the arm or leg is another: a possession, a thing external to the self that owns it. Since each body part has a name, this means that, in the image of language the illusion is formed that what you are is *not* the physical person/body, but some non-corporeal essence that ***has*** a body, an arm, a leg, an eye. This "self" possesses the body, therefore is not it.

Actually that language-created image might, at first, seem close to the true feeling of being alive. You do not feel like a leg. You don't look out into a world from the perspective of an arm. You don't feel like the eyes you look through, nor even the brain that would seem to house your consciousness. So, what are you that owns all these things or where?

Beyond linguistic effects, the traditional understanding of being human would recognize total ***physical self***, identifying with "being" a primate, advanced, more intelligent than other animals, but structured not unlike various apes. You see other people, see yourself in a mirror and presume yourself to be a living biological specimen like them. You've seen others die and disappear from the scene, so the image of the physical self seems temporal and defined. Traditional religions may add on undetectable features like a "soul" or spirit aspect; your view of your self may include those elements.

These glimpses of your essence are standard self-perceptions of our time. Never really taught, you picked them up from general cultural notions, perhaps enhanced in detail by a religion or biology course.

But this perceived self is an appearance created by definitions. Actually, beyond the artificial picture words create, your arm and your leg are ***a part*** of you, not something owned by a separate you. There is a major difference in reality between "being" and "possessing" – the latter creates a conceptual boundary between the possessor and possessed object. There is no boundary between you and your arm. Your arm is not a possessed object, but is clearly an aspect of you, **a part of the whole** – as is every defined portion of your body.

Similarly, looking at other aspects of your being, there is no boundary between you and your feelings. These, though less tangible, are no less real, no less vital to you. Likewise, no boundary lies between you and your creativity, your memories, your curiosity. Clearly these are **all** aspects of your Self, as is your capacity to love, to imagine. These ideas are pretty easily acceptable, but let's go a step farther: your accomplishments are an aspect of you, a reflection of your nature. Are not then your house, your pet and your car aspects of your Self, in that they reflect your very nature of abundance, your taste, your interests, your abilities? And your friends – are not they part of your greater, total Self? If you were different in character, your friends would not be the same people, as those relationships depend on your nature.

Keep going… Your environment, the hills, the plains, the air you breathe, the path you walk – each and every one of these ***constitutes a distinct image***, reflecting, in terms of value, some aspect of your Self integrally incorporated within the whole of what you are.

Language and traditional ideas create boundaries where there are none. You are not an isolated being of some physical dimension, inhabiting a world of distant objects that you may or not possess. You are the total essence of your life. What you are, the true and profound nature of your total Self, is seen in each and every aspect of the world, i.e., the events and relationships you encounter, however distant, however seemingly removed from the little, local "you" you are used to considering. Coming to perceive that clearly, growing Aware of the Oneness of you with all you encounter – this is the ultimate purpose of pondering the nature of life, the ultimate essence of Self Awareness and ***the*** essential aspect of Clear Awareness.

Clearly Aware of the Essence of Reality, when you look out into the world, you see only a reflection your Self. And you don't need a mirror.

On Language

Dicing the Carrot

Before we move away from language, it's worth another gander to see the profound effect it has on your world-view and thus, your awareness.

When your parents (or whoever) taught you to speak, it didn't take too long after mastering "ma-ma" and "da-da" for you to absorb a packaged notion of reality that was gift-wrapped in their beliefs and trimmed with a big, objective bow.

Your parents didn't say to you, hey, this is a portion of a total Oneness which you can use to sit on, crawl under, stand on to reach higher or conduct various other useful tasks, and we refer to it by the word "chair." They said: ***this is a chair.*** They didn't say: here is some organic, nutritious grain and vegetable matter for you to consume to continue the ongoing flow of sustenance and biological functionality. They said, ***eat your food***; quit spitting it out and making a mess! And those continuous lessons broke Reality into the objects represented by the words.

Life is inherently a subjective venture. There is a meaning to you in each phase, in virtually every element of your day. But language and our tradition are highly objective – rather than considering the impact of things in a real, live setting, language draws dotted lines around each object and brings focus on the conceptualized thing, not the use. In so doing, just as in the automobile analogy at the beginning of this Angle, language severs the world you encounter into a bunch of seemingly separate things. And the illusion is perpetrated that the things, the **objects**, are real, but meaning stemming from the interaction of those things is only consequential and peripheral. Indeed, in Reality, it is the other way around: the ***meaning*** is what's real, and objects only serve as props in playing out that meaning.

This effect leads to difficulty in communicating awareness to you. I'm always trying to prod you to see Reality as it flows in a concerted, fully interwoven fashion, forming patterns of meaning in your life. But I've only got a means of communication that absolutely invariably cuts this flowing Oneness into little pieces of being and action. And there is another problem…

On Words

Hear Ye, Hear Ye!

The words of a language are the only real tools I have to communicate with you. Hand gestures, body language, eyebrow twists and such, however helpful they would be should we be together, fade rapidly at the keyboard on which I am typing these very symbols of thought.

The meaning of a word is carried in a definition, a series of other word symbols that bring about in your mind a similar concept to that which was held in mine when I conjured up the word in the first place. So a word is a sound – or a series of letters codifying a sound – that symbolizes something, some real thing or action.

Picture a rock. Or go find one. It won't look exactly like the rock I'm picturing or holding, but it will reflect the word and we will both be satisfied to the point of agreement on what that rock is. Right?

Actually, ***no we won't!*** For you, that rock will be an object that exists – a solid thing, innate and of essence, in existence and unarguably real. For me it will be something quite different.

Nothing in all that exists remains fixed. Change is such a given in this Reality that it is the only absolute. That rock changes even as you hold it, absorbing sweat and oils from your hands, rubbing particles from your skin. Throw it, drop it, set it down, and it changes again, losing small flakes, changing position and thus the role it plays in its environment.

To you, conceptually, our example rock is an object. Once it is identified to your mind, you then treat it as a fixed commodity, a defined, static object. To me, that rock, however solid it appears, is a flowing, changing ***portion of all that is Real***. It finds no element of being unto itself, but fits into Reality only in meaningful context with all other things.

But that is only the beginning of the differences between what exists in my mind and what might exist in yours when we use the word "rock" to communicate! To me, living in Pennsylvania, the word will conjure up an image of a yellow-grayish, flat sedimentary rock I see all the time along creek beds in the forest. I might use it to build a stepping spot in a stream so I can cross it or use one to pound stakes into my garden to mark rows. If you live in Arizona, the word might bring to mind a red, sandy rock that would fracture if you tried to pound with it. If you live in Ireland, you will likely use the rocks themselves to mark rows!

Had you grown up in the mountains, rocks would be the most common of background materials. But, raised in a large city, you may never have seen, or at least handled, a rock at all. But again, in any of these instances, the concept of a rock is so embedded in your mind, so accepted, so much a part of the background of life, that you scarcely notice, hardly observe a real rock when you encounter one.

The point is this: a word, even as simple an example as “rock” brings a substantially different thing to mind for you than for me. How much more difficult is it, then, to communicate about complex intangibles like feelings and beliefs? How can I hope to describe for you the intimate perception of life’s interwoven Oneness, when each of the words I use will carry a different meaning into your mind than I intended in formulating it in my own?

Simply put, I can’t. And that’s why The Essence of Reality is not philosophy, not another attempted description of How Life Works, not a theological or theoretical treatise composed of definition and hard imagery. Given the unavoidable, innate limitation of person-to-person communication, I cannot, given all the words ever concocted in English – and presupposing appropriate cognitive ability on your part – tell you exactly How Life Works.

But what I can do, and what I do, in fact, in all the perspectives offered here, do, is use the language creatively to lead you to perceive Reality as it is.

The perception of the Oneness of Reality is an immediate, unrestrained experience in your range of awareness. That direct experience does not involve words in your mind at all. Indeed, awareness will be strongly inhibited by your identifying Reality’s elements through the mind-image, symbolic words you were taught or any I might try to impress upon you. So I

can only offer you perspectives that help you see through the illusions formed by words and other mental mechanisms, knowing that your sincere effort to grow in awareness will ultimately open up Clear Awareness by breaking down the inhibiting elements.

On My Status

Proper Classification: None

Many people feel more comfortable with a label to identify any source of interest. Should you be like that, I will offer up some semblance of clarification for what I am in rendering these perspectives and offering them to you.

Am I a mystic? In a way my vision of ***what is*** extends beyond the usually perceived aspects and apparent machinations of Reality so that I may bring them to your attention, depicting them with a pointed clarity. But, unlike your typical mystic, my awareness is such that esoteric, mysterious aspects of Being have faded, leaving a clear view, one that doesn't need to be wrapped in spiritualistic banter and presented in mystifying terms. You won't find me meditating in a cave, clad in a white robe, chanting odd phrases, burning incense or reciting supposedly sacred quotes.

So, while my words come out as de facto ***mystical*** by virtue of differing substantially from the common way of looking at things, they are always meant to demystify Reality, to clarify how it works, rather than present it in a specialized light.

Am I a mystic? Answer: yes and/or no, depending on how you look at it.

* * *

What about "guru" as a term describing my status, that being a traditional Hindi term for a personal teacher, mentor and spiritual guide. Let me cover all those concepts…

First, I am not really a teacher, since I don't pass along knowledge so much as perspective. My hope is not that, by virtue of my telling you something, that you will consequently begin to see things that way. Rather, by pointing out the artificiality of much of the knowledge you have already absorbed and by revealing the illusions your mind forms through its acceptance of that knowledge, I trust that you will see through and discard (or at lease deactivate) much of the definition and explanation you now carry.

I hope only that you will come to see things clearly ***as they are***. "Unteacher" would be a more accurate term.

As to the "spiritual guide" portion of the guru role…

Well, in a manner of speaking, should you listen to me and grow in awareness as a result, then ***yes*** would seem to be the correct answer to that descriptor. But I don't at all differentiate the "spiritual" from the real, the philosophical and ideal from the firm nature of daily event. Such a boundary is synthetic and deceiving, as your mindset, the ***quality*** of what might be termed spiritual content, yields the real events directly. There is no isolated spiritual realm beyond the ability of the mind to imagine one.

As for the "guide" part, I decline the position. It is for you to engender the personal recognition of your own innate integrity, personal power and individual fortitude to be your ***own*** guide. After all, I can only tell you how life appears from my perspective, perhaps relating how I got here – but in any case your path will be different and yours to find. So I absolutely don't want to guide you, though you might expect that.

So, does the title "guru" apply? Sort of, in that I talk about life, but not really.

* * *

How about "master"? I will say this: you will never attain Clear Awareness by bowing to any individual, living or dead, and that means conceding that he/she is somehow spiritually or mentally – or in any fashion – inherently superior to you. If you do so, you will form a self-image of a lesser status and inhibit your own potential, your own ability to grow.

I have never encountered a master, and I will not be one. I'm not even a master to my dog – more like a friend and partner, a caring helper. (Sorry if that sounds a bit trite, but I have no need to lord over any individual in any sort of relationship.)

So, am I a "master" of sorts? If I am farther along the path toward Self-realization than you, so that I might clarify some of the pitfalls to be found in the trail, then the term might seem applicable. But if you think of me in such terms, then you are missing my point entirely and will consequently inhibit your own growth.

* * *

Am I a philosopher? Well, again, in that I depict the workings of Reality, by the strict definition of the word, perhaps. But the typical philosopher sits in his chair and points out the window, describing in glowing terms and logical arguments how that world out there works. He can prove his conclusions, support his points with argument and perhaps offer up supporting conceptualizations from previous, hallowed philosophers who think the same or widely accepted belief structures that coincide with his ideas.

I never point out the window: I have no paradigm to describe, thus offer no proofs or arguments. I only tell you that what you hold in your mindset will become realized. Any argument to that effect – or against – is meaningless, since the realization of that mechanism is a point of awareness, of being conscious of how mind values combine to affect personally experienced events. Consciousness is not gained by elaborating on structured conceptualizations; thus, I don't intend to prove that or anything to you. My only effort is to point out aspects of common experience and how they appear from the standpoint of Clear Awareness, a clear perception of them in light of the Mind/Reality Oneness.

So, am I a philosopher? Well, maybe I seem to be, since I talk about life. But, in that I have totally integrated my viewpoint into my life, and in that I don't reduce the function of Reality to some paradigm, some rational, provable explanation, I only appear to be a philosopher ***if you don't under-***

stand what I'm getting at.

* * *

Prophet, maybe? Many like to latch onto that particular title. Predicting disasters, idealistic futures and such can draw a lot of attention and probably pick up followers from those full of fear and insecurity.

I don't need to predict major events, disastrous or creative. What will happen in your life is consistent with your own inner nature, and it will happen whether you are involved in or distant from large scale events. There will be no immaculate, miraculous change that overtakes humanity. The positive change that will happen to our culture will take place only as individuals change on a personal basis.

There is nothing to your immediate life that requires prophetic insight. So consider me a non-prophet entity.

* * *

And what about "Savior"? A big-time status, our culture has been looking for one of them for ages.

By and large, there is nothing you need to be saved from except your own old, worn-out beliefs and hidden assumptions. The problems you face, your fear of death, your pains and defeats in life are reflections of the limits you have of perceiving your own creative power and innate existence. You don't need a Savior to protect you from mind elements of your own, and there is no force in all Reality that inflicts an external will on you.

But if you hear my words and are helped along the way, haven't I been a sort of Savior?

If I drive from Pittsburgh to California, I benefit greatly from the Missouri road crew people who mounted direction signs along the way and Colorado construction workers who laid interstate pavement through rugged mountain terrain. But to get there, I've got to do the driving. They might have made it easier, but it is I who made the trip – and, given enough fortitude, I could have done so on horseback or by foot without even passing through Missouri or Colorado.

Likewise, it is you who must travel a path toward Clear Awareness. If I make it a bit easier, all the better. But it is you who must make your way. And you could do so, most likely, without my help, albeit at a much slower pace.

So, am I some sort of Savior? Not hardly. Save yourself the worry about needing to be saved from anything.

* * *

OK, so what does that leave? Who am I – or what – if none of the above, that I speak of life this way?

All the above niches are traditional roles being played in a cultural interaction that goes far back in our prehistory to the time when shamans chanted their phrases to invoke positive events from the gods they believed in. I play no such role. While my communication here can be seen in the ways listed above, truly I am none of those – as they each are outward indicators of the limited mindset of the Old Age, some being a bit fancier than others.

When you have outgrown that old mindset and no longer ***need*** a savior, a master, philosophers or a guru, you will realize that you don't need a title to depict what you are. So, for now, don't apply any label to me, because, whatever it is, ***I'm not one of 'em***. I'm just a real human, offering worthwhile perspectives gained by being open-minded, living a real life and having some fun.

As it is, the vital question you should be asking is not what I am, but what you yourself are.

Changing Focus

Looking from Another Angle – Right at You

Illusions remain to be revealed. But let's change the lighting slightly, and rotate our view to refocus away from life itself toward a more intimate angle and ponder…

EoR – The Second Angle: Your Journey

A Needed Change of Scenery

Imagine finding yourself sitting in prairie grassland of central Kansas, getting a bit bored watching amber waves of grain blowing in the wind. The great vista of the Grand Canyon might beckon. Or how about a dip in the Atlantic Ocean along a Carolina shore or perhaps a walk along the Freedom Trail through Boston's historic district?

To get from Kansas to somewhere preferable, you need to make a journey. That should be pretty obvious. Of course, you could watch a movie about some other place, read a book or just imagine one of those more exotic spots. But each of those alternatives presents an artificial substitute to the real thing – nothing like being there. Regardless of how you might trick the senses, you would still be in Kansas.

Your life, as measured in the experiential quality it engenders, is very much like Kansas: not too bad, but prone to be flat and rather predictable.

Certain things are happening all the time; these events hold some combination of rewarding emotional responses and disappointing ones. Your friends, colleagues, neighbors, family and other relationships yield a similar complex of positive and negative feelings. But without a doubt, you would like to improve on events and relationships so that any pain, rejection or health problems are replaced by joy, acceptance or energetic health.

Mostly, people hope and pray for the world to change around them for the better, trying their best, indeed **striving**, to manipulate people and situations to accomplish those things they desire. But while some elements of life might improve, others will wane, and the struggle goes on. And although some excitement and stimulation, some degree of escape, might be drawn from movies, books, alcohol or other synthetic means, when the sensory venture is over, your life is still what it is, still mired in an incarnational equivalent of Kansas.

* * *

Things don't just happen to you randomly, nor do they conform to an ethereal script, the dictates of a whimsical god or a devious fate. Events unfold in your life, and relationships evolve in specific, repeating patterns – all of which reflect your nature. The innate consequence of that is: if you want your life to change for the better, ***you need to change your own nature***, i.e., revise your inner mindset. And just like getting out of Kansas, that requires something of a journey, albeit, an inner venture wherein you first see clearly what your own nature entails and then change it.

If you don't leave Kansas, you won't see the Grand Canyon, the Freedom trail or any beach known to man. If you don't change inwardly, ***your life won't change***, in real effect, outwardly.

So, this Second Angle from which I illustrate How Life Works looks at Your Journey to get from where you are – where life is far from ideal – to where you want to be. That personal status would include: **Abundance** and the freedom that accompanies it, **Authority** wherein you determine your life's situation and your **Acceptance** by the world ***as you are***, without your having to compromise your nature to suit others' requirements. In that state, these three qualities are prime features of your life, not just molding fantasies in your dreams. And you are fully Aware of how those features came to be realized.

Engaged to fully explore your mindset, this inner venture will expose your fears and beliefs, your self-image and world-view, your very nature. If you can adequately come to view these elements of your Self, see the mechanisms by which they have become woven into the fabric of your life, then you can re-tailor that fabric, even **re-weave** it, to fundamentally improve your life in all aspects.

Making use of the means for improvement I illustrate here is completely up to you. But I would caution that, reading this section without applying the techniques via your own Journey, is like sitting in Kansas, looking at a picture of the Grand Canyon and deluding yourself into thinking you have seen the real thing. Of course, you can certainly opt to stay in your life's equivalent of Kansas. That's not really such a bad place, you may conclude – fields of corn, fresh air and, well, more fields of corn and more fresh air.

So the journey to a better place – i.e., ***making*** the journey and how far you go on it – is all up to you. I only ever offer perspectives here, never trying to convince you of anything or sell you a new religion. However, fully Aware of how life flows, clearly perceiving the source of real events and relationships, I sincerely offer a simple but valued notion: if you want to improve your life, you need to accomplish change within your Self.

Setting Out

A Long Hike, Not a Short Sprint

While the inner-outer flow is simple in essence, your mindset, as you will find, is exceptionally complex. Sitting with your attention focused on this page, you don't hold immediate cognition of the vast store of memories, of lessons and conclusions, of explanations, defined "facts," and beliefs, of significant and often emotional experiences, of hopes and fears, definitions and pre-set value judgments – all of which are there to be perceived, evaluated and, as desired, changed.

The prime caveat I present here is that the Inner Journey, like that trip from Kansas to any of the featured alternatives, is a long one, requiring many a single, measured step – much more a long hike than a short sprint. The Journey incorporates two gestures based on its and your very nature: first is a process of clarifying your awareness to perceive the Oneness, the inner-outer flow of values into real elements of life, and second is the measured jettison of inner elements that negate, neutralize and/or nullify your will.

These two build on each other as you proceed. With each cleansing step, you gain greater awareness of the Oneness and more confidence in your innate ability to affect the outer realm by altering the inner.

So beware the fast-track, automated alternatives invariably offered by vaunted authorities: belief in a savior, kundalini yoga, elimination of thought through meditation, occult insight, drug-induced awareness distortion, sensory deprivation and the like – all of which either manipulate the outer realm or scratch, but barely, the surface of it. These may get you out of Kansas, but you are likely to end up in Nebraska – or the Yukon.

In the Third Angle, I will consider numerous caveats that await you on Your Path. But for now, **four main considerations** pave the way in this Second Angle concerning Your (personal) Journey…

For one, I will review commonly available tools and techniques whereby you can begin to gain some level of perception of the inner self – showing strengths and values of each, but also indicating their shortcomings. Then I will illustrate Mechanisms of Mind – specific mechanisms by which you weave your nature into real events and relationships. These will be itemized and clarified here so you can begin to fathom what is going on within the broad value-body of intangible material that your mind holds. Based on that, then, third, will be explicit tools whereby you can focus inward to change it. And fourth, mixed in with all that, I will illustrate hierarchies of values that you embody and exhibit in all aspects of your life.

None of these is offered as definitive, but rather reflective. **My** journey to get where I am is not ***yours***. The purpose is not to present a slide show about my hike in the Grand Canyon, but to enable Your Journey to get there. You need, necessarily, to find and employ techniques that are effective ***for you***, a process involving ever-greater reliance on your Self, on your own inherent wisdom and trust to grow – and never come to depend on me or any other teacher to provide you that money-back-guaranteed path to enlightenment. So, while I provide here something of a map away from Kansas-ness, replete with many a road hazard warning along the many routes, it is, I repeat, ***you*** who must make the Journey.

Again: without change, those values you brought into this particular life format will remain stubbornly intact and continue to dictate the flow of your life's qualities. With no pointed effort, they will change only slowly; your life will proceed through its stages with little variance in quality-effect, subject to physical malady, failure, rejection and all man's other traditional ills.

With concentrated focus, however, you can decipher, understand and change your inner nature with its collection of values significantly and directly. By doing so, you will, at the same time, gain in awareness of your innate Oneness with all you encounter and come to shape those events and relationships, ever more positively, in line with your intent.

Direction Setting

Wither Ho

Picture yourself sailing a boat; let's say you are currently floating in mid-ocean. There is a steady wind, captain, and it's a fine day. You have plenty of food, necessary equipment, all you need…

So, where do you want to go?

In this simple metaphor for life, you may have specific goals you wish to head toward, but find headwinds and storms that always seem to inhibit progress. You might, by nature, go with the wind, regardless where it was headed; you may be driven by a vein of rebelliousness to tack against it. But like many humans, indicative of their approach to life, with no destination, no goal, you might drop the sails and just sit there.

Sitting in that figurative sailboat, like it or not, you will always be moving, nudged by wind and current, sails up or down. And so it is in life, whether or not you have a goal, you will be moving in **some** direction. The difference comes in intent: when sailing, with a destination in mind, you can sail ***toward*** that goal, provided you have some indication what direction to go and an understanding of ***how to sail the boat***. Likewise, in life, when you focus your intent – and understand How Life Works – you can move in that direction. For sure, even as you come to see life's interwoven flow, events may seem to hinder you at first. But, slowly, with determined focus on dispelling inner, inhibiting elements, life itself will begin to aid in realization of your goal.

So, then, what is your goal in life? What direction should you take? You set minor goals all the time when you focus intent on solving problems and achieving various things. But what should be the greatest goal in your life, more significant than a career accomplishment, more vital than a championship, wonderful partner or world record?

Turn your head away from these words and ***think about that*** until you think you know: what is the primary goal you should set in order to attain happiness, accomplish lesser, immediate goals, achieve health and abundance and generally experience good things?

* * *

Are you back now? Have you thought of the ultimate goal?

So, what is it: Enlightenment? Lots of Money? Realization of God? Political power? Self sacrifice? To find truth?

"Truth" is like a shiny paint job on a well-polished car. It fits the lines and sticks solidly to the defined body. It looks great – but without the car to mold itself around, paint lacks any innate substance; it is superficial and hollow. If you take away the car the paint crumbles into dust.

That proverbial car is like any defined belief system. Each one, each religion, philosophy or science, has a coating of truth that looks wonderful, shiny and polished like the big, fancy buildings that house their followers and the complex, agreed-upon paradigms that embody their explanations. But they look impressive only so long as the vehicle is present, i.e., so long as you believe in the defined system. Once the artificiality of the belief system is exposed as an illusion, the pretty paint of supposed truth flakes into dust.

So "truth" is not the goal, because it convincingly adorns whatever illusory vehicle it coats.

So, what do you think?

Should "oneness with God" be the goal? Whatever god you sign up with will seem to be real, so that won't get you anywhere. One plus zero equals one, and you're back where you started.

Money? Power? Illusory, fleeting and inconsequential, both, as we will consider later. Neither wealth nor influence can ***cause*** contentment, either in abundance or sufficiency and certainly not in lack.

What about their opposites: simplicity and servitude? These defy human nature; they undercut the very impulsive drives whose fulfillment provides the basis for engaging in an incarnation at all.

(In a discussion about abundance and possessions, a noted, intuitive teacher once pointed out to me, in order to emphasize the meaninglessness of worldly possessions, that Mohandas Ghandi, when he died, owned only a loincloth and a board for writing. My response was that a baboon owns even less than that at death, but that my objective in life was not to emulate either. Man's complex creativity embodies many items, well beyond the primitive scope of survival. Possessions are not external objects, owned and controlled, but part of the Self. While desire for ever more or grander physical possessions is neither a wise goal nor one ever able to be satiated, this Reality presents an enormous abundance, and the Aware individual will not be found lacking in quality things.)

Ascendance to astral planes or seventh heavens? When you go looking for any such esoteric effect, you'll find it – of course, you will have just created it according to expectations. Kundalini? Deliverance from sin? These only intensify the illusion they start with. Longevity? Many spend their whole lives seeking health and trying to maintain youth. But that gesture is like spending your whole career as a professional athlete practicing but never playing a game.

OK, enough suspense! Your singular goal can be only this: to **clearly understand *How Life Works***. (You should have guessed...) If you set sail in any other direction, you will make real the illusion that was the destination of your intent.

By setting your goal to clearly understand How Life Works, you will lead yourself toward Clear Awareness. Set it elsewhere, and you will not.

On the Term "Spiritual"

Heavenly Daze.

Many a treatise on Consciousness or New-Age thinking bandies about the term "Spiritual" with great alacrity.

But only with reluctance do I ever use that word here. Since there is no real dividing boundary between the Self and anything "external," conceptualizing something as spiritual creates an artificial line, a defined boundary, between spiritual stuff and other aspects of life, which then must be "non-spiritual."

Traditionally, spiritual things are set apart from "worldly," or material, real things. But the "real" – that is, ***Reality*** itself – is a physical manifestation of inner values, held in mind as concepts, qualities, values. While higher aspects of mind content – goodness, ethereal planes, heavenly blessed angelic stuff and all that – are usually given a special niche of superlative being that is thought of as spiritual, there **is really no such isolated quality** or realm or nature, without a conceptualized boundary to set it apart. Everything fits together to embody experienced values in the life forum, from brutal pain to ecstatic wonderment – the whole spectrum. Spirituality is not innately sectioned out from that wholeness; if your accepted notions artificially cull it out and set it apart, you will unavoidably distort your perception of the Essence.

Nor can the path toward "enlightenment" be termed spiritual – for the same reason. It is an all-encompassing journey into life replete with the mundane and the worst of man, seeing how and why those qualities come to be, not an endeavor into goody-goodyness while either ignoring, perpetuating or fleeing the negative.

So I use the term "spiritual" here, in EoR, not as a concession to traditional ways of looking at things, but in order to catch the reader's attention that ***ALL*** growth is spiritual, in essence, because your existence is spiritual

in basis and real in effect (as opposed to real in basis and experienced in effect). But that "spiritual" connotation can only with validity refer to the consciousness side of the Consciousness/Reality Oneness, not to any white-robed, ritual-laden, sacrosanct sham of traditionally conceptualized esoteric fantasy.

Tools and Means

Knapping Your Own Flint

The mind window of awareness is so central a part of your being that it may be difficult at first to orient mind function toward pondering its own essence – like spraying a garden hose with its own nozzle. In fact, at first, it may be difficult to focus your mind on ***anything***, so used it is to hosting a constant barrage of extraneous thoughts.

But, in order to accomplish change, one must focus specific attention effectively, for the mind and its content, with its many facets, its wide-ranging effects and its consistent mechanisms, is so complex that an unfocused view is destined to dart about with little penetration into core values.

If you were to undertake to examine an engine, explore the geological strata of a region, discern the light spectrum of a remote galaxy or skin and gut a mastodon, you would greatly enhance your abilities by using the right tools and techniques. Such is the case in the endeavor of introspection. The most effective tool for introspection needs to provide focus and the ability to delve into specific content.

What you hold in mind content, in terms of values, blends to become the real events and relationships you encounter, in terms of the values ***played out*** in your experience. All the pains, failures and sorrows, as well as the joys and successes, are a result of, a true reflection of, your inner complex: the self-image, the beliefs, the expectations, the evaluations, the fears and so forth which you hold in mind.

Your leverage, then, for changing your life for the better is not in trying ever greater means for manipulating the world out there, but in discerning elements of your mindset that contribute to undesirable aspects of your life and ***changing them***.

The good news is that you have access to all the information you ever need to know. It is all stored, every memory, every value, your entire self-image, all mechanisms for all effects in your life within the unbounded inner realm of your Consciousness.

The bad news is that you don't have ***easy*** access to it. Why not? Because all information pertinent to your life flow lies below your common, rational recognition in something generally called the "unconscious" or "subconscious."

Ah, but the good news is that the subconscious realm of your mind is only cut off from your ready access by your self-image! You have been taught that the self is limited to the intellect, the "rational mind." And you've absorbed, to some degree, that this rational mind (the "you," the ego-self which you generally feel yourself to be) is bounded by the reach of your senses and consists of only stockpiled, learned information, perhaps at best stacked on some rudimentary instincts.

In the greater picture of your inherent nature, that is not the case. But your mind and capability function that way – and seem ***to be*** that way – because (bad news again) you absorbed a cultural paradigm of existence that creates boundaries to your awareness by virtue of your ***holding limiting beliefs*** **within that model** as to your nature!

You are, indeed, psychically tied to all that you encounter, with access to unlimited information as to how your body is working in all ways at every moment, how your life is headed at every moment – indeed how everything that happens relates to you. But you cut off that information from your conscious attention because you were taught that such info is unknowable, out of your reach, murky and primitive, even evil and frightening.

SO...

In order to effectively perceive your nature and all its aspects, you need a technique that allows you to bypass your conceptual limitations to see elements of your mindset – at least until you've cleared away the restrictive mind elements that limit your view of pertinent details.

And that technique should embody the focus you need to discern specific inner elements without interference from a flood of extraneous thoughts.

With those needs in mind, let's consider some techniques to delve inwards for the purpose of improving your health and life. Understand that I will present an overview of each concern, with the expectation that your personal research will fill in more detail on any technique that you find of interest.

Meditation

I Think Not

Classic meditation forms the base of an age-old Eastern tradition of introspection, tied in with Hindu and Buddhist understanding for the nature of consciousness and life.

In general, meditation is meant to quiet the mind from its normal, semi-frazzled state, wherein extraneous thoughts pop into consciousness without cessation. During meditation, the individual seeks comfort in a characteristic sitting position – not so comfy as to fall asleep, however.

Then the mind is cleared. When thoughts come up, a "mantra" – a simple, typically meaningless word, which is often supplied by a guru ***who knows much more than you do about all things*** – is substituted by conscious gesture so that the thought stream is disrupted. With practice, that technique, by itself, can lead to serenity and initiate positive effects in life. But the ultimate goal is akin to the mystic experience I related earlier: for the quiet mind to perceive, directly and immediately, the Oneness, the flow of all that is within the scope of existence.

The inherent value to meditation is more than significant. The quiet focus is an integral part of any Inner Journey, for a troubled, garbled mind can scarcely make any progress.

However, the limitation to meditation as a tool for inner growth is as elemental as it is subtle. To see that limitation, you need only regard the nature of your existence…

You are not a physical entity whose consciousness results from brain function. You are the total Consciousness/Reality that experiences itself in a timeless Now moment, from the centered perspective of your being. ***You are*** the entire complex of values, of mind elements, of image and thought that constitutes the Consciousness side, and exactly that total picture is realized in the Reality side – ***but you are the whole***, functioning as a flow of inner element to outer effect.

Thoughts that come to your mind are not random annoyances to be discarded; they are not meaningless gurgitations from some stupid lower consciousness that erupt for no purpose. Each thought is reflective of some element or complex set of elements of your mindset – often reflective of the means you learned to manipulate what seem to be external forces and sources.

Eastern philosophy generally regards thought as a bad thing, to be squelched by the mantra so that, having shut off the "crazy monkey" of thought, the mind is at peace.

But such an approach is like having a bottle full of rotten, putrid organics, putting a cap on it and thinking you've cleaned up your problem. The rotten stuff is still in there, even though you don't smell it.

Likewise, your mind content, even with its spontaneous thought stream gagged by the mantra, ***will still contain its negating and neutralizing elements!*** They don't go away just by choking off the symptom of their existence: that stream of thoughts. And those detrimental aspects will still be woven into your life's real elements as painful events and failed relationships.

So meditation, as practiced and promoted by many a guru and yogi, might get you to the border of Kansas – a good first move – but not much farther. If the fields of corn and wheat no longer bother you, it's because you have relinquished your drive to fulfill your intent to experience greater things – not because you've reached the beach or, in the inner sense, the grand canyon of Nirvana.

On the plus side, if you meditate long enough, perhaps you will incite a mystic experience. Then you can move on to other techniques that will facilitate your cleaning out the stinky bottle instead of just capping it and proceed to get on out of Kansas.

Healing Techniques

Reiki, Reflexology, Acupuncture and Other Prodding

The practice of Reiki – literally, the "Universal Life Force Energy" – healing stems from rather recent times with Japanese roots, although I have to presume that its basis is likely much older.

Healing, according to Reiki, lies in what is described as "energy transfer" from an ***expert*** to an individual with some sort of problem, based on the notion of a universal energy "ki," as equated to the Chinese Chi or Qi, which is, as defined, a universal energy that permeates all things. In practice, the healer places his/her hands on the subject and, with no particular concentration or ritual, simply lets "energy" flow into the troubled body.

Reflexology, on the other hand (or foot), uses the feet as something of a lever to affect a healing. By massaging and otherwise manipulating the feet, the Reflexologist intends to restore order and trigger healing in other parts of the body, which are held to be intimately related to the feet in particular ways.

Acupuncture seeks to affect the flow of Qi through the body along channels called meridians by inserting long needles into key positions. This should restore balance in the yin and yang, which, according to that ancient oriental view, as traditional opposites, together compose the totality of all things. The notion here is that excessive masculine ***or*** feminine forms an imbalance, which leads to physical problems.

These healing gestures, along with traditional "laying on of hands" of Christian and other heritages, chiropractic technique, herbal remedies and ***all other*** alternative healing practices, while their approaches to healing seem unique and their techniques appear varied, all share a common notion. Indeed, their approach lies, in its general gist, not outside the scope of traditional medical science when seen from a vantage point beyond the personal belief structure that would lead one to utilize any of them.

Each of these healing techniques attributes the effect of ill health to something, specified or unspecified, manifesting itself in the body, some conceptualized, **external thing** attacking it or some isolated element(s) spontaneously out of whack – any of which need to be manipulated in some fashion ***known to the expert in the healing practice*** to get things back into order, thus to restore health.

Reiki healing looks at a person with symptoms of illness as needing an energy flow from somebody deemed to be whole and restorative. Medical Science sees a physical symptom from a stupid slab of flesh that doesn't have the sense to work properly and concludes a need to apply a chemical or manipulation to put it back in order.

Reflexology would apply pressure to sympathetic body areas to wrangle the affected places back into shape, while acupuncture would leverage the Qi flow. The Christian laying on of hands would somehow channel healing power of a deity (who apparently wasn't interested in providing health directly in the first place) toward healing – and is even rooted in the notion that invading evil spirits are responsible for illness.

Each of these takes a prescribed **action** to ***try to manipulate reality*** to accomplish health by applying some leverage based on the belief system the healing technique relies on. But each is caught in its own conceptual trap.

* * *

In essence, the body, at all times, is carrying out an enormously complex range of functions: passing oxygen and carbon dioxide back and forth to millions of cells, coordinating through complex muscular effort, nerve reaction and glandular secretion, an enormously complicated functionality, replacing cells as needed, healing tissue, processing nutrients and delivering them to each cell and so on. Each of those healing techniques disregards that, even if some symptom is present – sickness, back pain, you name it – 99% or more of body functionality is working ***just fine***.

And each of those healing techniques – along with many other variants – is blind to real causality in the emergence of any specific problem regarding the state of health.

In the interrelated Oneness with which this Reality unfolds in the direct experience of a conscious mind that encounters it, **there is no** yin or yang, no Shiva or Shakti, without somebody having defined them and without you buying into that paradigm. Within the functional Singularity of life, your life, ***all physical symptoms*** have a mind-based value equivalent from which they emerge.

If you want to counter unpleasant symptoms currently being experienced, you may well take action to restore chemical balances, kill viral invaders, reinforce ki, eliminate imagined evil spirits or take a couple aspirin. By all means, in the short term, do whatever your belief system requires to clear out the bad guys it features.

But if you want to deal with root causes of ill health ***so they don't happen again***, you need to see clearly how your body is a real reflection of your mindset, how specific mechanisms – primarily struggle and conflict – get woven into your real experience from their intangible, yet invariably effective roost in your belief structure.

So, all of the above healing techniques, while some may appear more spiritual and trendy New-Age than others, share the same fruitless gesture to accomplish health: an attempt to manipulate a symptom, which is really only an **effect** – in that the real world out there, with all its good and bad occurrences, is a ***realm of effect***, never of cause.

For the establishment of real, ongoing health, you need to begin to delve inward to clearly discern causal elements of mind and change them toward the positive. None of the above techniques do that; each conceptualizes a false cause, then proceeds to work with its own fallacious power source against its featured fantasy villain to achieve health. Each might be temporarily helpful to get you beyond your original ailment, should you share the prime illusion. And each might promote contact with caring practitioners who can help relieve you of your pains (and some of your money). But all are superficial and, in the end picture, ineffective, because the root, inner cause, specific elements of your mindset, not addressed at all, will yield either a recurrence of that ailment or some other resultant symptom.

Prayer

To Whom?

This inner gesture is a mixture of some positive and some negative. Basically, as practiced in Christianity, it involves silent (usually), concentrated thought on a particular entreaty to the Christian "God" (deemed to be the ultimate causal force) for positive things to happen, probably backed by thoughts of personal commitment as a reinforcement of worthiness in the supposed eye of that god.

The plus side is that, thinking positive things with a hopefulness of getting those positive things to happen, is a positive thing in itself.

The down side to prayer is simple: the Christian god (named "God") doesn't exist. So whatever you ask him (Him) for creates the overall picture of personal helplessness – and ***that's what gets realized*** in your life: **the helplessness**! Add to that the deficit that, in your own self-image – which is critical in the real emergence of events in your life – you are really so unconvinced that what you desire will actually happen, that you need some magical, divine intervention to make it so.

Angle Four will explore roots of the Christian deity in detail, but for now, note that Christianity wraps many inconsistent characteristics into one deity-package, however innately incompatible the attributes are. Thousands of such named deities have peppered man's past, been attributed grand powers and rich mythological cosmologies and have been worshipped by humans worldwide for ages. All of them share one real attribute – they exist only ever in the minds of people who believe in them. None of them can heal, because none of them are real.

So prayer, on the whole, is well into negative territory, because whatever god-image you pray to exists only in the rich imagination your parents and culture planted in the naïve, absorbing mind you held open in your early years.

Kinesiology

Flinching Your Way Closer

This healing program begins to delve into a biofeedback technique, wherein body responses are elicited to give the practitioner an indication of the patient's condition. The study grew out of chiropractic technique, but has grown in conventional terms through more-or-less scientific research into more holistic directions with "Applied Kinesiology" and other personalized sub-sections of that practice.

This technique looks into problematic conditions by testing muscular response – whether robust or weakened – as an indication of a healthy situation or an "out of balance" status. With direct questioning, the practitioner can query the subject as to the nature of the problem and get answers (ostensibly from the body, where reduced muscular response indicates a negative condition, but really from the subconscious) as to whether a physical or emotional cause is in play. Through repeated query and response, the effective practitioner can hone in on the problem and suggest corrective action.

Although that brief account hardly does justice to the effectiveness or widespread use of this practice, it suffices to indicate a value and a shortcoming. While Kinesiology begins to delve more deeply and analytically into the inner sources of health than the previous techniques, it does so only with the coarsest of filters for gathering information.

Kinesiology presents a tool capable of, at best, a dim grope into the subconscious for the purpose of identifying causal mind elements of an individual's physical symptom.

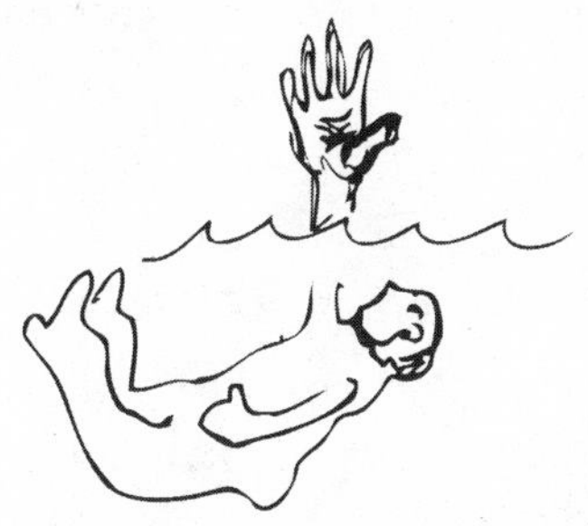

Understanding that, in the essence of things, i.e., the Oneness with which you, your body and your life function, every physical symptom has corresponding inner elements, it is clear that Kinesiology can only delve into the most shallow portions of mind. Thereby it would tend to affix causality onto aspects that are themselves only symptoms of deeper, more problematic elements of the mindset – elements inherently out of reach of this tool.

The second problem with this practice is simple: it requires you to pay somebody else, an expert schooled in the technique, to analyze you. In actuality, only ***you*** are capable of delving into the most profound, most intimate depths of your psyche. Any practice that requires some expert to straighten you out will have severe limitations on just how much benefit you will gain. (The practitioner, by the way, always gains, since you pay him/her for services, however ineffective.)

So, does Kinesiology have value for you as a useful technique in your Inner Journey? I don't know, because I don't know you, where you are coming from, where you are going or how you will get there. Only you know that – and only you have access to the totality of your Self to facilitate the endeavor.

Holism

One Plus One Plus One Equals ONE

My initial exposure to Holistic Health came at a major HH conference in San Diego, where many noted speakers at the time – Ram Dass, Joseph Chilton Pearce, Fritjof Capra, Ralph Nader and others – gave talks and workshops. As helpful and enlightening as it was, the concept of a Oneness of Mind, Body and Spirit, the hallmark of the movement, was puzzling to me within my understanding at the time (my early thirties).

How could ***mind***, an intangible thought process that clearly was part of my way of being, be "at one with" the ***body***, which was identifiably a real-world feature? And what did ***spirit*** have to do with it? That seemed to be way off, somewhere else, in some ethereal region or intangible dimension of reality clearly not equated to mind and body. In those days – and it is peculiar to think back on the questioning but puzzled mindset I carried into the search – I still had to filter things through a belief system I had yet to even perceive of, let alone understand to any extent, much less dispel.

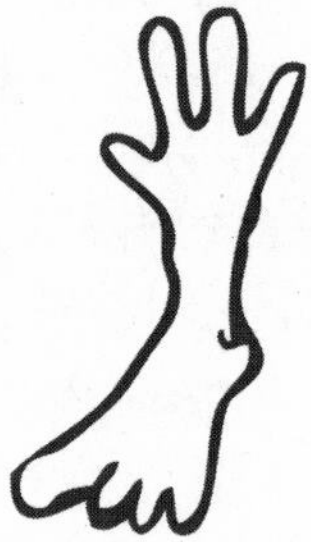

But, of course, **there is** an overriding Oneness to this life forum, as I would come to perceive. And Holism explores the functional system, with a significant caveat: the Oneness does not have boundaries. Thus, the Holistic movement and its many, many offshoots fall prey to the great, conceptual limitation of all philosophies – it's own paradigm.

Certainly Mind, Body and Spirit are all One, but dealing with those three words breaks them into separate, distinguishable pieces. What you ***are***, in simplified terms, is a grand collection of intangible, but discernable, value elements. The "mind" is your window inward or outward. It is your crosshairs to focus on any imagined scene, inner value, memory, dream concoction or other element of your mindset, but also can focus equally well on outer experiences in the "real" world. But the real world you encounter at all times, including your body, is, as I've emphasized repeatedly, a functional reflection of the totality of your inner Self – the same value reprise as the inner realm, just converted into events and relationships to be encountered. The "Spiritual" is, ***hey***, the same ball game (!), looked at from another angle, with a bunch of fancy cultural trappings of idealistic crepe paper and glitter to elevate its ethereal nature somewhat artificially.

So, Holism is absolutely on target, and the bull's eye it hits is itself, but with some artificial, conceptual rings spread out so it looks like a target. But its very core image breaks the Oneness into three components, which tends to shatter immediate perception of the whole Self, not clarify it.

Other Regimens

Lots of Packed Shelves to Choose From

In terms of techniques and disciplines, there exist many a path out there, offered for your benefit, mostly at a price. You'll find, if you go looking: Applied BioEnergetics, Gurdjieff's Fourth Way, Crystals, Siddha Yoga, Silva Mind Control, Aroma Therapy, Feng Shui, The Rosicrucian Order, Left-Brain/Right-Brain Theory, Edgar Cayce's Association of Research and Enlightenment, Transcendental Meditation, The Institute of Noetic Sciences, Dianetics, Pyramid Power, Kundalini Yoga, Homeopathy, Hari Krishna, Light Therapy, Avatar, Eckankar, Movement or Touch or Sound Therapies, QiGong and, oh, the list just goes on and on. (And that's not to touch on **religions**, each of which considers itself not simply the best, but the ***ONLY*** answer.)

Many of these – perhaps all of them to a degree – can be helpful to you.

Which ones would be best?

If you go to buy some shoes, you try them on first, check the price and how they look. If they feel comfy, you may purchase them and wear them for a while, continuing on your way until you tire of them or they wear out. Likewise, with all the above and the plethora of self-help, consciousness, New Age and other regimens, try them on, explore them see how they feel…

But, in terms of footwear, more important than the shoes are your feet. And in terms of Your Journey, more important than the discipline or the movement is ***you***. It is **your Self** you are seeking to find, to become aware of – and that Self can be colored and flavored in many illusory ways based on your accepted notions and the subtle definitions you carry along.

Thus, any discipline, any self-development scheme or sparkly, esoteric internalization technique can lead you to find, not your real nature, but a pseudo-self, supplanted by the process into some mystical nature that you aren't, but now seem to be.

The human mind seems innately comfortable if it pictures itself within a stable infrastructure. All philosophies and religions – and certainly science – create defined paradigms meant to represent Reality, typically picturing you embedded in an innate setting. If you've come to see that the image you absorbed while growing up is not valid, and you launch out on a prefabricated Journey, you are **most likely** to simply replace it with another, fancier paradigm – the mind is that easily fooled by its own base view. That new understanding may be much more intellectually pleasing, allow you a greatly improved quality of life and surround you with other people who all agree with your new truths. But, via any religion, any commercial self-development scheme, any esoteric enlightenment package, Eastern or American-made, you will not reach Clear Awareness – an unfettered view of your Self.

The real Journey is a personal venture into your own mind content. Nobody, not the greatest mystic, the most vaunted guru, the most hailed psychologist, though they might shuttle you along the trail for a ways, will get you there. Only you yourself can do that.

Hypnosis, Self-Hypnosis

Your Ayes are Getting Heavy

There is nothing mystical or super-natural about Hypnosis. (In fact, with nature being effectively all-inclusive, there is nothing "super-natural" about anything! There may, of course, be extensive misinterpretation of events based on limited awareness of How Life Works.)

A "Hypnotic" state is simply: totally focused awareness.

With an experienced hypnotist, a good subject will maintain an exclusive focus on whatever he/she is told, whether real or imaginary. But the same focus can be induced and directed by you yourself and held on values and concepts within the mind. Fundamentally, self-hypnosis is not a discipline like those specialized, esoteric ventures named above. It is simply a procedure to focus your attention, creating a state of concentration through which **you can achieve real change**.

This state of focus, when self-directed, can be used to locate and specify values and effects, to clarify their overall pattern in your mindset and resultant impact in your life. The same directed focus can then be used to clear away the undesirable, limiting value and place the desired effect in its stead.

(Remember: no hypnotist, no analyst, no psychologist, no psychic – ***no anybody*** – can look as deeply, as clearly and as effectively into your mind content as you can!)

I will return to self-hypnosis and some closely related techniques shortly. For now, I need to shift focus toward the inner elements that need to be dealt with. If you better appreciate your innate nature, you will realize just why the specificity of self-hypnosis is so vital to real progress in comparison to other techniques.

Elements of Mind: Interwoven, Hierarchical Structures

Components of What You Are

At the core of the western mindset is a default **objective interpretation** of reality: the world of quarks, sub-atomic particles, atoms, molecules, objects, planets, stars, galaxies and the vast universe in general is seen to exist inherently as substance. In this model, which you have pretty much absorbed through the culturally shared paradigm, you and all humans are partakers of this reality by virtue of one or the other mechanism (maybe both, depending on your beliefs): a god created you and placed you in this environment, or your progenitors, who evolved over ages with an increasing awareness based on ever expanding brain capacity, procreated you.

In either model, you lack significance.

If, by one account, a god made you, for whatever purpose, you are a feckless pawn in this celestial chess game, plodding ever forward by a space or two, while other pieces, seemingly with more power, bound about doing more significant things – but all controlled by the real mastermind player, some sort of god, moving pieces, making things happen, perhaps in conflict with a satanic opponent. If, though, you are simply an evolved creature whose consciousness rests on brain function, your engagement of this reality is arbitrary and inherently meaningless, in that you will pass out of existence at some point, so that whatever you do will inevitably decay to dust.

In the first, the creative god would be the only significant entity. In the second, the universe extant when you came into being via a near-randomly fertilized egg would have significance, while you, a small, fragile being scurrying about on the finite surface of a small planet in an unexceptional solar system in one of millions upon millions of galaxies have little or no value in the scheme of things.

Both of these notions rest on old, fallacious notions.

As you grow to perceive the unending, inter-related flow illustrated throughout EoR, you will realize that the life experience ***itself***, as embodied in real events and relationships, is of utmost significance for each conscious entity experiencing it – with ***you*** as the prime example. ***You are*** that creative entity that you've been looking for way up and out there in dedicated heavens and astral planes. And you are that Unified Field science has been trying to quantify – with the apparent, multi-galactic universe as a backdrop for the real events and emotional relationships that form your life.

Life is inherently meaningful. And the "inner" stamps specific meaning on the resultant "outer" with proclivity. **Meaning *itself***, as embedded in the values you hold, drives events into Reality – not an external judge or chaotic particle flows.

To discern working elements of your mind, it is vital to at least begin to understand that what happens to you is innately, invariably tied to your own nature.

In coming to grasp your basic nature, then, start with your ***will***. Things happen within the context of life as a human – meaningful things regarding your physical status, relationships, creative ventures, career aspects, etc. You want events and relationships that do take place to be consistent with your will, to satiate your desires. Typically, desired experiences would include: maintaining energetic, robust health, culturing true friends, finding and bonding with a loving, dependable partner in life, nurturing healthy children who grow to succeed in life, succeeding yourself in your career and other endeavors, encountering good weather when you are traveling and rain when your garden needs it.

It should be easy to identify your will. When events and relationships unfold in fulfillment of your will, you feel pleased about them: you smile, you relish the experience and apply the judgmental word "good." When your will is negated or neutralized, you feel pain, depression, rejection, down – and the word applied becomes "bad," or some equivalent.

In any case, what ***does*** happen to you in your life, the stream of real events and evolving relationships you encounter daily, is geared off your will. But (were I to venture a guess) that flow doesn't simply reflect your will by continuously fulfilling it in some sort of idealistic, heavenly enchantment. The flow of your life indeed reflects not your will, but ***your total self***. And that self, incorporated and specified in your mindset, includes hopes and fears, images and understandings, notions and beliefs, all of which, consistent with your overall self-image and world-view, contain negating and neutralizing mechanisms.

To affect the flow, then, you need to deal with aspects of your mindset – most specifically **finding** the elements that lead to negation and neutralization of your will and **eliminating them**. As stated, any rationally concocted ***action*** you take to manipulate the apparent forces in your life will only act out the artificial rules you were taught and, in the process, fulfill the struggle and conflict that are woven into your mindset.

To present a clearer view of how things flow in this integrated Oneness, I would illustrate this meaningful, interconnected Reality from a big picture downwards towards details.

Looked at in the most general of terms, life breaks down into these interwoven aspects: Love, Joy, Peace and Ease collectively, and Freedom.

These large-stroke elements form handy guidelines for delving into inner elements that restrict each area. If your will is being fulfilled in the course of your life, you will realize all those qualities. The degree to which your will is negated or neutralized, though, is the extent to which those overall value hierarchies are being compromised by elements of and mechanisms within your inner nature as specified in your mindset.

In that they differ somewhat in nature and effect, let's regard each…

Energizing the impetus to exist that renders the essence of all being is ***Love***, the core driving force behind the emergence of all Reality. To see that clearly, surgically remove (temporarily, at least) all the romantic, sexual, family oriented and other constricted senses of the word "love." Love, at its basis, can be equated to **non-judgmental acceptance**. As such, it is, really ***IS***, the driving force to all engenderment. It is the essential, core impetus to your base nature, driving to create a somethingness of experiential value out of blandness or neutrality.

So, Love, the basis of existence, i.e., your existence, ***all*** existence, is an innate positive quality which only takes on barnacles of negative pain in its restricted, effected contexts – the romantic, sexual, etc., side (which you can restore now or later, once you've seen the bigger picture).

Joy can appear as qualitatively different from Love as the sense of smell is to taste – related, complementary, but different in nature. Joy (need I define this?) is the exuberance, in variable degree, engendered by the fulfillment of Love as it drives a flow of positively meaningful experience into Reality. While Love is, overall, an absolute, an emerging essence, Joy is much more a reflective quality. As such, Joy is virtually the reciprocal of Love – i.e., the status of ***being loved***, embodied in events and relationships that reflect the will and thus reflect back a status of ***being accepted***.

Peace and Ease, however mild-mannered they might appear as common words, actually represent vital aspects to evaluating and living your life. Angle One introduced their opposites: Conflict and Struggle. Peace, in its base sense is not a state of mind wherein one ignores or tolerates the conflict and annoyances that emerge from relationships and environmental chaos. Rather Peace in its greatest essence embodies a pure state, which, once attained, disallows the **occurrence** of Conflict at all in directly encountered events and relationships.

In the framework of your will, Conflict occurs when your desire not only fails to be fulfilled in your experienced Reality via good, pleasing events and relationships, but it gets negated – yielding painful, "bad" ones. If Conflict is interwoven into some aspect of your life, you can realize your will in that regard only after engaging some opposing agent and winning.

Struggle, in this overall context, manifests when your will is fulfilled only after great effort, but without the opposition rendering damage to you or threatening to.

Picture driving down the highway: Conflict is like a headwind – not only slowing you down, but actually pushing you backwards. Struggle in this scenario is like friction in your car's tires and moving parts – not pushing back, but simply resisting going forward. Either one requires effort, making you burn more fuel to move forward, i.e., fulfill your desire.

Conflict functions to ***negate*** your will, turning your desire back against you with potentially damaging happenings; Struggle just ***neutralizes*** your will in emerging events, with basically nothing happening, neither fulfillment nor negation, without effort.

Peace and Ease are critical concepts to grasp in the flow of your life as Reality emerges in response to your will. If your mindset holds the bad boys, Conflict and Struggle, you will repeatedly encounter resultant life events and relationships that have negation and neutralization woven into them. In practical terms, without being fundamentally at Peace and at Ease, you will encounter annoying, troublesome, displeasing elements in your spouse, your boss, your children or parents, your neighbors and/or the events that surround your interaction with them. Negation and neutralization will recur in patterns, changing, wending, featuring different people through your life, but as soon as you solve one problem – so long as you carry C and S – another will come into your life.

The other overall value, Freedom, is a resultant effect that spans the gamut of all the above. So long as you imagine forces and sources outside your Self that hold some sway over you, you will not be Free – there will always be something or someone out there appearing to hold leverage over your actions and/or expression. So long as you entertain Struggle and/or Conflict, you will face inhibiting elements or opposing elements in your life, be they your finances, your health or people.

Being Free does ***not*** entail throwing off external control via rebellion. External control is an illusion. The first step toward personal Freedom is realizing that, in scope of the Oneness of things, your own inner nature is the driving impetus that formulates the emergence of your life elements, thus beginning to shed the notion that there is ***any force out there*** that holds sway over you. The remainder of complete Freedom is attained in the long and likely arduous process of ridding yourself of all inner elements that negate and neutralize your will.

Keep these overall value-effects in mind as we explore more specific structures affecting the emergence of your life's aspects. Much of the focus will revert back to Peace and Ease. Love, as the driving essence, is a given, a core attribute of your nature. It may be dampened by failure and rejection, but it can't be destroyed and will rekindle as you delve inwards and clear away the root causes of the failure and rejection.

Joy is a resultant of realizing your will. While not a characteristic to be leveraged or directly addressed, its presence or absence in your daily life will clearly and absolutely reflect – and thus gauge – your status. Likewise, Freedom is a measure of clarity in your awareness and cleansing of negating and neutralizing elements. Striving, rebelling, fighting for Freedom only realizes Struggle and Conflict as you battle illusory forces and sources. Eliminating Struggle and Conflict, while a complex undertaking always engaged inwardly, when completed, brings real Freedom.

In the complexity of life, mixing career considerations with social and creative aspects, life will present highly complex mixtures of good and bad, fulfillment of will mixed with negation and neutralization, many shades of gray instead of pure white or black. In bringing attention to the specific mechanisms in play as your life unfolds, the first focus needs to be on clarifying major aspects of life wherein those values become real…

The Three Bears

As I trudged, sprinted, hiked and occasionally crawled along on ***my*** Journey, I found a recurring dream to be a great help for clarifying significant inner structures that needed to be addressed. Of course, dreams embody symbols of inner elements – exposing a codified menu for the meal that will be served up in real events. Within sleeping consciousness can be found key clues to lesser and greater problem areas to your life.

On and off through the years, I had had variations on a dream in which three bears would appear. Mostly I would find myself in a varied, open setting doing whatever the dream had featured prior, until I would see three bears off in the distance. Invariably, the thought would occur that I didn't have to worry about those bears – they were far off and certainly wouldn't see me. No, I surely didn't have to worry…

But every time, without fail, they would come right toward me; I had to seek shelter and protection so they wouldn't get me.

Using inner exploratory techniques – yes, I'll get to them shortly – I deciphered the gist of those bears. In the meaningful symbolism of the dream reality, they represented three elements I was carrying with me, as in the other meaning of the word "bear": to carry.

And those three elements are the three main operative aspects of this life's format: Abundance, Authority and Acceptance. Each of these requires some attention, for it is within these areas that your level of Peace and Ease will be realized and result in Freedom and Joy – or not.

The first, Abundance, in actuality, translates into the ability to realize some level of wealth. Without adequate wealth, you have no freedom. Forced to carry out tasks you don't like in exchange for pay, without wealth you have neither Peace nor Ease.

There is a stylish, New-Age sort of adherence to simplicity and poverty, as though it is more spiritual to be without possessions than to have plenty. Contrary to that notion, in fact, nature is rife with abundance: in most natural settings, life forms flourish, surrounded by great abundance of all they need. And, no less than squirrels with nuts and seeds galore, birds with millions of bugs and even more seeds to peck, lions with vast herds of gnu and antelope or yeast with lots of carbs to consume, you should live in abundance, too. This is not to promote a bloated accumulation of wealth just for the sake of acquiring ever-fancier possessions – for there can be as great an unhappiness for one surrounded by wealth as devoid of it. But the natural state of being includes abundance and the person truly aware, at Peace and at Ease, is **not poor**.

Through much of my life, though, the "Dearth Bear" was after me, as I tried to succeed financially, but couldn't, regardless of any action I took – and my subconscious was clearly illustrating that.

Authority, in the sense of acceptable dominance in one's life status, is a vital attribute; its implicit meanings will be examined in the Third Angle. But without Authority as a cornerstone element to the self-image, neither health nor a fulfilling relationship will come to be. Violence, force, weaponry, medications, anger – these are all symptoms, not of authority, but severe ***lack of it*** – in one's personal self-image.

In any case, the "Subservient Bear" had plagued me much of my life. As a child, I was the younger son in a household where everybody – father, mother, brother, visiting adults, grandparents, aunts and uncles – absolutely everybody who came into view had authority over me. (I didn't even have a dog – and my little turtles didn't pay much attention to me!) By deciphering the real mechanisms in play for implanting that underling mentality, I outgrew a very intimidating bruin.

Those childhood patterns, perceived or not, left unchanged, will **continue to recur** through adult life. For much of my professional career (doing things I didn't want to do for money), I was supervised by people with less intelligence, know-how, creativity and just about every other desirable quality – but I had to kowtow to their authority. I couldn't break out of the recurring pattern until I found the underlying mechanisms and eliminated them.

As for the "Rejection Bear," he was probably the worst of the lot. Acceptance, as a quality incorporated in the self-image, leads to rewarding relationships, a fulfilling sex-life, success in imprinting one's desired endeavor into the career path and much more. Personal life status within society will always reflect one's self-image. The key to being accepted is to be found in eliminating all inner mechanisms that support rejection – not in trying to manipulate people to into liking you. And definitely not in compromising your own nature to gain acceptance!

(It's interesting that, having come to see these significant angles of one's life and their impact on quality of living, self-esteem, success and all things good, I read that the vows of a nun in the Catholic Church are to poverty, chastity and obedience – just the opposite of what fulfills one's typically natural inclinations. But religion, of course, is an unnatural compromise of one's Self – projecting authority and creative impulse out to a conceptualized externality, thus welcoming the three bears.)

My mother was quite religious, dreaming of this wonderful heaven where everything would be ideal – all the while disavowing all the key pleasure-based aspects of life that make ***this*** **Reality** worth living! If you suppress your sexual desire due to artificial, Victorian moral codes, waive abundance based on religious calls to simplicity, dampen your spirits into meek, pious servitude, you will have so thoroughly constricted your own nature that real Heaven – which can **only take place *Here and Now***, never later in some other idealized place – becomes no more than a fantasy, never to be realized in this lifetime. Nor will it improve in your next one, unless you come to shed those synthetic restrictions.

I've mentioned that, while the process of the inner-to-outer emergence of real events and relationships is extraordinarily simple, the inner realm, with its interwoven values, beliefs and definitions, cultural standards, expectations, hopes, fears, etc., is quite complex. I've illustrated some of the higher levels of easily discernable, overall effects of the mindset.

Peace and Ease, Conflict and Struggle – all will be found in prime aspects of life, Abundance, Authority and Acceptance, and these will be impregnated with fulfillment of your will mixed with negation or neutralization of your will according to your total nature. This engenders your health, your relationships, your degree of success – in short your capacity for resultant Joy and Freedom.

But these overall value-images break down into distinct mind elements. For, woven into the major swatches of cloth that constitute your unfurling life elements are specific mechanisms, the threads of causality to that life fabric. Following a look at these details of inner functionality, we can delve into tools through which you can specify all effects in your life, understand their nature and change them.

Mechanisms of Mind

Building Blocks of the Inner Structure

Plato, in pondering reality, put forth a conjectural model known as the Allegory of the Cave. He imagined a group of captives, chained deep in a cave, where their heads were held so that they could see one wall only. Behind them was a strong light source that shone on the wall. When puppets were made to move about in the light, they cast shadows on the wall. Dialogue among the puppeteers, bouncing off the wall, seemed to come from the shadows.

Plato figured that, if the only things the captives were able to see were the silhouettes, they would develop a default notion of reality regarding the shades, even name them and discuss perceived characteristics as though the shadows were "real." To the captives, unaware of the puppets and light source, the shades **would be** reality.

Avoiding the academic, conjectural aspects of the allegory, I would point out that it quite effectively pictures the standard condition of experienced reality.

The realm you perceive in everyday life is akin to the shadows on the wall. While people and things move about and appear to have an innate existence of their own, are indeed named and analyzed in depth – in essence, they function within the meaningful encounters of ***your life*** like silhouettes on a three-dimensional wall, acting out not random, meaningless events, not soap-opera plots of a hidden, divine puppeteer, but elements of your own nature.

Like the captives, who cannot turn attention to the real puppets and the source of light, but only have a fixed, overt perception of the resultant images, you cannot turn your focus to clearly, **directly** discern and quantify the emotion, expectation, hope, fear and other expansive, intangible elements of your mind. Yet, understanding How Life Works, you can interpret mind content clearly and specifically by discerning the ***effects*** of your inner state, woven into memories of real events and relationships, as they have emerged into outer, resultant patterns. Indeed, current memories of your life's significant passages reveal an exacting status of your nature: while you can't look directly at fear or abundance, those qualities are woven into the events and relationships that constitute your life.

From the moment you, as a conscious entity, engage in an incarnation, you stamp the flow of your life with your own characteristics. The following mechanisms illustrate comprehensively the building block aspects of your mindset, combining in ways I will illustrate to formulate the larger picture, incorporating Peace or Conflict, Abundance or Lack of it that I discussed above.

Bear in mind that your nature is complex, multi-faceted and inviolate – only potentialities consistent with your nature become realized in your life. Yet those characteristics that comprise the fully outfitted **you** can be changed, thus impelling change, subsequently, in the quality of your life's events and relationships.

In examining your life, you can regard conditions that exist **now** or refer back to memories of earlier times. Whatever your current mindset entails, memories of previous times will concur with it, showing patterns that repeat throughout. (The term in psychology for this process is Transference, as you "transfer" an effect, innate to your mindset, to different people and situations as you progress through life.) For specific deciphering, clearest understanding and easiest change, it is most effective to find specific mechanisms at their earliest point in your life – the childhood or infant stage when the effect "first" took place.

For now, understand: you brought your nature into this life; thus you will find reflections of that nature wrapped around childhood events and conditions, highly interwoven with effects from your early care-giver(s), with most likely your mother as central figure.

First: the mechanisms; then we'll see what to do with and about them.

Simple Mechanisms: Direct Experience

#1: Mimicking What You See

While you brought your nature into this incarnation, you did so with a blank slate of memory – which might be likened to bringing home a computer with an operating system and software installed at the factory, but with an empty database.

Subsequently, from birth on, you absorbed impressions from your environment and more-or-less installed them as your own functional understanding. Highest on this list of directly absorbed impressions is the process of copying – basically mimicking – the actions you observed as you watched people, animals and objects.

Much of what you do, think and intend **even now** is drawn directly from what you see, saw as a child and have ever seen others do, think and intend.

If you doubt the extent of this effect, watch a toddler for a while. You did the same thing, but you don't generally remember the details of your mimicry at age 1 or 2. (Actually the tendency doesn't abate with adulthood. Note how rapidly a comic phrase, a cool gesture or hit song permeates the culture, even the world scene, if it happens to catch on.)

In most cases this copying isn't a bad thing. Much of the richness of life grows from cultural aspects that are passed to new generations by visual cue. But negative stuff gets passed along, too. In psychological terms, you emulate the actions and nature of others. ***Emulation*** can be a powerful factor in your having taken on negative elements that you now seek to eliminate.

#2: Accepting What You Hear

Your world-view is formed as you learn to speak the language of your caretakers. The childhood lessons of learning to communicate carry a subtle, but extraordinarily powerful level of authority: when the large and ever present, seemingly all-knowing adults, who provide food and affection, clean you and remove various pains, explain something, generally you accept it. In fact, you accept it from early times as the very basis of definition for **what is**.

As you grow, absorbing ever more input from a wider circle of your neighborhood realm, that set of parentally implanted perspectives is reinforced by other – probably ***all*** other – sources of info. It becomes your worldview, with many subtle aspects never fully clarified or even explicitly stated. Your parents didn't explain, "This is a part of the flowing Oneness of Reality that we sit at to eat or play games, lean on, set flowers on for decoration, that reflects our social and financial status, that enhances our experience." They extracted it from that Oneness by defining it: "This is a table." And you absorbed that and a plethora of other definitions and explanations – including gods, fate, chance and luck – as "facts."

Again, this isn't entirely a bad thing. In the process, you come to communicate with others and gain a set of rules and expectations to operate by. But it can be exceptionally bad when self-defeating, intent-negating, illusory elements are built into those definitions – ***and they were*** without question.

This mechanism will be referred to by its common psychological term, ***Suggestion.***

#3: A Major Emotional Event

As we consider these mechanisms, much of the focus will be on negative things, elements of your inner self that yield the bad experiences – illness, emotional pain, failure and so forth. Basically the ***good*** things – aspects of your life that fulfill your will – don't require any attention and certainly don't demand to be changed.

So, in uncovering effects that directly impact your psychological posture, you will be concerned not only about the mundane elements Emulation and Suggestion, which were oft repeated during daily childhood activities, but also with a single episode or ***Impact Event*** that carries a strong emotional charge that adversely affected you: sexual or physical abuse, the death of a parent, a traumatic fall or auto accident.

Key Mechanism: Direct Transfer

#4: Literally Yours

The most direct mind-to-body connection is with a literal display of a symptom channeled through a verbal expression. This can be found in earlier life episodes like the other mechanisms, but is probably just as easily noted in the present.

Simply illustrated, you can display an expression: likening someone or something to a "pain in the neck" or a "pain in the ass," as two common expressions can channel a negative state directly to neck pains or hemorrhoids. Silly as it might sound, it is a direct, often frequently reinforced, gesture of autosuggestion. And it gets more serious when the phrase is "loser," "idiot," or some other derogatory label you were confronted with as a child.

This mechanism may be found less commonly than the others, but if any ***Literal Display*** is there, you'd do well to find it and eliminate it!

Complex Mechanisms: More Subtle Effects

How simple it would be if your mindset consisted of a batch of simple, straightforward childhood impressions that just needed to be untangled for you to greatly improve things! But added to the list above are several, somewhat more complex mechanisms that you doubtless carry in your baggage, whose end effect is also to twist the creative power of your will into undesirable events and relationships.

#5: A Negative with a Positive Attached

"A spoonful of sugar," sang Mary Poppins in the old musical, "makes the medicine go down…" as she programmed little tykes to repeat sickness.

Your parents (again, probably your mother or mother-figure, but I hate to appear so accusative of motherhood) passed along some strongly negating effects by rewarding painful things with added cuddling and care.

When you fell and scratched your knee, pinched your finger or just got sick, you likely received special treatment, including more attention and extra nurturing. Later, when sick, you could stay home from school thereby avoiding annoying things like tests or bullies. That mechanism, established during childhood converts into injury or illness as an adult, where you can likewise legitimately avoid going to work.

The mechanism consists of connecting a positive, pleasing reward with a negative occurrence or situation. As such it is more complex than suggestion and requires some degree of understanding for who did it, when and how. But the effect is this: unconsciously you bring on the negative just to realize the reward. This mechanism is referred to as Conditioning or ***Motivation***, where you are motivated to entertain a negative situation by a potential reward.

#6: A Positive with a Negative Attached

In superimposing cultural values on little you, the toddler or terrible-two-year-old you used to be, parents may well have punished you for "doing something bad," with the judgment rendered according to their specs and the execution according to their rules. The difficulty is that the message, while ostensibly intended to keep you headed in the right direction, was that **pain would be attached** to your self-expression **if it differed from what the authority considered acceptable**.

And the gist to that was, you needed to learn rational, culturally accepted behavioral patterns that you had to employ even when your nature led you to do otherwise. (And that helped create the **rational override** that plagues your unsettled mind, wherein it constantly second-guesses natural impulses with a rational comparison to all the rules you've accumulated for how to manipulate, what is acceptable, what is punishable, etc.)

Now the problem is: you are no longer toddling your way through forbidden living room vases and lamps. You are trying to live a life and succeed financially and in a relationship. Yet the mechanism of ***Punishment*** can still be there, functional and universally applied by your subconscious as basic ***Self-Punishment*** when, via guilt or self-deprecation, you judge your actions – or even thoughts – to be against the parental rules now welded into structures of your mindset. (There are other ways in which you might engage punishment, but you'll need to find them.)

Discerning this insidious mechanism can be tricky, as it can be indeed complex, based often on rules that were never clearly presented and tied with motivations or other mechanisms that further dim the process.

#7: Imposed Pseudo-Nature

Some patterns echoing into your current makeup were imposed on you either forcefully by parental edict or via subtle, situational conditions. There were aspects of your life wherein you ***had to*** do something, a step beyond punishment or threat of punishment where you at least had the option to violate rules first.

That coercion or ***Force*** might have been fairly active, wherein you had to go to church, had to take care of siblings, had to clean the house. Or it might have been quite subtle, where due to the ongoing situation, your preferred action or status was simply not available – say, for example, you desired to have friends, but grew up in a remote location with nobody around to play with. This mechanism, which I call the ***Subtle Force***, can be difficult to identify, since there is no culprit, no overt force causing you to be, in this example, alone.

Of the two, the Subtle Force will have left damaging effects somewhat trickier to identify and eliminate.

#8: Trying to Be Somebody Else

One step beyond mimicking your parents or others as a small child is trying to ***be like*** some other figure with a greater degree of complexity based on a later stage of youth in recognizing qualities of culture, toughness, attitude, whatever.

As you come to recognize your cultural group or subgroup, you will have taken on traits associated with others in it, qualities considered somehow desirable. You may idealize yourself as some movie star, associate your own being with a sports hero figure, a parent or other family member and strongly imagine yourself with that person's qualities. This process is referred to as ***Identification***, wherein you, by psychologically associating yourself with some other person, build their characteristics into your own self-image.

Again, that might not seem too bad if the figure is a positive character. But first, even then it can carry along some negative characteristics of that other. And second, you are **your own person** with your own set of qualities. It inherently demeans your own being by relegating your esteem to second place in your own mind.

#9 and #10: Toughing it Out

Here we are back to negation and neutralization as base elements for cultural function, as we had noted in Angle One. But now we will see them at a much more personal level…

Understand that cultural attributes don't exist hovering in space over a particular geographical region – they exist only in the mindset of each individual within a culture. So it shouldn't be too surprising that the outer symptoms of ***Struggle*** and ***Conflict***, found everywhere from large-scale international relationships down through neighborhood squabbles to spousal difficulties rest rooted in core elements for each individual's personal mindset. That includes yours.

From the time of birth, you've been exposed to these two traits in the world around you, woven into actions, health, news, parental interaction, sibling and peer interplay – pretty much everything you've encountered. Until you get rid of each and every aspect of your mindset that they are attached to, you will continue to encounter them. And I scarcely have to speculate: S and C are intimately attached to many elements of your mindset and thus, many aspects of your life.

Tailoring Your Nature

Repairing the Fabric

The above mechanisms, wherever present in your mindset, are like flawed threads in the interwoven events and relationships that form the fabric that is your life. Each and every physical symptom, each painful encounter or failed project, every swatch of your life that deviates from the fulfillment of **your will** contains frayed strands in its fabric containing one or more of these mechanisms.

Your task, integral to and of the Inner Journey, is to find those frayed threads by seeing clearly how they are spun from detractive mechanisms. Then you remove the threads and replace them with good ones by changing your mindset to conform to your intent. As you do so, patterns of your life formed by the resultant fabric change in consequence, always for the better. And with each step, delving ever deeper into more meaningful aspects of your life, you grow more and more confident in your innate ability to affect change in your life, more and more aware of the functional Oneness with which life works.

The only creative force capable of causally revising your experienced reality is ***your power to change your Self.***

In order to accomplish inner

change, you need a proper technique to see very clearly just how any such mechanisms are involved in life events and relationships. And that brings us back to the specifics of your Inner Journey: tools and techniques you might engage to accomplish change.

Angle Two began by regarding many techniques and disciplines to engender healing, to delve inward into life looking for some sort of enlightenment or betterment. While each might bring some small value, none of them can dispel the Overt Sequential Causality state of mind you inhabit (remember Kansas?), because none of them is equipped with the focus or technique necessary to approach the core building blocks, the base mechanisms, which comprise your mindset. At best, each can only shift the illusory cause to some other conceptualized force. You can fiddle with Qi, energy flow, whimsical gods, genetic structures, crystals and esoteric notions all you want, but if you hold negating and neutralizing elements in your mindset, you will experience illness, flawed relationships, failure or pain.

And there is ***NO WAY AROUND THAT:*** your nature gets imprinted onto the events and relationships you encounter. The flow of Reality initiating within that mindset contains inviolable propensities: qualities that ***will be*** realized, regardless of any rational interference on your part or the advised expertise of any source – physician, Reiki practitioner, Shaman, Priest or Preacher, anybody. What you ***are*** is what gets woven into the fabric of your life. What you ***do*** – in terms of rationally concocted actions – is not causal, however much you are used to planning, thinking, scheming and acting in conventionally manipulative ways. Because your life is a reflection of your inner Self, causality comes exclusively in changing your own nature, not trying to change the external world out there by manipulating it.

Ways and Means of Introspection

Reflection of Self – Without the Mirror

The basic mechanisms reviewed above are commonly worked with in the field of psychology. I did neither invent nor discover them (with the partial exception of Struggle, which I came to differentiate from Conflict, and Force/Subtle Force which I found within). What I have done, however, has been to take common, useful concepts of psychological analysis, scrape away boundaries and limitations formulated by scientific notions in the objective, expert-induced practice of psychoanalysis and leverage my personal perception of life's flowing Oneness. Slowly, over many years of subjective introspection, using exacting technique, I enhanced my awareness and cleared away prior mechanisms that were feeding the three bears and restricting my life – all the while clarifying to my perception the functionality of the mechanisms. With each step, my life improved: health issues, career steps, relationship conflicts and many other aspects of my life cleared up once I had eliminated their root, inner causes – no Qi to divert, no god to pray to, no foot to reflexologize and no expert to pay.

So what I present here are tools known to and used in the field of psychology as means of delving into significant emotional problems. But in your Inner Journey, it is not severe behavioral issues you seek to examine, ***but all aspects of life***. The psychologist is interested in clearing up major problems (and making money). My interest has been clearing up every annoying, limiting aspect of my life so I could be free and successful.

So the procedure here for finding and changing any aspect of your life consists of several steps:

1. Isolate a specific illness or other undesirable condition in your life to be changed,
2. Picture it back through your life by eliciting memories of similar events or conditions, of equivalent patterns – most effectively, trace it back to the first such instance as early as you find it,
3. Relate the real event to its root mind element(s), by becoming aware of any mechanism (from the above group) involved and by clarifying all aspects of the inner source, then
4. Change that inner state through autosuggestion.

At your disposal for accomplishing steps 1 through 3 are several valuable

Tools/Techniques that, if used with commitment and determination, will help to effectively discern the mind roots to negating effects. Each has its own value; each provides a unique view into the psyche:

- **Meditation**
- **Self-Hypnosis**
- **Ideomotor Response**
- **Automatic Writing**
- **Dream Interpretation**

To which is added the one and only means of accomplishing step 4, revising the inner:

- **Autosuggestion**

Each of the techniques can play a role in the overall scheme, but the driving force is you, through determination and intent.

Here's a closer look…

Meditation

Temporary Respite from Thought

While I pointed out the shortcoming for classic eastern meditation earlier – stifling thought does not eliminate underlying mechanisms that generate specific thoughts – there is definitely a need for relaxing and disengaging the mind.

You learned through a raft of childhood lessons, simple and complex, how to manipulate reality to accomplish what you want. As noted since Angle One, however, events flow from within, not in response to actions taken. But still holding notions of manipulation and external causality – including fear and worry about your security, health and all sorts of things – your mind will produce a stream of thoughts inquiring after information, processing it and formulating actions to take. All these thoughts will run consistent with your belief structure of how to accomplish what you want. And they will never let up, based on your ingrained need to manipulate things.

To really quiet the mind, you will need to disengage each of those prepackaged, rational data-receiving and action-planning processes, one at a time. But to just begin the Journey of introspection necessary to clear out that psychological debris, you need to establish some semblance of quieted mind, at least for periodic sessions, during which you can directly sense the flow of Reality.

Meditation How-TO

Gurus, Self-Help Experts – lots of people out there are real experts on meditation techniques. Go explore what they have to say; then try some of their concepts on for size.

If you already have tried them out and didn't get anywhere or don't want to bother, then just sit down in a quiet place, on a chair, on the floor, on a rock – it doesn't matter. Find a comfortable, upright position that you can maintain without dozing off.

Clear your mind of all thoughts – and when the next one appears, just jettison it down an imaginary chute. With your eyes closed, become aware of the sounds you can hear – not judging them or evaluating them, as those are thoughts that go down your chute.

Or open your eyes and, without moving, look around you – ***seeing*** things that are there, things you quit paying attention to long ago. Just watch. If a thought comes, dump it. Just watch.

As the next thought comes, reassure yourself that whatever that thought concerned isn't important now. It can be dealt with later. Drop it down the chute and resume, continuing for some time as you directly pay attention to what is around you, rather than on extraneous thoughts that come into mind…

Note: there is nothing magical or mystical about meditation. Despite esoteric claims by various sources – most of whom would like to have you donate money to their specialized cause – there is no far off, exotic realm of other-dimensionality that you are seeking. There are two realms to which you have access under any and all conditions: the real and the imaginary. Astral planes, seventh heavens populated with angels and archangels, alternate planes – these are all constructs in the unbounded realm of the imagination. Via meditation, you are seeking a preliminary quietude of mind that will aid in getting past the onslaught of thoughts that impede your focus on substantial, meaningful inner elements that need to be dealt with via the following techniques.

Self-Hypnosis

Specified Focus

Where Meditation quiets the mind, self-hypnosis pinpoints the focus of attention so that you are thinking precisely about the subject at hand, thereby allowing no gaps for other strands of thought to emerge.

With the inner self, in a Journey to clarify undesirable elements and change them, you are of needs dealing with information, meaningful impressions woven into memories and value judgments concerning those perceived events. Through a comfortable technique and practice, you can maintain that focus to the exclusion of unwanted, intrusive thoughts – and without falling asleep. Self-hypnosis is really only **conscious focus**, and you need that to discern critical mind elements that reveal your own nature.

Self-Hypnosis How-TO

There are hypnotists and hypnotherapists galore who have written books, offer courses or provide websites that will tell you how to induce a hypnotic state. Explore them. Find a technique that you can use effectively.

Or…

Find a quiet place where you will not be interrupted. Sit down in a chair with your back straight and comfy, hands on your lap.

At this point, eyes closed, you need to imagine a descending series of numbers – one classic example: picture the control panel of an elevator as it drops down from the 12th floor to the 11th. At each floor, you repeat to yourself quietly, inwardly, that you are going ever deeper, becoming ever more relaxed.

You pass the tenth floor, ever more relaxed; you feel your body release any tension… As you come to the ninth floor, you are even more relaxed. You feel your shoulders droop, your arms lay loose…

Proceed down through the floors, each after the other until, by the time you reach the basement, you are totally relaxed, with pointed focus on what you determine.

An alternate common technique: imagine by picturing in your mind each part of your body, starting with your scalp, your forehead, your eyes, and with focus on that part, relax it totally. Progress downward, reminding each muscle to relax as you come to that part of your body.

Note: hypnosis is about as simple as that, except that ***you have to do it***. Through practice you get better as you go. Once you have reached a full, focused state of hypnosis, you can turn your attention to the subject matter you need to work on. As you get better at it, perfecting this and perhaps the following ideomotor tools to delve into mind content, you will ultimately not need the formal induction procedure. The point and value is ***focus on meaning***.

Early, formal procedures to focus attention through a technique like the above will one day become unnecessary. You will find your normal waking state free of extraneous thoughts and able to focus on the task at hand.

Ideomotor Response

Hey, You – Get Out of the Way

Your Consciousness is unbounded. There is no inherent limit to what you can become aware of in terms of mind content related to personal experience. Indeed, there is no limit at all in perceptiveness, save for those subtle boundaries formed artificially by your self-image and those necessary constraints inherent to the format of engaging a life as a human.

However, the fundamental, contemporary, cultural paradigm for mind and consciousness includes only the rational mind – the intellect or "ego." Without some delving to acquaint yourself with your own depth of consciousness, this notion of intellect, as self-aware and containing stored knowledge, will be regarded as shallow, stacked on hidden, shadowy instincts and drives (called the "id"). The ego, as cultural notions have taught you, is generally what **you perceive yourself to be** – a thinking machine somehow contained in a complex computer grid of your brain, with its data stored as synapses or chemical notation.

That notion of a self-image – a lonely, brain-based ego riding a batch of stored survival mechanisms – is no more workable in reality than a paradigm based on an external, free-floating god conjuring things into being. (Indeed, that your vast complex of feeling and responsiveness, of enormous creative capability, imagination, etc., could ride the DNA structure of your cells into existence, is utterly absurd. That your great store of literally thousands of moments of vivid memory, complex conclusions, music, law, philosophy, etc., stored as chemical or electric signals in a physical brain is laughable as a workable paradigm. But, of course, workability has never deterred people from believing in something.)

Anyway, that whole default notion projects the subconscious or unconscious mind into a nether-realm "below" the rational, i.e., somehow deeper, out of reach of the commonly conscious mind. According to common regard of the nebulous subconscious, some other functional rationale should be dominant in these lower regions – animalistic drives, survival instincts, urges to do harm that need to be countered by civilized rules, etc.

According to the field of psychology, those deeper regions share space with the superego and may, depending on the model, either form a body of information isolated from everything else or tie into a Collective Unconscious, where it shares archetypes, symbols and information with all other consciousness.

In reality, the attribute of consciousness regarded as the sub- or unconscious is really only a **store** – an unbounded store, indeed, but essentially a repository – of information and value judgment. But it ***functions***, based on the inner-outer flow, to effectively regulate the body, to hold symbolic and meaningful aspects of Self and by virtue of the nature of the specific info and value set, to basically control other functions of physical and emotional well-being.

While the subconscious has been regarded by various cultures as anything from god-like and all-powerful to primitive and scarcely controllable, has been delved into with exotic rituals, potions, trances and chanting or has been totally ignored, this aspect of Self holds the sea of information on which you sail through life. It engenders dreams, initiates urges and supplies to the conscious self events and relationships exactly reflective of what is asked for.

(But caution: "what is asked for" is not to be confused with what you desire! **Exactly what** you are beseeching, due to noted mechanisms, includes a lot of things you don't really want. For example, if you pray to a god for something, the message to the subconscious is that you are helpless and powerless to accomplish that request. So the subconscious fulfills your self-image with recycled powerlessness, setting into the flow precisely that lack of authority you have basically requested – which was likely, along with struggle and conflict, already there, or you wouldn't have been praying in the first place.)

There is no "other self" to the unconscious, no independent entity with its own agenda; it is only information and stored value relationships – a broad array of raw information that undergirds the more superficial "knowledge" learned through rational processes and impacts in all ways the emerging Reality that each conscious Self encounters.

(Don't confuse "information" in this sense with knowledge. Subconscious information covers all aspects of your being, your unfathomably complex body function and your intimate interrelationship with all else. Knowledge, by contrast, is a shallow, illusory and often distorted collection of notions you have accumulated from your cultural exposure. Information, in this regard, is precise in reflection of ***what is*** and thus vital to your ongoing life function. Knowledge, while vital to interaction in a life scenario, can be highly flawed and generally ***gets in the way*** of that function – which is why you are delving into these depths in the first place: to clear out the flawed notions.)

In actuality, no boundary exists between the conscious mind, i.e., the thinking self that you feel yourself to be in your waking state and the subconscious. But a functional separation is made effectual by **the very definition** and ***its incorporation in your perceived self***. The cultural paradigm inherited through the close of the twentieth century pictures the self ***as only*** the rational intellect; it shuts off the rest into a murky dungeon of undefined functionality.

An enormous amount of information in "the works" flows continuously, the vast bulk of which you need not be aware of – ever. When, for example, did you last worry about, and thus interfere with, the function of your pancreatic islets of Langerhans? Yet those cells work just fine to do what they need to do. However, insofar as your body and your life **do not** work right – that is, fulfill your will, rather than negate or neutralize it – there is vital information, operative via the mechanisms mentioned above, that you absolutely need to elicit into conscious attention. You can ***and should*** become privy to whatever aspect of Self you need know so that you can revise it.

The most effective means to conveniently bypass this artificial conscious/subconscious boundary is through querying ideomotor responses – involuntary movements that can reflect subconscious content.

The two most commonly used ideomotor tools are the pendulum and finger movements. These techniques elicit yes or no answers via the movement of a dangling weight on the end of a string (held in the hand, but not consciously deflected), through movement of certain fingers or other body motions to indicate, in response to questions, affirmative or negative. Once such a technique is mastered – through use and reinforcement by self-hypnosis – **all meaningful information in the subconscious becomes accessible**.

Given the need to discern life's functional Oneness, this technique allows invaluable perspective on the complex of Self that underlies your superficial cultural notion of your nature. As such, coupled with self-hypnosis technique to focus your attention, it should comprise your gesture to delve into mind content – far surpassing any tool, technique or discipline listed above to provide a window into your meaningful Self.

Ideomotor Response How-TO

The pendulum is a simple devise used to query the subconscious for information while bypassing conscious interference. There is much written on this subject that you could find, but the procedure is simple…

Draw a cross on a paper and lay it in front of you. Leaning lightly on your elbow, with your forearm upright and hand extended over the cross, hold a string with a weight on the end of it so that it dangles above the center of the cross. Don't move the pendulum.

With your visual focus intent on the pendulum, ask your subconscious to give you a "yes" answer by deflecting the weight along one axis of the cross – either back and forth to the left and right or toward and away from you. You may need to clear the mind with self-hypnosis prior to this, but generally you will elicit a response fairly easily.

Once you have a yes direction, ask for a "no" response as the other direction of the cross. Complete the potential arrangement by asking for a response for "unknown" and "don't want to answer" as circular clockwise or counter-clockwise movement of the pendulum.

(These provide an outlet in case you approach subjects that are too emotionally charged to deal with at the time. Generally, as you proceed to address ever-deeper subject matter, you will encounter these resistance responses less and less frequently. Also, based on how you ask a question, you may get a "yes and no" answer by having the pendulum alternate between your yes and no directions.)

As an alternate, you may find finger movement to be preferable. In this technique, you can elicit a self-hypnosis session with your hands laying flat on the arms of your chair. Patiently reinforce the desire to work with subconscious information and focus on the concept of affirmative. Ask the subconscious to lift a finger as a response meaning "yes." As one finger twitches upward, note that this will be the yes response and move on to "no" "unknown," and "don't want to answer."

After you have become comfortable in querying and receiving responses by either means or some other body movement you have found workable, you can begin to address specific problems and receive insights on the inner mechanisms involved. Bear in mind your subconscious stores **inner information** meaningful to you, not outer data, like the numbers to today's lottery or how others think about you. (So the unconscious, via pendulum response, can't give you today's winning numbers, but can tell you why you lack abundance such that you think you need to win it. It can't reveal how others regard you, but can help you absolutely specify your self-image, which is the design to which others will respond.)

The outer realm always flows from the inner: the key to effective use of ideomotor responses is to focus on specification of inner mechanisms, based on memory and meaning, so that elements leading to undesirable aspects of your life can be changed. If you clear away self-restricting elements, you won't need to win the lottery to gain abundance, nor have to impress your friends to gain their favor.

Automatic Writing

Let It Out

Akin to simple "doodling," this tool/technique can be used to bring inner elements to your conscious attention by letting your hand draw without any particular thought in mind. The drawings must then be interpreted and deciphered by means of making sense out of the symbolic images you just drew.

Automatic Writing is less explicit than clear ideomotor responses, but the latter can be used to fully interpret the meaning of the images recorded.

Your need for such aids as Automatic Writing may fade as you become more accustomed with dealing with mind content at any level and more confident in your understanding of aspects of mind you previously didn't recognize as part of the Self. But the symbolic writing, for many who are more artistically or visually oriented, may provide a valued channel for inner info to find its way out into conscious recognition.

Automatic Writing How-TO

With a tablet or sheet of paper in front of you and a pencil in your hand, establish a focus via self-hypnosis. Focus intently on a particular problem you want to deal with or just clear your mind and let the subconscious produce the subject matter.

With your eyes open and without any conscious effort let your hand draw on the paper.

If the image is unclear, use your ideomotor technique to clarify what it means and to delve deeper into it.

Dream Interpretation

The Soft Underbelly of Reality

Dreams constitute a clear, symbolic display of your inner content. Your dream-state consciousness is every bit as vital to your total Self as that of your time awake engaged with the real – and equally valid. The two are intrinsically, intimately conjoined, such that events unfolding in the course of your real life are enfolded, symbolically and without the time constraint of consecutive regard, in dream content. Your inner nature, replete with fears and expectations, limits, hopes and all else, will be on display in the menagerie of settings and often illogical, morphing events that constitute your dreams.

Whether or not you understand the symbolic, pictorial language of dreams, they transpire on a nightly basis, weaving things important and (seemingly) trivial into the dreamscape. But understanding them is vital: all angles of your Inner Journey are enhanced by your active engagement of dreams – understanding your inner nature and how it works, specifying inner details behind outer manifestations and clearing out negating and neutralizing elements so your life improves.

Nightly dreaming, as a process, provides for the emergence of major inner values into conscious attention, there to be reviewed for their content and meaning. Precisely this natural flow can be used to great advantage in perceiving the diverse, meaningful elements of mind you are looking for via the above tools. Vital to using dreams for your benefit, then, is a growing awareness of the nature of dream elements and their symbolic representation of real aspects of your life.

Understand first that real events in your life are very much **symbols** for the essence of their energy/emotional equivalent in your mind elements. Your argument with your spouse ***symbolizes*** conflict; your automobile and your house ***symbolize*** your degree of abundance and other status elements. It should not be surprising that the same elements appear likewise as symbols in your dream state.

Dream Analysis How-TO

There are untold volumes of writing out there concerning dreams: web sites, books, self-help guides, biographies of Freud and Jung, on and on. Unlike the previous How-TO suggestions concerning other tools, I can't get into extensive dream consideration here and keep focus on the big picture, but I will provide some general comments – presuming you will explore other sources.

Your dreams really are the unfettered, direct encounter with the subconscious elements that you have to engage and understand in order to bring about change in the Self and thus in the physical extension, your life.

Dreams are foremost **meaningful**. The seemingly crazy (when viewed from waking reality) kaleidoscope of events and encounters that take place during the dream state contain ***only ever*** meaningful insights into your core nature. The trick is to fully grasp what that meaning is by being able to interpret the dreams.

Many sources of dream analysis put forth a dictionary of what the elements of a dream mean. Because some aspects of life carry clear cultural, contextual meaning, generally shared across society, there can be a value to that. But the key to understanding dreams in the specific scope of your life – which is the only real value to you – is to reliably interpret the meaning a dream has ***to you***, personally and in terms of events and relationships taking place in your life ***now***.

The most useful tool for doing that, for translating the symbolic, intuitive, morphing elements of a dream into the more solid concepts of waking consideration is once again, ideomotor response as covered earlier. The meaningful thrust of dream content derives from the same meaningful elements of your psyche as the yes/no answers to posed questions. In order to detect and deal with those elements, perceive the meaning and practically change your mindset in response to the lessons learned, you have to accurately interpret what they are all about. The pendulum or finger response technique can reference the core, inner self and allow you to clarify real meaning amid otherwise cryptic information.

* * *

As to **Ways and Means** thus far, you have the capability, using the above means of delving, to become aware of any aspect of mind leading to any effect in your life – health, relationships, success, everything. Having become aware of an undesirable aspect of your life, you can come to see the mechanisms by which this effect is realized using those tools. Having clarified the root, inner elements to your life's problems, you will subsequently wish to change them...

Autosuggestion

Your Lever for Moving the World

You've been subjected to ***suggestion*** since the earliest moments of your life. As noted above, influence from parents and other early sources was a major – **probably *the primary*** – source of your whole mindset, including notions of what you are and what you should be.

Even now, commercials and advertising seek not to just inform you of what is available to consume, but subtly, strongly, with humor, sex and attention-grabbing effects, suggest what you should buy, hoping all the while to implant in your mind the desire to buy it. Politicians, charities, non-profit organizations for arts and other good works – all these use suggestion on you as well, all the time.

Suggestion works because the mind is interactive and dynamic. Like the Reality that reflects its mindset, the mind, a window to Self and meaningful content, is always somewhat open, changing and flowing with evolving meaning in your life.

As you come to regard that content, understanding the pure, innate relationship between Self and emerging Reality, you will see that ***your sole leverage*** towards steering your life in desirable directions is in formulating the suggestion that goes into and **becomes** that mindset. Indeed, as you regard the Mechanisms listed above and how they apply to your experience, you will realize how, through them, the large body of your belief structure and definition set built up through childhood. But when you see them in place functionally in your mindset, you will also realize that trying to emulate, motivate, force, struggle or punish yourself into betterment is **just not**

doable.

But you are very open to suggestion and it makes a lot of sense for ***you*** to do your own suggesting.

So the five means to discern mind content, self-hypnosis, ideomotor indications, dream analysis, etc., are various tools to discern the negating and neutralizing elements of your being. You may need them all to some degree to decipher your often-cryptic nature.

But once you've **clearly identified all aspects of a particular issue** – ***then you have dominion over it***.

When, and only when, you clearly see the **inner roots** to **an outer condition**, you can change them and thus it. And your single, effective means to revise that inner realm is ***Autosuggestion*** – with you providing the directions to dispel previous programming and superimpose desired aspects.

Autosuggestion How-TO

Having discerned all inner elements as roots of a particular problem, including the earliest appearance, who was involved and which mechanisms, you are ready to eliminate it and replace it with a positive effect.

In a focused state, you silently review the inner elements of the outer symptom. You tell yourself in some fashion, "I see clearly these roots to the problem of _____. Now I dispel and discard those elements. They serve no more purpose, and I leave them in the past. Now I am _____." And there you fill in the desired status with a positive effect.

That can be reviewed and repeated for a week or so, two or three times a day – depending on the severity, magnitude, complexity, etc., of the problem/symptom. Those negative symptoms will abate over time. Depending on the instance, though, there may be more aspects to the problem you have yet to see. Other inner elements related to your focus symptom may go deeper – or other problems may be related that must also be dealt with to eliminate a symptom completely.

Never underestimate the complexity of a problem, particularly when dealing with aspects of life deeply important to you. You will come to understand that interrelatedness as you get a feel for the inner realm.

I will reiterate, for this is the most important concept of The Essence of Reality…

The key realization to delving inwards to deal with the roots of outer symptoms is this: once you have clearly identified the core, inner roots to a problem, ***you then have authority over the situation***. It is only a question of change via autosuggestion to revise your causal, root mindset.

If, though, you never delve within, seeking to manipulate the outer world by treating your body, manipulating your antagonists, praying to a deity, psychically affecting the Qi or any other gesture, you will only ***at best*** shift the symptom to some other form. If you do not address the core problems resident in your mindset, you will not eliminate the inner source of the problem and thus never fully extinguish the external symptom.

Proceeding on the Journey

Making It So

On the Inner Journey, then, you are seeking to discern elements of value and meaning which comprise your mindset – with particular focus on those which result not in fulfillment of your will, but in negation/neutralization, for those specifically are in need of change.

Much more than your physical self, more than your intellectual self, your cultural role, your occupational character, much more than any aspect of personality or identity you are used to considering yourself to be, you consist of an expansive range of intangible values and concept elements. You ***are*** those values you hold in mind, and those values become real in your health and all the events and relationships you encounter.

To be clear about it, you exist ***NOW*** in a discernible state of interwoven values. You have changed a bit from yesterday, and you will evolve a tad by tomorrow. But ***now***, your nature is a specific blend of values, flowing as described in Angle One, from within into real effects. As you look into your memories, your **current** nature is stamped, clearly and invariably, on the resultant values your life contained at any past point. Thus, when you consider past events, your current nature is to be seen faithfully brought to memory there, in the values intertwined in past situations.

The "past" is generally considered to be a hardened trail of events, recorded in memory or in word, and immutable. You will find, however, that a "solidified" past is an illusion. As you change by reprogramming mind elements, the past changes to reflect the current self, the values you hold ***now***.

Of course, events, per se, don't suddenly alter their historical course and revise in essence, but their **meaning** changes, along with their ***impact on your life*** and the perceived value of the experience – which is the only thing in a meaningful existence that really matters.

Likewise, the unfolding potential commonly called the "future" is stacked with events exactly reflective of that same meaning-based mind content you hold currently. No event, no encounter, no injury, no "coincidence" ever occurs by accident. Each fulfills a value cognate you hold within.

So, in effect, the past and the future both extend outward from this moment, each in reflection of the current state of mind you hold ***now***. When you change your current nature, both past (as you interpret it) and future (which will ensue) change to suit. Perceiving this functional Oneness and how it works is highly significant! You are not, first of all, locked into a personal nature that is fixed and predetermined, unalterable. You are not branded by a concrete past whose events and quality reflections are somehow limiting to your current status and future accomplishments. Nor are you preset to encounter events fixed by any external plan, by mysterious forces of fate, fortune, some deity, planet alignment or destiny.

In fact, your creative potential to shed past limitations and move toward freedom of expression and action is bounded only by your ability ***to perceive your own nature***. For that freedom can be realized ***only*** through revision of that realm which causes the engendering of events – the inner realm of mind elements as it exists ***now***. And it is realized most effectively by consciously eliminating the restrictive conceptualizations you hold now. After you've accomplished such inner change, the elements of meaning that you comprise in the new ***now*** moment will be reflected in past situations you recall from your childhood and will be the meaning-based outcome of upcoming events.

There is no other force, no other determining factor, no external cause to the cohesive unfolding of your life's episodes – only ***your composite inner nature***. Change that and you change your life.

* * *

Within EoR, I present perspectives that can help free your self-perception and tools whereby you can direct and energize that change. But for all I can say here, the impetus to change and the degree to which you can accomplish that change are yours alone. Just reading EoR can help loosen the old, rusty conceptual chains of beliefs and misunderstanding. But you shed those shackles by using the tools and techniques I discuss here in a determined effort on an ongoing basis – ***only that*** can bring true Awareness and true change for the better.

Sit Still and Get Going

Years ago, while living in San Diego, I attended a talk by Joseph Chilton Pearce, who had recently authored *The Crack in the Cosmic Egg*. He was, at the time, a proponent of Siddha Yoga and rather promoted its prime leader, Swami Muktananda.

Pearce made the point that Muktananda was an exceptional being, capable of bestowing "shaktipat" on a sincere follower. That exotic gesture should infuse the seeker with energy and promote Kundalini, itself a release of cosmic energy from the base chakra.

I asked him, why couldn't a sincere, perceptive individual attain that state on one's own?

Pearce commented that he didn't think the "bootstrap technique" was possible – referring to the concept of pulling oneself up into the air by pulling on one's own bootstraps. He said that an advanced mystic like Muktananda was necessary to channel such energy. But somebody must have done that in the first place, I said, otherwise there wouldn't have been anybody to bestow it. The discussion didn't go much further than that.

I was never out after glittery, glowing special effects. I pursued Muktananda's recommended chanting, "Om Namah Shivaya," a Siddha mantra, with sincerity. But after a time, sitting and om-ing away, I concluded that life offered more than whatever it was Mukti was seeking. People who followed him seemed to fit neatly into his package, content to revere him as superhuman, donate to his movement and remain happy in a little world of retreat.

About 32 at that time, I already realized that life ***did*** present much more than that. But it took many a year and a lot of delving to confirm that the bootstrap technique, indeed, ***is the only one possible*** to reach a Clear Awareness of what's happening here! Nobody is going to save you, hand you enlightenment on a platter, affix a halo or bestow Clear Awareness on your rationally oriented mind. You have to do it yourself.

And here is basically how…

Symptom Solving

Since the effects of your life that lead to pain and annoyance are always consequences of inner elements, what you commonly regard as "problems" are more accurately seen as outer ***symptoms*** of inner, causal problems. The practical approach is to begin looking at those specific aspects of your life that are not as you desire to find their source, rooted in your mindset.

You wouldn't start a career as a builder by taking on a 14 story castle, but rather work at some carpentry and plumbing tasks until you get pretty good at them, then move on to siding, roof construction, concrete pouring, etc. Similarly, you wouldn't start your inner reconstruction with major, earth shattering, personally intimidating elements, but rather with simpler, less emotionally charged annoyances. Having cleaned up minor things and mastered the technique, you work your way up to the big stuff.

The values and effects of your life might be likened to a bowl of spaghetti, whose interwoven strands you wish to consume. You don't stuff all the spaghetti into your mouth at once – you would choke on the sheer volume. Likewise, in dealing with inner roots to outer problems, you take them one at a time, as though pulling out one strand of spaghetti, regard it thoroughly, chew it up and swallow, then move on to the next. What you are looking for is a clean plate, and you may well have a big bowl with many, interwoven strands to deal with.

So start with simple problems (i.e., symptoms): physical annoyances as experienced in minor health problems would be a good place to look.

The advantage to an initial focus on health issues is twofold: first, it is conceptually easier to comprehend and accept the mind-body connection than more complex situations that entail relationships with others. And second, your health is of primary importance if you want make significant progress through ***this*** incarnation. It wouldn't be too wise to clear up all your relationship problems, set yourself on a marvelous career path, attain great abundance, then die young of physical maladies that you didn't clear up early along the trail.

So ponder a simple, annoying symptom and use the tools at your disposal to address the key, inner mechanisms involved.

* * *

One of the early issues I recall approaching was a nervous foot kick. Living in Munich and then San Diego, I had been doing some creative writing. But I found that, whenever concentrating on typing, my leg would start kicking, bouncing up and down – you've seen folks with that habit or maybe have it yourself.

In any case, I could, of course, stop it if I focused on that leg. But when my attention shifted to writing or some other activity, the leg started kicking.

That was the first simple symptom I addressed as I began to use self-hypnosis and the pendulum. I had been schooled in a very helpful self-hypnosis seminar, given by friend and fellow Mensan, Jack Mirowitz. And ideomotor technique I learned from the noted book, *Self-Hypnotism* – by Leslie M. LeCron, a pioneer of such technique. (LeCron nicely articulated many of the mechanisms above and had delved deeply into inner causality. The only limitation there is scope. Not only one's health, but **all of life** is to be addressed via the inner self!)

Using simple yes/no questioning, I came to the root of the symptom. Having already gotten comfortable with self-hypnosis, I ushered myself into a comfy spot and put concentrated focus on the pendulum. Then I queried my subconscious in the following manner – to show my thought train, first is my question/thought, then the pendulum answer (swinging left to right for no, back and forth away from me for yes). It went something like this:

I want to concentrate on my nervous leg kick. Is it a good time to look at this. ***P: Yes***

Does the leg kick go back to an earlier time in my life? ***P: Yes***

Did this start before the age of six? ***P: Yes***

Before the age of 2? ***P: Yes***

Before the age of 1? ***P: No***

So, I began to kick my leg sometime while I was one year old? ***P: Yes***

Was anybody else involved in this condition? ***P: Yes***

Was my mother involved? ***P: Yes***

My father? ***P: No***
Was anybody else involved: ***P: Yes***
Was this person a family member: ***P: Yes***

At that point, it popped into my mind that my brother, 4 ½ years older, used to pick on me and certainly was already intimidating to a 2-year-old.

Was my brother involved in my leg kick? ***P: Yes***
Were there any of the mechanisms involved? ***P: Yes***

I went down through the list mentioned above – Suggestion, Motivation, etc. – getting a ***No*** response for everything but Conflict. And the pieces of the puzzle started to fall into place.

Was the conflict with my mother? ***P: No***
With my brother? ***P: Yes***

And it became clear: my brother was a threat to hurt me, but if my mother was present, I was safe. By that point in my life, my brother had long since ceased to be a menace and my mother had died several years prior. To the subconscious, however, which engages mechanisms in this timeless ***now moment***, those things didn't matter! What mattered was this situation: my mother was not present, and my brother (though living 2500 miles away) was thus a threat – so I was in danger and the leg kick was an outlet for the tension.

Having correlated the outer effect to its inner roots clearly, I then could proceed to disengage that mechanism. For several days following that, a couple times a day, I would do a simple self-hypnosis session during which I would tell myself: "I see the mechanism behind my leg kick. I see clearly the conflict involved, but I no longer need that. Now I release and dispel the conflict and tension, as my brother is no longer a threat. Now I leave that symptom in the past, and my leg is relaxed."

Within a few days, the nervous kick left, never to return.

* * *

Another ongoing health problem worth illustrating concerned frequently recurring colds, sore throats and various sinus problems I'd experienced since childhood. Later, as my confidence in the efficacy of the pendulum and autosuggestion grew, I took on this more major symptom…

Is this a good time to explore my recurring colds and sore throats?
P: Yes

Through a series of questions, I determined the starting point for this frequent illness as age 5, then proceeded to find that my mother was involved. So I began to look for the mechanisms…

Is Suggestion involved in this situation? ***P: Yes***
Do I emulate anybody in having frequent colds? ***P: No***

Running down through the list, I found that Motivation and Conflict got a positive response, while Punishment, Struggle, Force and the others were not involved. So I needed a clearer picture concerning the three mechanisms underlying this symptom…

Are there more points of Suggestion than just one involved here? ***P: Yes***
Did the Suggestion come from my mother (I queried, already coming to a dim understanding of her thoughts on causality.) ***P: Yes***

So, pondering the past and confirming my memory with the pendulum response, I came up with many of the standard notions common to folk wisdom that my mother had told me: colds are ***caused by*** bacteria or virus. Sickness could come on when I was exposed to those "germs," via contact with a sick person or getting sneezed on. If I sat in a draft or, in winter, got my feet wet or wasn't dressed warmly enough ("You'll catch your death of cold," a motherly phrase that clearly echoed back to my grandmother from

Belfast), I was likely to "catch a cold." Of course, that phrase itself is highly suggestive to a child – presenting the image of something out there ready to attack you and inflict pain.

And I recalled all the great length of medical wonder that was mobilized to save me from these evil bacteria: antibiotics like penicillin, nose spray and antihistamines to open up my clogged nasal passages, a vaporizer spewing medicated water vapor into the nighttime bedroom air to help me breath and sleep, mouthwash to gargle with and kill all those bad germs in my throat, aspirin and other pain relievers to ease physical symptoms. All in all, the great weaponry of medical science, even in those days, the 1950s, was more than enough to suggest to the 5-year-old how dangerous life was, how inept the body was in "fighting" off such invasive bacteria and how much I had to rationally beware of such conditions as would bring on the next infection.

Did the Motivation involve my mother? ***P: Yes***

This didn't require much input from the depths of my subconscious. When I got sick, I got special care and attention from Mom. She would make me a cup of tea and toast to dip in it, spend more time with me, checking on things – and ultimately, the big bonus, I could stay home from school! And, talk about motivation, I not only got extra protection from my brother, but even ***he*** was less likely to poke me or pinch me if I was sick.

That left the third mechanism involved, Conflict, which was clearly my interest and desire for health vs. these evil bacteria and threatening conditions out there – all out to get me.

Having clarified all these factors, I set out to reprogram the inner software: "I see clearly the mechanisms leading to my recurring illness. I see the conflict involved, but I no longer need that. So I release and dispel the conflict involved in my colds. And I see the suggestion as to external causes. But I see that bacteria and conditions do not cause my illness, so I dispel the suggestion and leave that in the past. And I see the Motivation. But I see that my mother is no longer here, and I don't need the extra attention, so I dispel that mechanism and leave it in the past. Now I am healthy, with clear breathing and open sinuses."

* * *

Now this particular symptom was considerably more complex and ingrained than the simple leg kick. So it took a while longer and more focus. Through time, as I got sick less and less, I could revisit the scene and make sure these three mechanisms were thoroughly cleared. In recent times, I rarely get sick in any way – and then the illness always has to do with current, considerably deeper issues that I had been dealing with finding their way out through symptomatic expression.

As I became ever more comfortable delving within, I approached other physical symptoms and dealt with them: knee pain while running, allergies, skin problems, etc. Fully comfortable (at that time, through my 30s) with the concept that the mind and body were absolutely connected in the causal relationship of inner nature to outer effect, I came to fully grasp – as mentioned, based on further inner delving, added exposure to greater perspectives via reading and the experience of giving psychic reading – that there was ***no boundary*** between my perceived self and all that I encountered. Each element of my life – success, personal relationships, abundance – was as intimately related to my inner nature as my immediate health.

So I turned focus on the inner plane to personal problems – career questions, relationship annoyances, rejection in specific ways, elements inhibiting what I wanted to accomplish. Always, the key to understanding was similar to those early physical improvements: isolate the problem, break it down into elements – mechanisms involved, time frame of earliest encounter and who was involved – then reprogram it via autosuggestion.

In the more major elements, dreams came to be significant factor. With a current focus on a particular part of life that needed attention, my dreams would weave the subject matter into symbolic occurrences. For example, I recall a dream in which I was at my grandmother's house – she lived next door as I grew up – and I was somehow picked up and turned over by an invisible force, which I couldn't resist.

As I delved into this dream's meaning, I could easily discern what it meant. Most of the trail of physical and life symptoms had involved Struggle and/or Conflict as key mechanisms. As noted already, negating and neutralizing elements are deeply woven into our mindsets by intrinsic cultural values and notions. This dream graphically noted how these factors had originated in my "grandmother's house," that is, of course, not the physical building, but the mindset that my grandmother brought from Belfast, passed along to my mother and thus to me. Turning me upside-down was symbolic of inverting my desires and intent.

My mother was a loving, caring person – one of the kindest and best people I have ever encountered. But in passing along these inner limitations, her intent and love were only able to intensify the negative effects, for her mindset was bound up in religious dogma and rational control. Thus, her every gesture, however well-wishing she was, passed along self-doubt and an invariable propensity toward illness or injury with the **need to control** body function, rather than simple trust of my body's ability to work. She was exceptionally prudish, harkening back to church-founded relation of sex to sin and was thoroughly unable, as are most strongly religious people, to see the shortcomings of archaic beliefs – both conceptual and practical, as her health suffered enormously from her guilt and inner Conflict.

In your self-examination, it is not ever necessary to psychoanalyze your mother or any other critical character who influenced your early life. I mention these things to provide the perspective that, however good the intent of a parent or guardian in your upbringing, they will pass along their restricting mechanisms without fail.

It is vital to recognize that you bring ***your*** nature – the mindset and its many interwoven values – into this incarnation. Just as in a dream, you will find yourself surrounded by a setting with all the potentials for positive and negative experience. Indeed, from this moment forward, a vast array of potential happenings might unfold. But, quite precisely, the course that ***will become real*** is the one reflective of what your nature, your mindset, holds.

For me as it will for you, each positive change entailed another step on the long Journey inward, clearing out one element at a time, struggling until I had cleared Struggle out of various health and other avenues of life, fighting with my body, my vehicles, house problems, etc., until I had cleared out Conflict.

Each step was similar to the examples above: clarify the issue, then get rid of it and replace it with a positive notion.

Through self-hypnosis and ideomotor responses, you can explore every nook of your life.

* * *

After many years of picking apart the various minor ailments and frustrations in life, I had come to see the Three Bears noted above, representing lack of Abundance, Authority and Acceptance – and wasn't nearly satisfied in my status of any of those at that stage of my life. Efforts to succeed in financial matters always seemed to lead, not to budding success, nor even failure, but just never to where I wanted to be. And even for that, I had to struggle all the way. In terms of authority, as that personal sway over one's life would be evaluated, I encountered resistance and conflict in every way but health, which I had pretty well cleared up. In terms of Acceptance, I still couldn't be who I really was and meet glowing friendship and openness. So I shaved away at them, with focus on one aspect at a time, one strand of spaghetti, until the plate was empty. Now my life works very well indeed…

As you proceed on Your Journey inward, and as you clear out items of significance which you are sure are the major stumbling block to your happiness, if your life doesn't improve as you expect – just keep going, keep looking, keep clearing away the debris of restricting mind elements. If your life still isn't as you want it to be, ***just keep delving***, with optimism, seeking improvement. It may be a long Journey, but your only options are to give in and accept the current status or keep moving in the direction of a better life.

As You Change – The Healing Process

The Immediate Consequences

So you understand by now that problems and conditions you face in life – whether concerning your health, your economic status, your relationships, your ability to succeed or ***anything else*** – are rooted in your own psyche. You have begun to delve into aspects of Self, for that is the only way to functionally as well as practically grow in awareness of this inner-outer Oneness. Having done so, you begin to experience the healing, the improvement of the condition you are addressing.

What should you expect? Is it that easy, that simple?

It is indeed, simple. The inner-outer relationship is intrinsic and inviolable, based on the Essence of Reality riding on value and meaning, all of which initiate within and emerge outward. If inhibiting Mechanisms are deleted, thus revising your inner mindset, ***you*** change both inwardly and, consequently, outwardly – as embodied in the quality of your experiences, the essence of your relationships.

"Simple," however, should not imply always "easy." As you approach very meaningful aspects of your life, your emotions will be riding those horses you'll be trying to run out of the corral.

You should be aware of the distinct process that plays itself out during healing. With effects of lesser importance, it isn't critical. But when you go after major aspects of your life – career, relationship, financial or other such biggies – **it will be!**

The Compression of Effect

Dealing with those lesser effects – nervous twitches, colds, allergies, etc. – you can eliminate symptoms in a fairly straightforward manner. As you delve deeper and gain confidence in your innate power to change, the procedure actually gets easier: despite your delving into ever deeper, more meaningful inner values, you will come to know with ever more confidence that **you are** the source of all qualities.

But there exist effective hierarchies of value in the whole of your mind structure. Aspects of Freedom, Joy and Peace are such over-riding values, almost measurable in their overall experienced expression in your life such that you might consider ***degree*** of Freedom and Peace as a direct consequence of your comprehensive mind image.

For example, suppose you find that your propensity to catch colds easily is based on several mechanisms, as illustrated above and you proceed to eliminate these. Subsequently, your tendency to catch colds dissipates. Your nose and throat now function as they should. That's great, but, in addition to the direct correlation of symptomatic consequence, those physical effects also represented a portion of conflict in your life, of struggle with your body, your sinuses and perhaps even with others in your work environment. These are symptoms representing your level of Peace and to a degree your feelings of Joy and your realization of Freedom. If no deeper venture is undertaken to address these over-riding values, then, even as your colds clear up, **other symptoms** will emerge into your life experience to fill in the gap of conflict and struggle where you used to display those negative effects in body function. That is, if you don't address your general philosophical outlook, such that you still value courage and fortitude, then eliminating the struggle against illness will require the realization of struggle against ***something else***!

I refer to that as Compression of Effect. You've eliminated some elements wherein struggle and conflict are reconciled, but you haven't really delved deeply enough to root out ***the need for*** struggle and conflict in your life. So S & C get compressed into other avenues of your experience.

It is wise to understand, based on the above, that a ***partial*** journey can leave some aspects of life improved and others, unaddressed, worse off. If you clear up surface conflict in your relationship with your spouse, for example, by finding the roots within yourself for continuing such strife, but you haven't delved deeper, you may find the conflict simply shifting into your relationship with your parents or children, with your boss or your neighbors. If the propensity toward conflict exists within you, and you haven't delved deeply enough to clean it out, it ***will come out somewhere*** in the events and relationships of your life.

Short-Term Intensification of Symptom

As you approach and address a particular symptom, finding and eliminating it at its roots, you may find that the symptom intensifies for a bit before it wanes and ultimately ceases to be – much like a fever as your body heals from an illness. Have you experienced a fever? It builds and builds until it rapidly breaks and dissipates, the infection having been cleared up.

Inner healing can work like that, with the symptom first intensifying before dissipating.

The Release

A further aspect to note here – highly significant – brings an effect that also comes ever more to the fore as deeper and ever more significant values are addressed.

As you change, you are emerging from one mindset into a new one, having "reprogrammed" some undesirable element that more justly reflects your intent. In that process comes a consequential ***release of emotional energy***. With you as the **totality** of what exists in your inner realm, movement toward the positive, in terms of fulfillment of your will, ***will neces-***

sarily release the negative. That release is a distinct ejection of emotionally charged baggage.

So, as that healing takes place, you may encounter various "**Release Symptoms**" as you wrest your mind free of negating mechanisms. One or a combination could emerge – then pass – as the new mindset settles in. I will describe them in some detail so you might anticipate the emotional adjustment period:

- **Emotional Pain**
    - When you encounter effects in your life that embody painful experience and eliminate them inwardly, as your mindset shifts in overall nature, a direct experience of pain-response can result.

- **The Crunch**
    - Imagine a child "throwing a tantrum," his/her body stiffened in frustrated defiance over some real or perceived inequity. The "Crunch" is a similar effect of clenched muscles and feelings of frustration.
    - As negating Mechanisms are perceived and released, the mind will focus on the highly meaningful, mostly intimate and powerful values that are involved. Through the process of healing, i.e., moving toward a cleaner mind state, emotion can swamp the mind with negative thoughts very much in the vein of the negation that had been cleared out, with the Crunch as a natural – though passing – response.

- **The Wipe-Out**
    - During the healing process you might experience a totally drained feeling, a loss of immediate vigor, interest and motivation to do anything.
    - This might be recognized as "depression." Indeed, depression is clearly indicative of powerlessness and frustration in realizing the will. In this case, though, as inner roots are dealt with and

eliminated, the Wipe-Out will pass if and as all elements are dispelled.

- **The Shake**
  - With release of negating Mechanisms, one might experience an energetically shaking hand or foot or tendency to rock back and forth.
  - Again, the emotional energy must dissipate. Given the configuration of the human body, there are limited movements through which to drain this release of energy.

- **Crying/Grimacing**
  - What more human trait is there for the process of exhausting emotional energy than crying? The grimace is an equal translation of emotional distress into facial expression. The exit of painful inner elements can certainly follow a path through tear ducts.

With experience, each of these will be recognized as a fleeting episode of emotional/physical release following the flush of negating mechanisms. All such Release Symptoms will pass and take the long term suffering along with them – provided you have found and dispelled all mechanisms involved.

Understand that whatever discomfort you encounter with the release of inhibiting elements, it is ***a great deal better*** than continuing to experience the pain of whatever the mechanism as its patterned stamp on your experience and relationships repeats itself indefinitely! (If, though, you have difficulty with any Release Symptom as too intense or unyielding, simply stop the inner cleansing, at least for a time, to let the emotional state settle.)

The Second Angle

Summing It Up

Your Journey inwards is a private venture. As you travel into the depths of Self, into the values, mechanisms and intangibles of mind, others who are not on their journey – at least not consciously, for exactly this journey is what life is ***for*** – will not understand your focus, your pointed conscious effort in the process. Interference by others or trying to convince them of the benefits of the inner venture – even loved ones with whom you would share your new understandings – may only deter Your Journey without benefiting the other. To delve very deeply, resolve your inner state, then display Crying, the Crunch or the Wipe-Out in front of others invites interference and questioning you may not find helpful.

So I will pass along an observation I made long ago: the whole of the Inner Journey is a very private venture. Proceed on your own – discuss life openly if you wish to, but delve inward on your own and release your counter-energy in private. You will understand what is happening; others might not.

Your Journey, Your Path

As I introduced you to tools and disciplines that were available to gain real improvement in your life – travel from the inner version of Kansas' flat plains to a place of more diversity and scenic interest – I showed you the basic limitations of each. Now you hold some degree of awareness for the mechanisms functioning, intangibly and subtly, during every moment of your life. And you recognize that delving to the inner roots is needed to really elicit change in your mindset and thus in your life.

So you **can** proceed towards real Freedom and Abundance, realize personal Authority in your life and bring yourself Joy – should you choose.

But if indeed you undertake the Inner Journey, you need to be wary of rocks, moss and roots you might trip on along Your Path. So let's expose some of them up front…

EoR – The Third Angle: Your Path

Hazards Along the Way

Imagine you enter an unfamiliar room where strangers are currently engaged in playing a board game. A seat is open. So you sit down and find yourself included in the action with your game piece placed on the board and moving about, although you don't know the rules...

Some of the other players who were playing before you joined in turn to you occasionally and explain with great assuredness what the purpose of the game is, how it is to be played, what is right and wrong, a good move or a bad one – but their descriptions are conflicting and confusing. The game proceeds even though you are unsure what is happening.

Often, even though you follow the players' advice faithfully, you find that you are penalized and lose points. Very often, doing exactly what you were told and planning out the cleverest of strategies based on what you know, you fail. You notice that some people succeed no matter what they do, while others can't do anything right. You try to copy how some of the others play, but it doesn't work the same for you.

Finally, you are abruptly informed you are out of the game – not really sure if you'd won or lost or even what constituted winning!

* * *

However frustrating and annoying that scenario seems – sounding much more like a nightmare than a game – if you look at what's happening in your life, that situation is pretty much what you have faced for as long as you can remember.

Since your earliest days in this life, you have been told by parents, by preachers and teachers, by the media, by older generations and by peers just what this game of life is about, how to play, how to win. Even worse, every story, every literary work or media expression has subtly communicated, and thus reinforced, core assumptions and cultural standards that you have also absorbed and woven into your world view – **mostly because *there was no alternate way available to look at things***!

Through that paradigm, passed on through countless generations, you learned very early that reality had to be manipulated to make it work how you wanted it to, learned generally to manipulate your mother (or other early care-giver) and expanded on explicit and implicit lessons as to how to manipulate people and things to get your way. Pray, struggle, work hard, get an education, threaten, force, take medicine and vitamins, listen to experts, cheat if you have to, compete, motivate people, dress and act in certain ways to impress others, protect yourself from bacteria and virus, kiss butt, conform, impress your superiors, obtain money to have power – these and a thousand other ways you were taught to control others and manipulate reality.

Think about it! Just as in the game above, you do all those things as you were taught, yet you still have troubles, illnesses, emotional pain, failures, frustrations. You are still unfree, never completely at ease, never truly at peace. You don't control your life in any way – your destiny is dictated by other people, by your body's spurious health, by your own shortcomings, by chance and accident and by a host of other apparent forces.

Looking at life in the previous Angle, considering your personal Journey inward to discern elements of your complex mindset and clear them out, I presented **specific steps** to take toward seeing the real flow, the inner-outer emergence of your nature into real events and relationships. As you make that Journey, however, Your Path will be wrought with many a subtle, illusory effect – like the mysterious game above – creating false truths, synthetic accomplishments and other hazards that may ***seem*** to be the next great, solid wonderment. Gurus and followers of ancient masters, guys in white robes with candles and religious leaders dressed up in red outfits and carrying scepters, self-help experts who have sold millions of books will be telling you how to play this game. But each discipline – many just noted in Angle Two – and each glittery, spiritual teacher will turn out to be just the next lesson, the next self-assured, advice-giving expert as in the hypothetical game above – and consequently will direct you down yet another dead end street.

One option you have is to wander off on your own, find those pseudo-truths and fall for them, one at a time, thereby learning your own lessons. You may, quite on your own, come to see through the phony explanations to perceive clearly how this game works.

The second option: I can just point out many of the false trails to you, expose the fallacious explanations and illusory notions, thereby saving you a lot of effort, disappointment and frustration.

That second option is what this Angle, Your Path, is about. The same caveats apply as earlier – my perspectives will likely differ from your notions. You can accept what Mom, Dad, the preacher and the scientist told you. Or you can expand your view well beyond their scope to see things **as they are**.

I would remind you that the most convincing illusions are the ones that appear most real – otherwise they wouldn't be illusory, and people would have long since figured out How Life Works. Fallacies underlying those illusions are equally difficult to detect until you see the constrained validity of the underlying precepts.

In any case, as you journey along, delving into the convolutions and complexities of your mindset, keep an eye out for the following hazards on Your Path…

The Pedestal

A Real Bust on Top

If you picture other people as superior to yourself, you will realize that mental image.

Putting a preacher, a saint, a prophet, an expert or ***anybody*** up on a pedestal in your personal view, fundamentally accomplishes nothing but the

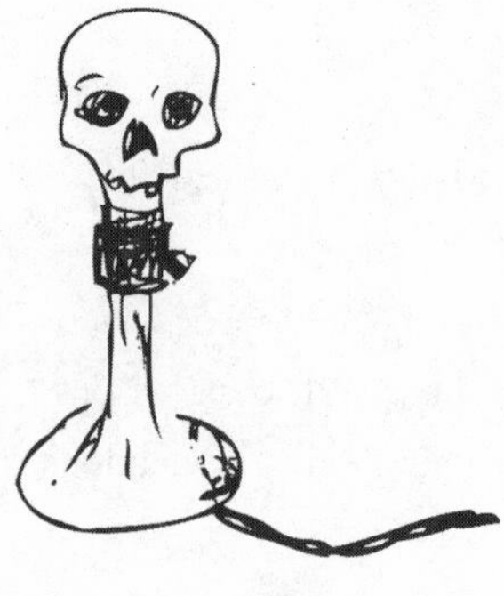

effect of putting ***you*** in a pit.

No human has a greater inherent capability of awareness than you have. There may be those who have come to a clearer perception of the nature and status of the Self than you. (A group that includes me, otherwise I ought to be reading your book!) But Your Path towards that greater perception is never promoted by bowing in subjugation to **any of them**, regardless of their perceived, outward status – ***never*** – not even if they, themselves, have promoted their own elevated position, presenting academic degrees, esoteric titles, overt spiritual paraphernalia and grandiose proofs of their status.

I'm not proposing you deceive yourself into an artificial, spiritual level you don't feel you have attained. I'm not saying to place yourself above others who seem so at ease, so spiritually together that they appear to be where you aspire to be.

But I must emphasize that the status you foment in your own mind, whether absolute or relative to others you evaluate, creates the course on which Your Journey will proceed. If you place that focus high, with emphasis on **your** innate value and natural endowed capabilities – which, again, are as complete and powerful as anybody's – you will promote a Journey that moves you through the pitfalls and illusions that appear along the way.

But if you enshrine somebody else as special, in some way superior, you yourself pale in your own view. And the path created by that notion leads toward an innate mediocrity in the self-image you hold.

The only one who truly belongs on a pedestal in your hall of fame is you, i.e., ***you***! It is the very self-image of confidence and value that will necessarily direct Your Path towards a rightful spot precisely on top of that pedestal.

Feelings of humility, piety and conservatism, whether sincere or feigned in order to fit into some spiritual model or to emulate niceties you were taught as a child, incorporate their own set of subtle restrictions and limitations into your life and Your Path. And that will be the case, should you choose to continue them or should you be so programmed by dogma you absorbed during youth that you have little apparent choice. Nature and the flow of natural events on this planet have no such shyness, no such reluctance to exhibit power and creative force.

So your playing a role of humility in reverence to – or emulation of – a perceived guru, teacher, preacher, master or god-incarnate savior is in vain, a self-defeating gesture.

Be **yourself**; trust in that Self to express your inner feelings and direct Your Path toward peace, self-realization and accomplishment. And never put that Self, within your own mental image, in a subservient position, bowing beneath some vaunted figure sitting up on a pedestal.

On the Conceptual Chamber

Trapped by the Trap

Subscribing to a religion typically creates an enclosed conceptual chamber within your belief structure that is extremely difficult to break out of. Indeed adhering to ***any*** stated philosophical paradigm creates an artificial chamber of comfort and definition that is difficult to escape, but religions tend to be much more emotionally ingrained than contemplative philosophies, based on their typically inherent, exclusive self-evaluation.

Understand that your belief system was well solidified during your childhood, formed in part by impressions of how Reality worked and in part by indoctrinating explanations by adults in your environment. Basically, the world-view that they held and lived by, you absorbed. Given no alternate explanation, it would have been extremely difficult for you to independently conceive of life working in a way radically different from the one your elders and their culture presented – and often enough, enforced with punishment and the threat of ostracizing you.

The nature of the psychological enclosure is quite subtle, but highly effective. Religions, principally the main, Middle Eastern-rooted versions,

Christianity, Judaism and Islam, typically state that events in your life are impelled by a higher power, a god figure. This power source is regarded as able to inflict on you reward or punishment – which may or may not happen until after your death. Many deeds may be regarded as though this god has prescribed them as forbidden and punishable – but a prime listing on the divine black list is ***the very act of questioning***.

Thus are you frozen into a mental chamber of religious thought: you were taught to fear the consequences of the very act of intellectual exploration that **could lead you to think** freely enough to actually see the fallacy of the original belief! You were indoctrinated into accepting a belief system that precludes the simple gesture of questioning its basic assumption. It's no wonder such religions carry on for ages. It takes considerable courage and self-esteem, plus some degree of initial Self-Awareness for any individual to break out.

In essence, there ***is*** no external judge to punish you, either now or after your death. There is no third-person, Supreme Being that sits offstage as sublime puppeteer, pulling strings, causing you troubles as punishment or otherwise afflicting your life with problems for any purpose. There is a mechanism to Reality, but it responds only to your nature, not the whims of an independent, ethereal consciousness with its own ego, its own agenda. Notions in the direction of such a god-figure are based in ancient superstitions and myths, age-old concepts that our ancestors of tens of thousands of years ago began by picturing god-like powers as causes of the natural effects around them.

You are free to think as you wish. The negative events that you encounter, ones that produce pain and suffering for you, are direct consequences of that same belief structure you hold in mind. Ultimately, that belief structure is within your power to change, when you come to perceive it and gain trust in your own ability to revise it. This means that, in the final scheme of things, you ***and only you*** are in ultimate control of your life.

But to make use of that control, you must come to perceive and deal with – i.e., change – the values and assumptions that constitute your belief structure. Among these comes first, without fail, breaking out of the conceptual trap that your beliefs may well have locked you into. If you do not do so, you will always encounter subtle doubts and fears that will keep you from perceiving your own nature, your own Self, your own innate creative power.

Elimination of Restrictive Beliefs

Cleaning House

The ability to believe something is the mental capacity to accept an ***idea*** in place of direct perception of the real thing. You don't need to "believe in" a hill or a tree, in pain or happiness, because you experience them. You perceive them as part of the Reality you encounter and the conscious Self that encounters it. You do need to believe in a god or in subatomic particles, because you don't perceive either of them directly. Basically, you have to accept somebody's explanation that they exist and their definitions as to the nature of those conceptualizations.

If you do accept the requisite explanations and definitions, then either a god or subatomic particles can **seem** to exist. They then supplant the Real in your perception – the ongoing encounter with events and relationships that is your life – and become a pseudo-reality, an illusion. If you stop believing in them, however – literally dispel them from your mindset – they cease to be. God is a conceptualization, an imagined source of what is really just a mechanism of inner-outer flow. And subatomic particles aren't real, solid particles at all, but relative energy-force subdivisions of apparent matter that exist only in context with their surroundings, their existence being based on ignoring all the interactive aspects of the rest of surrounding matter.

One vital aspect in the Path toward Clear Awareness is the beginning of differentiation between belief-induced appearance and Reality. In many ways I can illustrate illusions and point out artificial concepts that are commonly accepted as real, but the onus of recognition is for you to come to see these things as what they are. You will find illusions formed by your beliefs to be of two basic kinds: flat out **misinterpretations** of real world phenomena or **portions of Reality**, synthetically culled out of the entire Singular whole by ***being defined***.

Subtly but significantly, all of the illusions you currently hold appear real, many unquestionably so. So long as that remains the case, you will remain at your level and encounter the same problems and the same woes, perhaps in different forms, indefinitely.

The differentiation and subsequent purge of illusions you hold as real can only be accomplished by first recognizing the artificiality of the concept, then quietly acknowledging to yourself that it is indeed an illusion, not real – much in the same way as discerning any inner mechanism using techniques illustrated earlier.

Dealing with beliefs, however, can be psychologically difficult when your self-image rests on the illusion, when the childhood lessons that underlie the veracity of the belief lie embedded in the comfort of motherly assurance, the underlying threat of fatherly punishment or some other emotionally charged peripheral element.

Your Path depends on your fortitude in disengaging your mind from all the artificial images it holds in regards to Reality. The flow of Reality is an extraordinarily simple stream, however complex its ripples and eddies, cycled constantly from mind-content into real events back into mind via perception and experience. Any other perceived mechanism is a mind construct based on belief – in effect, an illusion.

You will not grow to Clear Awareness until you, as part and parcel of Your Path, consciously seek out and shed the beliefs that destroy that clarity of perception.

Focus on Reading and Media

Watch Where You Point Your Nose

It's impossible to take a good shower while standing knee deep in mud. You might get the top part of yourself clean, but a lot of you – including some rather significant parts – will still be mighty dirty when you are finished.

The Reality you need to become aware of is the one you directly encounter – the events and relationships of your life. Yet, very often, in an age where communication is so widespread that information is constantly available, you tend to dwell on an external barrage of facts, music, updates, warnings and expertise that are well removed from you. You process a near constant influx of information from the outside; it grasps your attention and points your conscious focus continuously toward information that has little or no bearing on your personal existence.

If all you ever hear is news about one disaster or another, the latest murder or rape, insurgency or famine, your trust in your environment and your potential well-being suffers. If your entertainment constantly depicts murder and crime, conflict and synthetic, contrived plots, your whole outlook suffers.

For every real murder in a city during the course of a year, two million people go home safely every night, love their families and help their neighbors. For every rape a million people make love and for every fire, a hundred houses are built. Good feelings, good intent, good people and progress surround you – yet the message abounding to your ready attention is one of negativity, of despair.

If you wish to use this lifetime in a constructive fashion, in the only life focus of real value to Your Path, you will turn your attention away from the constant negativity of remote events reported by the media to inform you, but which really only divert your attention away from that which is Real. That Reality, consisting of the events you encounter firsthand and the relationships you maintain in ongoing days, is your prime concern. If problems are encountered there, those problems are indicative of real elements of you that need attention. The problems of the extended world that do not impact you directly are **not you**.

Understand, those problems, the famines and disasters, warfare and injustice of the world, all indicative of widespread addiction to Struggle and Conflict, all symptomatic of separation of Self from Reality, will always be there – at least until major portions of humanity outgrow their restricted, conflict-based vision of the workings of Reality. Certainly you cannot solve the world's ills, cannot divert their problematic energies by your focus on their details. Only the problems you encounter in the daily course of your life can you deal with – and to dispense with those, in that they reflect your inner state, you must delve into their roots within yourself.

As you journey inward to clean your mind of its limiting values, if you focus your attention on the crud and debris of the world's disasters, you will be effectively taking a shower while standing deep in muck. A critical part of Your Path is the disengagement of your attention on the negative events as reported far and wide in a media that dwells in the negative and a refocus on aspects of your own life.

Accepted Sources of Information

Veracity 101

The scientific paradigm tells you that consciousness is based on brain function. This explanation holds that memories are stored by some synaptic or chemical means, and that your consciousness evolved that way through a long course of natural selection. Implications are that, when the brain dies, so you, the resultant self-identity, must cease to exist.

(It doesn't matter to science that the vast amount of information stored as memory – visual and audio, experiential, meaningful facts and knowledge, etc., over 50 years, i.e. over a billion waking seconds of time, including great detail of a three-dimensional visual field of diverse colors and impressions – is simply too much data for a simple biological unit to store, all the while allowing immediate access to any detail.)

At the same time, religion, for millennia the core basis of our evolving culture's world-view, speaks of your existence being at the hand of an independent consciousness, a god with the creative power to conjure you out of nothingness. Intrinsic within this view is a whole raft of consequences affecting you and your destination in this journey of life – purpose, meaning, judgment, consequence to your actions, etc.

(It doesn't matter to religion that the level of power and complexity of a god capable of conjuring up a universe with untold millions of galaxies, containing billions of stars and untold gazillions of planets, asteroids, etc., capable of monitoring all thoughts of all conscious entities so that he (He?) might judge those thoughts against an arbitrary moral scheme, would be vastly greater than any possible mindset predisposed to ***even care*** about what they thought – particularly when he (He!!) would have created them with those predispositions in the first place!)

You can be sure, regardless of your acknowledged beliefs, that your self-image and world perception include elements of ***both*** the scientific and religious views, for many aspects of these views are subtly built into cultural axioms and shared assumptions.

Unfortunately, both science and religion are loaded with fallacy in their views of how Reality works – as we will explore in Angle Four. But you hold them and their notions as valid, thus leaving you on the journey of life in rather dire straits – not only unaware of your destination, but also deceived as to the nature of your vehicle, puzzled as to the route, unaware of your abilities to avert or solve problems along the way and clueless as to what you should be doing to best arrive at what ***should be*** your destination. Clueless, that is, prior to encountering EoR…

* * *

One prime hindrance to your growth in awareness consequent to your exposure to these new ideas is your predisposition toward "expertise" – a conceptual quality endowed upon people who have been trained in specific endeavors. Understand that degreed people, those sporting doctorate degrees as evidence of expertise and accumulation of knowledge in some vein of man's conglomerate database of facts, got that recognition ***from other people***. Those other people held similar views and judged the bestowal of that degree based on the ability to absorb knowledge and reflect it back satisfactorily. The entire academic realm of our culture is based on shared imagery of commonly held views that are deemed valid and thus considered to be "knowledge."

This is not to look critically at the educational scheme of our traditional scholarly arena, but to point out that knowledge and communication of it, while a vital and valuable traditional accumulation through time, is ***not the key to understanding how your life works***. Knowledge is great in the shared experience of virtually unlimited aspects to the rich life forum we experience, but – if held as unquestionable "fact" – it does nothing but hinder a clear consciousness of your personal, intimate engagement of the real aspects of your life.

So be wary of whom you consider an expert. Becoming enamored with knowledge and the experts who teach the details will lead you ***off*** Your Path, not down it. By all means, study, read, communicate. But realize that all the "facts" you encounter, while they enhance life in providing depth and substance to experience, do not clarify your understanding of life's Flow. Clear Awareness of Reality is founded on undefined perception. Knowledge is pure definition. The two are not mutually destructive, so long as you remain aware that knowledge requires breaking Reality into a multitude of pieces by defining them and is thus a synthetic view, however useful.

Aware, all the while, that Reality is an interrelated Singularity, aware that all aspects function as a whole within the scope of your experience, aware that all events and relationships respond to your own mind content, you can freely enjoy the exposure to knowledge. But if your Consciousness is shattered into an objective viewpoint – sacred truths guaranteed by some expert – in which items and events seem separate, driven by chance or outside forces, then your orientation toward knowledge is a major **deterrent** on Your Path toward Clear Awareness.

Be Your Own Guide

The Following Message...

If you take a guided tour during your first visit to a museum – as opposed to wandering about on your own – you will cover a lot of the most interesting things. The guide will surely point out the more popular exhibits and cover many of the main features. He may, of course, without even noticing, focus on areas of his own particular interest. In a limited period of time, though, a guided tour will likely present a more rounded experience, touching on more of what the museum offers, than might be possible on your own.

But given the time – plus motivation and interest – you can delve much more deeply into detail, expanding in depth and breadth, by going about on your own. Without other tourists to distract and spend time on areas not of such interest to you, without the bias of the guide, without the time constraints of the tour, you can explore every aspect of every display you find compelling.

Life, in the exploration of its outer intricacies and the introspection into the inner mind that perceives it, is much like that museum. You can easily latch onto a preacher, guru or philosopher and get a guided tour – they're all more than willing to guide you for a price. There you will encounter much of interest and of value. But, much as with the museum tour, you will have the certain, if often subtle, bias of the guide presenting his particular angle on things. You will have the interference of the others of the group, not only distracting, but also interjecting their own views along the way.

Life, like the museum, can only be fully explored with the freedom to wander about unperturbed. You may listen to a guide as you go, refer to notes as may be helpful, but in the museum of Reality, you can only explore fully and clearly on your own.

You can never gain Clear Awareness by following anybody. The spiritual leader, dressed in fancy robes, burning incense and chanting esoteric phrases, reciting his rituals, is as lost in perceiving Reality and his role here as you. There may be value in his message, but the greater value is to be had from seeing clearly what he is – an individual who followed his own authoritative teachers right down the same path. So devoted was he to his museum guide that he became a living exhibit.

Without question, a yogi, preacher or philosopher might present isolated gems of wisdom beneficial to listeners less experienced in focusing on truth and meaning in life. But gems can be plucked from the mountain without having to first buy the mountain. Hear their truths, ponder them, then move on – what you are seeking is a perception of Self: who you are, **what**

you are. This Essence of Self is perceptible only by you. The more you absorb of the teacher's perspective, the farther away from Self you travel towards that person's stock paradigm.

No teacher, mystic, philosopher, priest, pope, yogi, psychologist, guru, seer or metaphysician ever had **innate qualities** of higher consciousness than you. Consciousness, as a full perceptive quality of sensing the surrounding Reality, is not a variable to be quantified, like strength of muscle or intelligence. Consciousness, as awareness of an engaged Reality, is an inherent attribute of ***what you are***. A mystic may have cleared, intensified or – more likely – simply reoriented his awareness in some fashion so that he appears elevated in spiritual qualities. But undoubtedly, if he presents himself to you as a master, speaking of higher planes of awareness and spiritual realms, he has only traded his old illusions for a fancy, esoteric new set. In any case, he has no greater inherent quality of **absolute awareness** than you have.

How can you ever grow beyond the level of the model you set your ideal to? How can you become ever wiser if you consciously build into your self-image that across from you sits one who is magnificently wiser? How can you hope to see exhibits outside the guide's itinerary?

You can never attain Clear Awareness by following anybody, only by following your own Self. By setting clearly in your mind an intent that you are examining life and **leading yourself** will you travel down a path right for you. Only by learning to trust your inner impulses and your own innate wisdom will you travel surely down the path towards clearly ***seeing*** and ***being*** your natural Self.

Explore the living museum that is your life. Do so, in no hurry and on your own. No other guide, not real, not spiritual, not external, can present you with the essence of what you are.

A Table of Contents

What do You Have in Mind?

As oft observed, your only true leverage in determining the nature of the events you encounter is your ability to affect the content, i.e., the comprehensive quality state, of your mind – the values, the self-image, the world-image you hold. Thus, gaining perspective on specifically what "mind content" encompasses enables Your Journey toward an awareness of how mind contents become realized – thereby shedding some light onto Your Path.

Your mind contains an enormous accumulation of impressions and understandings. Forming a highly cohesive (if not always internally consistent) set, these value-aspects comprise the structure through which you view Reality and via which you interpret what you encounter – a complex of mental imagery that is often referred to here as "belief system." All impressions you absorb through your senses are filtered through this structure for interpretation, which leads to how you perceive and evaluate it, how you react to it and thus, how you formulate a response to it. That response, either **in line with** or **overriding** your natural impulses, will derive from the total nature of content of this inner structure.

While many fundamental aspects of mind have been touched upon, an organized overview should be helpful. The inner realm contains:

- **Core Functional Information**
    - **Subconscious store** – all information pertaining to your current life, body function, interaction with environment and others – not learned, but undergirding your existence through this (and any) life venture.
    - **Vital data** – information being processed from the ongoing flow, absorbed, insofar as is applicable, by the subconscious store.

- **Knowledge**
    - **Beliefs** – illusory mental constructs, generally put into place by

influential authorities during childhood, as to many aspects of how life is supposed to work.

- **Facts and Figures** – learned information pertaining to all aspects of life, accumulated throughout a lifetime, valid within the confines of the incarnation, at best, totally invalid at worst.

- **Definitions**
  - **Descriptions** – portions of reality conceptualized as things, actions, words, etc., held as real and appearing so, ***based on acceptance of the definition***, such as…
    - ✓ Complex paradigms meant to explain the workings of reality.
    - ✓ Agents "out there", depicted within the definitions, which seem to function as forces in powering reality or sources of creative impact.
  - **Language Capabilities** – a complex set of rules for converting concepts rapidly into symbolized form, either verbal utterances or physical script.
    - ✓ This transliteration from pure conceptualization into expressed notion can take place considerably more rapidly than the ability to actually express the words.
    - ✓ Built-in, causal illusions influence your way of thinking, in that every language carries a stylized formulation of notions and a constricted, finite field of potential event-understanding.
  - **Images** – formulated visions in your mind-view.
    - ✓ Your own nature and all details about your physical and emotional self, abilities, talents, as elements of your self-image.
    - ✓ Your role in society, family and peer groups including hierarchical references as to how you and your culture fit into the greater scheme of things – all forming your world-view.
    - ✓ Other sources of power – including purely imaginary ones, like gods and external forces.
    - ✓ Appended evaluations, by hope and judgment, as to what all those elements **should be** or could be, as opposed to clearly are.

- **Value Judgments** – meaning-based regard for various aspects of reality, covering the whole of experience in evaluating its meaning, pertinence and impact.
- **Assumptions** – underlying yet generally unfounded mind connections supporting how Reality works within your immediate understanding.
  - ✓ Often very subtle, these typically cultural standards, support your belief structure with highly illusory, generally synthetic and typically unworkable notions.
  - ✓ Insubstantial and nefarious to begin with, assumptions are generally camouflaged ***by the beliefs they support***.
- **Means to Manipulate** – learned procedures for initiating actions towards objects or other people, considered to cause a desired outcome.
- **Hopes** – focal points of desire that you want to realize, but which seem to lie outside of your realm of control (also tied into your world-view of what forces and sources affect reality).
- **Fears** – discomforting mind elements resulting from definitions, beliefs and self-image, wherein some element is perceived as an external source out of the realm of your "control," and thus threatening.
  - ✓ These will be subtly, but powerfully, tied into whatever forces you believe impel reality and whatever sources of authority you imagine are out there exercising those forces.
  - ✓ Again these fears may be directed at purely imaginary forces or at perceived sources that are actually not self-initiating sources.
- **Authorities** – defined sources, whether individuals or groups, whose:
  - ✓ Sources of explanations you accept as true and/or,
  - ✓ Apparent power holds sway over your action and being.
- **Mysteries** – areas of life you don't understand or can't explain, i.e., which accepted beliefs and assumptions noted above don't cover or in which they are inherently conflictual or mutually exclusive.

- **Memories** – current versions of life experiences that carry a value and a compiled, but changeable, meaning.
  - **Variability** –
    - ✓ While "recall" can access ***all events of your life***, memories are considerably more variable and flexible than often regarded.
    - ✓ In that they are highly oriented to your current mindset, memories evolve through your life, adapting in elicited effect to reflect your state of mind in the present.
    - ✓ Although reflective of explicit events, memories' flexibility allows for much redirection in the present to nullify any ongoing negative impact from memories of undesirable aspects of life.
  - **Access** – ability to "get at" any of the above, in that various inner mechanisms such as fear or restrictive elements of self-image can block or repress recall. (But all memories are ***there*** and can certainly be retrieved through Angle Two's methods.)
- **Intent** – the object of your will, but often compromised by your self-image and other inner elements to fall short of your Hopes.

(**Tastes**, inherent leanings toward certain music and art forms, interests in hobbies and various other specialized avenues of culture, and **propensities**, character traits that comprehensively embody your nature, are innate characteristics of the total Self as oriented in this incarnation. They transcend the mindset per se, but the latter will reflect their orientation.)

Regardless of your intelligence or aptitude, the above element types exist in a structured scheme within your mind. Most of the underlying elements were put into place as you grew through childhood; these were generally cemented there by enhancements along the way conforming with the shared core definitions and reinforcing them.

It is worthy to reemphasize that your current world-view can contain elements that are absolutely inconsistent with each other: You may believe in a god who makes things happen in a way meaningful to his (her?) plan, yet accept that there can be accidental events outside the scope of that plan. You may accept that bacteria and virus cause illness, but that some gesture can be made to affect the flow of energy to counteract that. You may believe that Jesus of Nazareth was god incarnate, yet fundamentally disregard in practice what his teachings contain.

In pondering this inner Table of Contents, you will see that there are no solid dividers between them – beyond Core Information, all the rest are based on meaning and value pertaining to you and the world you encounter. Knowledge and Definition both stem from learned input, meaning accumulated from the earliest time of your life. Memory is a personal regard for experienced events and relationships interpreted through the value orientation of the belief structure held. And Intent will formulate, consistent with tastes and propensities, based on all the rest.

Looked at as a whole, then, it must be clear that **all aspects of mind** center on ***meaning and value***. Thus, your existence, at its base nature of being, its core Essence, consists of elements of meaning, of interrelated value.

As you begin to grasp the full implication of that, it should reinforce the direction Your Path takes towards clearly discerning not only the whole of your Self, but in delving into each aspect as illustrated in Angle Two. For clearly, if your base nature consists entirely and absolutely of meaning and value, all of man's illusory quests to glorify defined gods, refine ever more elaborate paradigms and engender ever more convoluted schemes to manipulate a resultant reality are a cosmic waste of time.

Notice, too, that "thought" is not on the list. Each thought is an assemblage of meaning and value entering or leaving the mindset. While thoughts are unbounded in scope, types of thoughts are surprisingly few: A thought may result from outward mind-focus as it either compares encountered events to its underlying belief structure, i.e., evaluates real experience or formulates a response based on understandings set by that structure. A thought may reflect inward focus, as the mind entertains purely imaginative regard, eclipsing the real with pure imagery. A given thought may pull together memories and knowledge to fulfill the pointed meaning query of the thinker or may spontaneously erupt from within, based on meaningful requirements etched into that Table of Contents.

So the act of thinking – however frequent, however intense, effective or focused – is purely oriented by of the whole of mind content.

So, when you began to read The Essence of Reality, what did you have in mind? Well, structurally it's still there. But it might already have changed a bit in quality.

Money, The Measure, not the Measurer

Cash in Your Chips

Money is not the great corrupter it is made out to be, nor is it the source of power and influence. Money is not causal at all, but rather, along with the entire role it plays in your life, is a reflection of your nature – purely an ***effect***. While it beckons, enticing, as the goal of so many people's lives, in actuality, it is but an ever-glittering mirage, an illusion, hollow but virtually parasitic to the superficial and imperceptive mind.

Your level of wealth is a cumulative effect of your mindset. Many of the pertinent aspects relate to your personal complex of values, but some are essentially universal, shared among individuals at a cultural level. Without question, the amount of money you control indicates a measure of your personal estimate of your power and status in the community. Your money, how you obtain it and how ***easily*** you obtain it reflect aspects of self-confidence, your view of the nature, fairness and function of the cultural environment around you. Those inner aspects can be seen clearly if you just observe your thoughts and feelings – and understand what you are looking for.

A complex, ongoing dialogue takes place within your mind when you encounter the need or opportunity to spend money, whether for the usual purchase of a necessity, for entertainment, for non-essential items or whatever. Listen to yourself think on these occasions, and you will see what I mean. This dialogue contains many of the factors that money represents to you, mixed with your self-image – and the results of the dialogue reinforce the effect, whatever it is.

Suppose you need a pair of shoes and start looking in a shoe store. You see a pair you like and immediately check the price. "Too much money," you think and look for a pair on sale. In that fleeting episode, much indeed is revealed about the self-imposed limits to your wealth. For the implication is not only confining to the expression, let alone fulfillment, of your desires, but solidly reinforces the personal evaluation that you are too poor to afford something you want. And ***that*** evaluation mixes in with your whole self-image of your capability and cleverness.

It is the total image that gets translated into the events and relationships that constitute your life. With evaluatory thoughts like that simple consideration of shoes, you reinforce the very nature of your lack of abundance.

Old Age thinking pits you ***against*** reality. Taught all your life to see the world as separate and removed from you, you believe you must manipulate elements of your environment to survive or prosper. With that mentality, you must economize, must scrimp to extend the money you have. As you outgrow the Old Age, you come to realize that ***the very mentality*** of economizing and efficiently managing your money promulgates limits to your wealth.

Carrying the old mentality, you lead yourself into events that drain your resources. Enhancing your mindset by eliminating restrictive inner elements, you will spur your creativity to lead toward paths of abundance – particularly since that growth, as indicated here in EoR, ***requires*** consideration of and elimination of the limiting mechanisms. But having traveled that Journey, you will encounter relationships that promote your benefit, you will succeed with your plans, and you will not have to count your pennies to do so.

So look at your life, then listen to your thoughts. Do you skimp and save, constantly telling yourself you can't afford to buy or do things you want to? Do you always look for bargains, pirated software, discount tickets; do you skimp on "luxuries" and seek things for free? Or do you buy what you want, pay for shareware and packaged programs, buy things rather than look to get them cheaper?

All these things reveal your nature in action. The way to outgrow them, of course, is not to engage in inner conflict or self-denial as to the presence of limiting inner elements – but rather to find the roots in your mindset, just as with all restrictive inner mechanisms and eliminate them via autosuggestion, instead of continually recycling them via autosuggestion.

As you grow in the process, coming to perceive your stance embedded in a Reality that reflects that inner nature, you will shed those limiting perceptions and spur your ability to enjoy the abundance that is imminently available.

You are the cause of all things you experience. Money is only ever an effect, but, so being, it is a clear, profound reflection of your self-perception and self-image, of your total inner picture of Self and Reality.

On Passing Awareness to Your Children

What You Are Trumps What You Say

Clear Awareness, as I have emphasized often, is not an aggregation of greater knowledge. It is not a study in philosophical precepts that I can teach you by means of explanation. Quite the opposite: Awareness is a direct, immediate perception of life that is only ***hindered by*** the rational side with its grasp clinched on any such account. Thus, any explanation offered here is oriented to broaden the reader's perspective, not narrow it, to break down restrictive definitions, not to create a new set of them.

So how, given that you at least appreciate the value of such Awareness, can you be sure to communicate this attribute to your children, even as you endeavor to grow on a personal level? You certainly want to pass on as little as possible of the personal limitations and cultural hang-ups you learned along the way, for you wish only the best for your children. But how do you assure them of the greatest gift of all: Consciousness, an attribute that will set them on a path toward freedom, toward uncompromised love, toward satiation of their desires and fulfillment of their potential?

Much of your interaction with others in daily life emerges from a need to control the events of your unfolding experience. You've learned many,

many mechanisms for getting others in your life to do things that will lead to an outcome you desire. A great deal of that is built on relationships within the cultural standards our civilization holds. You have certain control over others in a workplace setting, in a community setting, in a family setting. Likewise, others can control you within the scope of various relationships you maintain on an ongoing basis.

Your children fall into a natural relationship scenario with you. There are obvious ways in which you control (or ***try*** to control) them. There are subtle ways in which they have learned to manipulate your actions. The relationship is indeed subtle in most meaningful ways – much of the control and attempted control happens in non-verbal communication, and much has been already thoroughly established at a very early time of the childhood phase of your offspring, while you yourself are steeped in your own traits that go back to your early life.

Within the scope of your relationships with your children, you communicate very much information and pass equally strong effects. But little of it is done verbally in a sense of teaching a literal lesson. Much more is played out in the whole picture, most of which again is unobserved by either you or your children.

When you try to control your children for whatever rational purpose by strictly enforcing a set of imposed rules, you only teach them ***control*** as a means, with conflict and force (remember the inner Mechanisms of Angle Two?) as background. You pass the unmitigated message that ***forces*** outside of them – namely you at that point – can control their actions, can force them to do something inconsistent with their own will.

Ultimately, you will have unconsciously passed your fears, beliefs and cultural attitudes along to your offspring by installing those inner Mechanisms – Suggestion, Force, Motivation, etc. – just as you hold them. The controlling "you," now meting out punishment for yet again slopping food all over the kitchen, in later phases of their lives, becomes their teacher, their spouse, their boss penalizing them – for it is the ***pattern*** that gets imprinted, not the simple verbal lesson you would like to communicate.

When you compromise your child's integrity by inflicting pain, the lesson is that it is a justifiable means of control; that invariably engenders a corresponding inner Mechanism in their mindset. Whatever you have punished them for is irrelevant – it is the act of force and punishment that constitute the lesson. If you reward them for being "good" (as defined by you), the delivered bundle is more palatable, but the message is the same, although the Mechanism becomes Motivation. In any case, the message is ***control***, for you manipulate them to conform to your rules, society's standards or other factors in bypassing their own natural impulses and drives.

* * *

So how do you teach your kids Awareness – to trust in themselves, to love without judging, to expect health without having to manipulate their bodies with drugs, to expect and accept abundance, not eternal struggle? Simply put: ***you can't*** – unless you have that Awareness yourself. In that case, you don't have to "do" anything – just be yourself.

What you ***are*** attracts the quality of events and relationships into your life. Your children reflect your nature as much as any other aspect of your life – likely more intensely and intimately so. Once they have come into your life, your children reflect your nature in its many aspects: they will live out your pains; they will form your conflict, formulate your frustration, embody your struggle – if you comprise those qualities. Or they will lift your spirits and fulfill your joy, if you are that.

What you teach your children in facts and equations can enhance their engagement of the cultural experience, but it has little effect on their character and total mindset in comparison to **what you are**. For ***what you are*** is what gets communicated to your offspring from the birth moment of suddenly being intertwined in each other's lives, through every gesture, every act, every moment of relationship.

So the **only** way to induce clarity of Awareness to your children is to ***have it***. Given a clear view of Self, all your actions, all your values, all your breadth and depth of heart and love will be communicated in every gesture, every act. And given that, control and punishment are never needed.

Wise Old Teachings

Are They?

Walking through a Pennsylvania forest late in the year, you will pass an abundance of trees, treading over the countless leaves they've shed in the past couple months. The shapes of these fallen leaves are sundry, and the variations on those shapes are unlimited – indeed no two leaves are identical. Still, the maple, the ash, the chestnut, the oak – each has its characteristic quality.

Suppose, though, you seek to find one of the grandest of trees: say, an elm. Standing bare in the stark, gray dampness of nearing winter, the elm looks much like all the others. How would you ever discern one from all the other varieties?

Right – you look for some elm leaves! Despite the long churning by the

Autumn winds, the elm leaves will likely be clustered near to their source. And the one thing you can be absolutely sure of is that elm leaves only ever fall from an elm tree.

So finding an elm turns out to be pretty simple. Hmmm – except for one thing: you have to know what an elm leaf looks like…

* * *

Humans have been recording their thoughts in written form for a good three thousand years. Oral traditions in the form of myths, tales and epic stories – many with a moral or other values interwoven into their text – carry thoughts from even older times. Within all the accounts from all the voices that survive to echo about our cultural awareness many clear and pertinent thoughts from many perceptive individuals have passed through generation after generation relatively intact. But a lot of invalid drivel has survived as well – indeed a lot more of ***that*** than the perceptive reflections.

So how do you tell the difference? Suppose Plotinus had a clearer, more intimate view of How Life Works than did Mohammed, but just wasn't as good at expressing it? Or he didn't have the aggressiveness to spread his views with as much vigor. Suppose Anaximander had been wiser than Socrates or Spinoza, but his words, misunderstood by his contemporaries, were not recorded clearly and survive only in ancient Greek texts covered with dust in a museum somewhere.

What would it be like to have actual texts composed by Jesus of Nazareth, instead of dim accounts, recorded by third parties several decades after Jesus spoke them? How different would they be – how much more perceptive? And, indeed, how could you even judge that?

On the other hand, words from Gautama the Buddha survive pretty much intact. These are revered by millions of his followers to this day. Does that make them right? Does that assure they are wise? By the way, who translated them into your language? Was he perceptive enough to grasp Gautama's real meaning?

Wise men... Many have come, spoken and gone their way. Lao Tzu,

Whitman, Plato, Nietzsche, Thales, Yepes, Krishnamurti, Eckhart, Descartes, Aristotle, Shakespeare, Augustine, Confuscius, Kant, Böhme, Merton, Dante... They saw with varying degrees of clear vision, spoke with the voice they had to those who would listen and passed through the exit gate. But however perceptive they were, for every one of them were a thousand who spoke as loud or louder, despite seeing **much less clearly**.

* * *

For every elm leaf on the forest floor lie a thousand larger, more visible other leaves. How, then, do you find the elm leaf to discern the elm tree with certainty?

An elm tree really isn't an "elm tree." That's just a name, just a verbally uttered sound we use to represent it. Each elm is really a portion of Reality that exists within the context of the other trees, along with the soil, the air, the rain, the seasons on earth and an ecology that blends all that in an ongoing, ever-changing form. In the Spring, the tilt of the earth brings Pennsylvania into a more direct angle of sunlight, warming its ecosystem in a timeless flow that brings slumbering, living juices from storage in the roots up through the grand trunks of such trees as the elm – and leaves sprout forth to greet and absorb this renewed energy.

If you walk the Pennsylvania forest in the spring, you will see that reawakening. Having seen and breathed and experienced, you will become a part of it. And if you walk again in summer, you will know intimately the leaves of the elm. They are small, elongated, jagged on the edge, but unique of all the great trees. Having seen them form, having watched them drip from the early rains, unfurl with the lengthening days, then simmer in the humidity of the hot summer day, you will know them when they fall as those days wane in length and warmth.

Wisdom in the words of others is like those leaves: you can recognize it only by knowing yourself how it appears, by identifying it through the inherent wisdom **you hold within**. If you understand life by living it, seeing clearly how Reality unfolds in your experience and perceiving the Self who you are ***just as clearly***, only then will you know, of the multitude of both wise and foolish who went before, who it was who could see clearly as well.

If you do not see clearly yourself, you can only judge blindly based on the hazy opinions of others, on popularity, on catchy or poetic phrasing, on the power of presentation or other superficial qualities, who was truly wise and perceptive.

And the consequence to that is, you can never **attain** a Clear Awareness of life's flow by absorbing and following Old Teachings, however revered by our culture, however vaunted by institutions and fancy buildings, however nice they sound, because you must already hold adequate wisdom in order to even identify it. Unless you can tell which expressions are wise **because you are aware of life's nature *yourself*,** you will invariably be soundly, profoundly fooled.

Authority

The Subject is You

The word "Authority" refers to two rather differentiated aspects of life. Both, as interpreted by you and integrated into your mindset, are vitally important to the quality incorporated into events and relationships you encounter.

In one usage, Authority indicates a determinative, causal direction of power from a personal standpoint. In this regard, your level of authority reflects your inherent ability to imprint your desired effects on the experiences you encounter. The other meaning attached to the word "Authority" refers to an expertise, an extensive familiarity with the subject at hand.

The power directive angle has a lot to do with you creating your life, but would be better examined after the expertise side is looked into…

* * *

The story has it in New Testament documents, that chief priests and elders of the establishment of the time approached Jesus of Nazareth, querying on what authority he was acting and who gave him that authority. They were looking, as do most closed-minded adherents in any particular field, for reference to sources they accepted as "experts" – in this instance, sources in the teachings that had been passed down to them from prophets who had gone before.

Therein lies a reference to validity that spans our traditional ways of considering any subject with the intent to accept or reject it. **Who is *an accepted authority* in the field**, an expert, and based on what credentials? They wanted Jesus to show them that he had studied all the accepted references to the traditional Law and Prophets, such that he could reiterate what they already believed.

This has been the great barrier to acceptance, by their peers, of the teachings from any of the masters who have come along – breaking the listeners away from archaic understandings that inhibit their ability to see clearly. (Jesus, in that account, was too clever to fall for their ploy; he gave them back a question he knew they would be reluctant to answer, then simply withheld his own answer to their original demand. In effect, as we will soon explore, Jesus' authoritativeness was based on seeing things more clearly than his peers.)

It is necessary, if one wants to proceed toward clarity of perception, to understand the shallow and synthetic nature of "knowledge" in any field and therefore the thinness of expertise that any authority on any subject would have.

If you consider the subject of history, for example, knowledge consists of a collection of supposed "facts," including dates, descriptions and interpretations of events significant to the flow of culture. But those descriptions, while often given de facto consideration as reliable if commonly accepted in a particular culture, originated ***only ever*** in **personal accounts**, either passed on by verbal description or written some time subsequent to the event. These accounts are ***always*** oriented and colored to some degree – and possibly extensively – by the bias of the observer and pick up subsequent distortion by any later turnover through translation or compilation. As cultural attitudes and values evolve, such accounts will be again revised to suit newer interpretations.

History, in other words, is not the carved-in-granite collection of objectively gleaned accounts and factual depictions it would seem. It is a collection of passed-on, subjectively perceived and interpreted experiences, often retold numerous times and invariably revised according to the latest reteller, thus subjected to his/her bias and currently fashionable historical perspectives.

Thus, history is rather ***an illusion*** **of established fact**, based on accepted sources. You will note that historical accounts vary widely from country to country according to the perspective and, again, change regularly in any given culture based on current values. It's not just that different people see history differently, i.e., interpret facts differently – it's that **subjective accounts** ***are all that really exist!*** There is no absolute truth about history, no objective record of events, no real "facts" – only personal accounts.

Try to grasp that fully before you proceed. History, as a recording of facts, is an illusion. It is a compilation of subjective accounts, nothing more.

Now, ***any*** such field can be so considered, whether a scientific endeavor, a philosophical genre or any other. They each consist of accounts and definitions, reported and often recorded in great volumes of tomes. But each word of each account in each subject was written by a human, based on a mixture of reports and concepts from other sources along with, perhaps, some personally encountered or observed experience – ultimately a subjective account.

Thus, an authority in any of these fields, is someone who has absorbed a great deal of other accounts, subtly or overtly adding to the mixture yet another bias – his/her own. It does not matter in the least what academic honors, advanced degrees or exhaustive research went into the authoritative expertise of an individual in any field of "knowledge." All that knowledge is a reiteration of the personal report – however complex, however universally acknowledged, however ordained or proven or verified – of other humans. A doctorate degree is granted, based on the agreement/opinion of a team of individuals who sit in judgment; it is awarded by an institution (which consists of individuals) empowered by cultural consensus (given by other people) to grant such a degree. That doctorate doesn't signify anything but an agreement that the awardee fits into the accepted pattern of expertise.

Now, if ***any*** subject matter is susceptible to the vagaries of distortion and the illusion of authority, it is the consideration of the life experience itself, as revealed in the documentation of philosophy, religion and science.

It is in this regard that the queries of the establishment of Jesus' time would question his authority. It was **they**, the priesthood of the time, who considered ***themselves*** to be the only authorities, based on their extensive study of the traditional, esteemed teachings of their predecessors and, of course, their corner on the rather lucrative market of colloquial priesthood.

And here, of course, the illusion forms. The chief priests, teachers of the law and elders who questioned Jesus were not authorities on **How Life Works**; they were only experts on a body of traditionally accepted, but artificially generated, laws, rules and definitions passed down to them. None of those laws or truths originated from any god, Yahweh or otherwise, but from individuals who ***believed*** themselves to be spokespersons for that conceptualized deity (probably, or else they were just bilking the system) and had the charisma to be so accepted among their peers.

A clear perception of this condition is vital to opening your mind to new perspectives. Revelations and supposed insights into the "nature of god" are personal accounts, totally biased by the belief structure held by the saint or prophet. The course of religious development of, in this instance, the ancient Hebrews, was a process of building on ever more complex concepts of what their god-notion incorporated (see Angle Four), ever more defined dogma and ritual, ever more ingrained cultural biases. Expansion of that mind-image continued to build, generation after generation.

Jesus' authority rested solely on an ability to see life somewhat clearer than his peers. He was trying to communicate to them something about how life worked beyond their archaic rituals and primitive views of the life experience. The priests and elders – certainly the most intense adherents to the traditional paradigm in that culture (and direct beneficiaries of the power behind the religious organization) – would ***never*** have accepted Jesus' clearer views, nor his self-professed status of authority.

* * *

In this same regard, you or others might question ***my*** authority to speak about life. Where, after all, is my doctorate in philosophy? Where is my training in psychology? How can I question the theologians, whose scholarly training and advanced theological degrees lend such credence to their status, while I have no such formal training in the esoteric, inner studies of church archives? How can I speak openly about aspects of mind not even considered by psychology subdivisions of medical science?

In terms of understanding life, all those knowledge-based compilations rest entirely on belief structures; as such, as synthetic tidbits of mindset, relying on shared, agreed-upon veracity, they ***interfere with perception*** – they don't enhance it. The preacher, priest, shaman, rabbi or guru is trained, not to see life clearly, but to absorb vaunted accounts held as the only truth, the base definition on which to rely. Thus, none of these "authorities" report on How Life Works; they single-mindedly reiterate accepted, pre-conceived paradigms. The psychologist, the historian – any academic in any field – does the same and is rewarded with a degree granted by others who accept the same paradigm, believe the same illusions, honor the same authority.

(Of course, in religious studies the adherence to accepted teachings is ***particularly*** intense, since it doesn't have to rely on verifiable tenets.)

Passing their learned material on to you, they implant on your mind image an artificial paradigm that, once accepted, will become the defining scope of veracity ***for you*** – whatever it may be. The bush native of Africa or Australia will have his explanation in mind, just like the nuclear scientist or Christian Theologian does, just like the Hindi guru or the Eskimo shaman does, and it will appear to work in terms of his relationship to his life format, just as well as the others do.

In fact, **there is no *functional* difference** between these mind-image-explanations, however they differ in apparent meaning.

But my accounts here differ from any such body of religious doctrine, definition of particle interaction or philosophical treatise. I don't define, don't reiterate any prior expert as an authority, don't submit proofs to satisfy some previously established and accepted paradigm, don't re-establish artificial concepts. I have come to see through all that for the synthetic quality of the wisdom it would present itself to be. My authority in speaking comes from a direct and clear perception of what's going on in life, having eliminated psychological adherence to all the many artificial images commonly accepted.

So, will any of the "chief priests" or "elders" of my time acknowledge my authority to speak about life? Hardly. And those authorities have multiplied considerably in number during the two millennia from Jesus' culture to mine. At that time, singular religious institutions had come to dominate most cultures, with but a few isolated areas where freer philosophical expressions could be uttered. Now, numbered among the experts are many realms of scientists, innumerable religions, both eastern and western in origin and bent, and a philosophical backdrop of shared beliefs that subtly draw concepts from many traditions.

But there ***are*** those whose intent is to come to see clearly How Life Works – with perhaps you among them. These words serve to accelerate their (your) Journey through the hazards of growth that offer up illusions in their path.

But it is never so much for you, the reader, to acknowledge ***my*** status of authority on life, but for you to become an authority ***on your own***. And that is done, not by memorizing my accounts, nor by emulating my state of mind (whatever you imagine that to be), nor by following me as somebody special, but by clearing away debris clouding your own awareness. Within that debris, our traditional reverence to accepted, venerated authorities is one of the greatest hindrances to awareness that exists.

* * *

The human never walked the face of this planet who saw life more clearly than I. But I didn't grow into that level of Clear Awareness by accepting anybody or any body of knowledge as an authority. And you won't get there at all until you can dispose of your attachments to authoritative figures whose aura of expertise is an illusion.

Authority, Another Angle

Surreal or Imaginary – Take Your Pick

Man's traditional quest to understand life carries some other odd angles that are vital to make note of on Your Path. Having considered main-line, accepted academic and religious authorities, several sources of "enlightenment" other than compiled rational explanations commonly recur in various cultures and at various times. Some of these might be rolled into formal religions or religious attitudes, while others might provide a springboard away from traditional thinking, at least ostensibly.

I will list these and proceed to consider the level of reliability offered by these sources of apparent authority generally – and if need be, specifically.

- **Spirit World** – often revelations, channeled by mediums or revealed through occult practices like Ouija boards or crystal balls, or via contact with the "spirit world" are given great authority by virtue of their mystic source.
- **Unconscious mind** – much can be attributed to powers of mind, reached through some esoteric trance or exotic paraphernalia, that are seemingly deeper than the normal, waking intellect can reach, i.e., more perceptive than the normally considered self.
- **Higher Force/God** – religions have been founded on dictation from individuals who have claimed to directly channel the word of some god or other.
- **Ancient peoples** – old accounts seem to carry enormous weight in the minds of some and gain authority over generations as their story evolves in cultural basis.

Let's consider:

Spirit Sources

When you go swimming you exercise, have fun, splash water on your friends, whatever. Then you get out of the pool. But when you get out, you can't race the other swimmers, can't splash them anymore. It's time to go shower, dry off and head home. You can go back into the water and swim another day.

When you die you certainly don't cease to exist, but you cease to operate under the identity you held during that lifetime. In effect, you hop out of the pool. The time comes for that. You've played your games, finished your races, splashed your friends. It's time to dry off and head home. What you take with you is significant – your love, your growth, your essence in terms of value and meaning. But you leave the pool behind and leave the people in it.

The life format provides extraordinary interplay with others during the lifetime – exchange of ideas and emotional encounters, accomplishment, teamwork, positive and negative interaction. But communication with those who have left the pool can be illusory. Yes, your loved ones still exist, but not as they were in the temporal space, in the pool.

If you go looking for Spirit Guides, for lost loved ones, for guidance from Jesus, for Ouija answers, for angels or whatever non-corporeal sources, you will encounter an illusion constructed of your own mind's image of reality. The input you receive will be built on your hopes and expectations less than on functional Reality. (By the same token, if your world-view – perhaps more accurately "other-worldly-view" – features evil spirits out to do you harm, that input can be equally negative based on your fears alone!)

Still, people often place great reliance on dictates produced by communication with spirits or other disembodied souls. Indeed, some such channeled information has provided significant insight into the mind and workings of reality. But much more has been distorted fallacy, curiously reminiscent of the mindset of the spiritualist. Did that channeled info really come from another entity or just deeper portions of the subconscious of the one channeling? In any case, does it make an observation more valid if viewed from a spirit's perspective? It might appear so to an imagination steeped in generations of superstition and misunderstanding. It would seem that the dead can see more clearly without the limitations of sensory perception and a focus biased toward the "real."

But when we leave the pool, we carry our fins and snorkels along. Running Bear, the trusted Indian Spirit Guide, is no farther along the trail than when he arrived at the Happy Hunting Grounds – and if he still imagines himself, now disincarnated, to be an Indian, he would hardly be worth listening to. In reality, though, ***can*** he tell you anything right now? The expectation that he can will certainly create a very convincing appearance of it.

Would my perspectives on life, communicated here, seem to you more valid if I told you I was channeling a spirit guide? If the answer to that is "yes," then you have a problem.

If that Spirit Guide, whatever its claimed identity, is so broadly aware and wise, why doesn't it incarnate and reveal his/her truths personally? Why hide behind a shade and spout unverifiable – and thus undeniable – truths for which that supposed entity makes no personal statement of veracity? In Reality, you do not know – **cannot** know – whether channeled information originated in the ether-levitating entity who claims some ethereal identity or in the deeper belief structures of the individual whose mouth formulates the words.

But you can judge the wisdom of the message – and you should do that warily, from your own store of perspective, whatever the source.

The Unconscious

When you ride a bicycle you don't pay much attention to what's going on underneath you. The gears, as you shift, switch your peddling leverage smoothly, allowing efficient climbs and speedy cruising. The bearings roll rapidly about the axle, negating friction and requiring minimal energy input, thus reducing effort from your legs. The chassis flexes, absorbing shock. The tires take their share of shock, too, all the while gripping the surface and keeping you headed where you aim.

While that's happening, your lungs are providing oxygen to your blood as it circulates throughout your body. Muscles compress, pulling against the leverage of the complex knee joint and even more complex ankle, with both driven by the buttocks and back muscles to propel the whole package forward. Meanwhile, your liver is cleaning the blood, and your brain is carrying out its complex task of interfacing body communications with your ever-present mind focus.

While all that transpires, you, the conscious, aware Self that you are, can be planning the next turn – or tomorrow's dinner or yesterday's trophy. You ride that body and that bike so smoothly that you needn't ponder much of anything involving the mechanism of movement to accomplish it. Yet, you ***can*** ponder any aspect of that mechanism...

The "sub-" or "unconscious" mind is not unlike the body/bike you ride in the above example.

Coordination of body function is an extraordinarily complex task, from simple muscle flexing – which requires precisely balanced flexing of many sets of muscles – to the communication of problems through pain, to hunger, to need for waste elimination, to a whole realm of other aspects of existence maintenance. This is all coordinated and communicated by your unconscious, along with much deeper functionality serving as an interface with all the elements you will encounter as you proceed. But you ride that functionality, like the bike and the body on it, without the need to pay much attention to it. You can, if you want to focus on such things, perceive much of the detail of life function, just like you could focus on your bike's derailleur – but that's not the prime value of your surface consciousness. If you do that while riding the bike, you are likely to crash. Your focus is needed on the overall ride.

And likewise, the detail of body functionality and life functionality is best left in the deeper elements of mind content that you ***don't have to think about!*** Your conscious focus is most suited to experiencing life and reacting to it. The grunt work of functionality is carried out in the unconscious, i.e., at levels you simply need not be generally conscious of (unless delving into the inner roots of specific problems).

The unconscious mind, however, is ***not*** an oracle for revealing wondrous truths. It is an extension of your being – the portion storing information and values to transfer when needed – on which you ride. It is not separate from you, but integral; information within the unconscious can be accessed directly (thereby making it conscious, i.e., pulling it into conscious focus) but need not be drawn into your focus for functionality of the normal state.

Nor is the unconscious an alter-ego making willful decisions, stuck to your self-aware Self like an eel on a shark. It is a body of info, an accumulation of meaning- and function-based value elements, to which you have access, and which is vital to recognize on Your Path to Awareness.

In any case, you need to come to a level of awareness of the availability of unconscious information, an understanding for its purely functional nature and a distinct level of confidence in information you can derive from within. But with common, popular distortions of what the unconscious is, you could easily make it out to be an external entity, an ultimate source of esoteric info, a greater "pseudo-self" somehow superior to you and thus an oracle or diviner in supplying information to you.

It isn't any of that and shouldn't be sought out as a guide. That would be like asking your bike which way you should be going.

Oh, and, as with Spirit Guides, would my perspectives here seem more valid if I had to go into a trance to retrieve them from the depths of my subconscious or some collective unconscious?

The Word of God

Or would my words ring truer if I claimed, like, say, Mohammed, that they came directly from some god and thus couldn't be questioned?

There is no god sitting in the wings of this stage, pulling strings, sending in hooks, controlling the scenery, chopping lines, providing props, writing the play or even directing it. There simply is no such external consciousness that dictates the flow of events and relationships in the life of any individual, including you.

Vocal cords are not rental units. No Hebrew prophet, nor Mohammed, nor any founder of any cult or religion ever spoke the words of anybody but themselves. Certainly, though, each would have held a mental makeup that revised the nature of their words spoken from an "altered state" to fit the belief structure of themselves and their peers, so that the quotes might have

seemed to come from a god they all believed in. But appearance and Reality differ when tinged by beliefs into a status of illusion.

No real god ever gave dictation. That's because none ever existed, save in the mind of a believer.

Ancient Accounts

Age seems to contribute a great deal of veracity to philosophical and religious accounts.

There is certainly an evolutionary effect in place, wherein generations of teaching children the dogma of any particular belief structure will enhance its acceptance among the population, along with the veneration of its original founders.

But if you look at the world's "great" religions, you find the culture present at the time of origin – the Middle East of 30AD or 600AD, China, India or even Greece of 500BC – to be rather primitive in nature. In ancient times people had little exposure to the world in general, to other cultures or geographical regions, to any but a most limited, single view of reality. They had little cognizance, e.g., of the solar system and how it functioned, associating the planets with gods, had no recognition of interactive ecological systems or body function. Daily life was rife with fear of nature and fear of invasion from external armies, not to mention fear of the ruling head (if not also the priesthood) of their own state. Far from being deeply attuned to spiritual connection with their god, they were strongly programmed from childhood into believing in whatever local pantheon or cosmology their culture imagined to exist.

I'm amazed at the fuss made over ancient documents like the Dead Sea Scrolls. These were accounts written by some sect or other, espousing their superstitious views of the world, not holy documents revealing eternal truths – though they may appear to be the latter if you have bought into the same definitions and explanations that the originators believed in.

I don't propose to simply disregard ancient accounts and old religions. They provide excellent examples of how a belief structure, commonly held, will create a common religious system, common deceptions and common illusions. Much can be gained from seeing this mechanism clearly. But in holding these old accounts to be somehow sacred, somehow more insightful than modern perspectives, even more will be lost.

Simply put, the relative age of a philosophical perspective has nothing to do with its veracity. It is pure illusion to imagine that just because a view of life was held and put to words long ago, that it is more valid. Because of prevailing limits to cultural understanding of life in ancient times, the reverse is **enormously** more likely…

So, in pondering what sort of authority on life you should accept, beware all the above illusory sources. None is any more valid an authority than you are – or rather, **can be** and ***should be*** if you proceed along Your Path with assurance.

Authority, Part Three

Take Me to Your Leader

A very significant element of your self-image is tied up with an additional meaning to the concept of Authority: the **determinative power** ***to imprint your will*** on the events and relationships that make up your life.

Seeking dictatorial power, i.e., a magical force it would take to order your imagined will into real experience, is an illusory quest. All the traditional schemes to manipulate the world, and there are many, are but mirages on the dry landscape of intellectual, rational control.

It is the invariable function of Reality to translate your inner qualities into outer experience – with exacting precision. The very **attempt** to rationally control events in your life propagates a cycle of the inherent control limiters: negation and neutralization. Realizing these will inevitably require **further** control, further manipulation, as the aspects of conflict you ***hold within*** continue to be built into ongoing experience. That subsequent experience can be the same, ongoing unsolvable situation or condition, or it can evolve and migrate into other events involving other aspects of your life and other people.

The simple point here is that Your Path requires refocus, within your mind scope, from the very concept of power or control over something to terms of personal ***authority*** as an element of your self-image.

You may be used to projecting creative power out to a god. You may have been taught to pray in a fashion that conceptually places power for the initiation of events and relationships in the source of that deity, which exists as a separate entity, with a will unlike your own. Since there is no such controlling, external source, your mental image will ***automatically*** translate into unfolding events that do not reflect your will!

Do you get the point? There is no external, embodied "power" source that forces events into existence.

The engendering of real events and relationships is **automatic**! It is a simple process of mind image becoming real. To stop that process from incorporating events and relationships contrary to your will, it is necessary, first, to clearly see the myths you were taught through religious training, plus the many default assumptions you absorbed through all the stories and fairy tales and traditional literary plot structures that permeate our cultural understandings. Once you see them, you need to drop them in much the same manner you use to reprogram the various Mechanisms of Mind in Angle Two.

But, in the gesture of reprogramming, it is decidedly ***not*** effective to ponder, "I see clearly how I projected power out to such-and-such a source (fate, god, luck, coincidence, parents, wealthy people, etc.), but now I am the power." You are not really the power, not in control, not the force behind the realization of will or opposition of will.

Indeed, ***there is no such power***! Translation of mind state into realized happening is simply how the Consciousness-Reality singularity works, how value flows from mindset to the real. Thus, it is neither power nor control you are seeking to engage as part of your self-image, but ***authority***.

You see, the process of authority, incorporated into your self-image is one of direction-setting – you are not so much the captain of your life, barking out orders, as the navigator with the whole thing on automatic pilot to follow your course.

* * *

But even authority in this sense requires some explanation. As you passed through childhood, virtually everybody in your small realm had authority over you – parents, older siblings, other relatives, teachers, neighbors, preachers. You had no authority. Even **they** had no real authority, as they had inherited the commonly deficient self-image of powerlessness prevalent in traditional culture, passing it along to you intact through their gestures to control your behavior. Having absorbed it, as you aged, you transferred that submissiveness from parents to other replacement sources – your spouse, your boss, police, lawyers, government officials and other authority figures.

And in the big picture, you also incorporated ways you learned to manipulate your parents (craftily circumventing their authoritative control) to all of those replacement authorities. By holding onto your learned **means of control**, you simply reinforce the mechanism of ***lack of authority*** characteristic of your own innate nature **then**, as a child. The clear implication here is that you are undoubtedly ***still*** manipulating people using the same mechanisms you did to control your parents.

Changing that ongoing state, thus implanting authority as a characteristic of your self-image, is like changing any facet of your nature. Come to see the effect clearly, identifying the people, events and mechanisms involved, then revise your mindset, reshaping it into a desired state including Authority.

But, in the case of instilling Authority into the mix, you needn't hammer the self-suggestion, "Now I am in authority in my life." Having seen and dispelled the parental authority, the teacher authority, the conceptualized god's authority, the sibling authority and any other, one-by-one as they are found and having delved into many other mind mechanisms such that you clearly see the Inner-Outer connection, you gain a simple recognition of your own inviolate authority within the scope of your life. "Now I **see**

clearly that I am the authority in my life," would be the more useful autosuggestion.

You ***are*** the only real authority in your life, but you yield that status to so many externals by believing in them, by having been punished or forced into accepting them. You lost that rank by projecting the determinative elements of your creativity out onto other people or conceptualized forces and sources. And you can regain it only by coming to see your nature as central to all causality.

Home Stretch

Where Your Notions Came From

Hazards along Your Path – the above should expose some hindrances to your progress, but your Journey is enhanced by your coming to recognize others on your own.

The Fourth Angle will instill further insight into notions of authority, looking in depth at great teachers and culturally sustained notions from the past. The purpose will be to find value or expose invalidity wherever either is to be found.

Better buckle your psyche's seatbelt. It's liable to get a little rough down the home stretch…

EoR – The Fourth Angle: Other Teachings

Seen in the Light of Day

The focus here remains exclusively on life – not superimposing my cherished opinion, philosophy or conjecture about how it works, but viewing the process of Reality without those inhibiting conceptual structures. By this time you will have explored from three Angles the view I present of the Essence of Reality. One remains.

Mystics, sages, philosophers, visionaries – such individuals have come and gone through the ages who have seen Reality somewhat more clearly than their contemporaries, glimpsing to some degree the Oneness that I have illustrated from three Angles. Their accounts are available, should you go looking. Read and perceived for what they are, they can only benefit you through the exposure.

However, several specific aspects of visionary messages temper their validity and thus limit their effectiveness – a caveat always to be aware of.

First, many highly regarded teachers were not very aware of the flow of Reality in the first place. A visionary's message can only be as perceptive as that person's level of awareness; the greatest of visionaries still carried core beliefs and cultural notions that compromised their clear view.

Second, many perspectives originating with man's great teachers were set to words by others, individuals of lesser vision than the originator and often much later in time. Such third-party accounts will necessarily suffer distortion – should an elementary school student explain Einstein's General Theory of Relativity to you, it will certainly lack the original nuances of vision and will at least partially, perhaps totally, distort the original base meaning. The degree of clarity of any reiterated message is unavoidably bounded by the writer/translator.

The greatest teachers invariably suffer the hazard of trying to pass along ideas that are, by their innate visionary nature, beyond the ken of their contemporaries. Often, given the closed-minded attitude of past timeframes, the insightful message may have been not only well beyond the grasp of most, but even into forbidden territory of taboo expression. So the reputation of the original speaker may have been overblown into mythic proportions or condemned by contemporaries – or both!

Third, writing deeply penetrating perspectives in the richest, most flexible of languages, current English, is difficult enough. Expressing complex perspectives in primitive tongues, limited in vocabulary, flexibility of grammar and figures of speech is just not possible.

(Then, too, the most aware of seers may not have been the best of writers. For every Gautama, Plato, Dante, Shakespeare or Whitman, how many could see more clearly than their peers, but could not explain it very well?)

But even for those who recorded their views with alacrity and precision, a major fourth caveat exists: those original teachings fade in clarity by virtue of change through time of the original language, by subsequent translation and by evolving background cultural understanding. Add to that inherent distortion the misguided efforts of small-minded functionaries through the ages who ***intentionally*** changed the meaning to suit current political and bureaucratic interests.

Then mix **all that** distortion in with a lot of flack – teachers, often charismatic, who were basically clueless as to the real function of Reality, but wrote eloquently and convincingly in myth-based and fallacious idioms. And add to that the heavy indoctrination – and thus deep emotional attachment – religious accounts typically receive by each coming generation at the hands of older generations with great conviction and little awareness.

What you end up with is a situation in the recording of religious and philosophical perspectives prone to – indeed virtually guaranteed to – promulgate distorted vision and illusory notions. As you have begun to see, if you've been looking inward at your own beliefs, it doesn't take much to destroy clarity of vision. Valued concepts, once issued from a visionary, easily convert into superstitious garble when processed by lesser men.

* * *

My presumption is you will not have read this far without, at the very least, a sincere, open-minded attitude. You will realize that I am not presenting you with a tidy model of reality that you can buy into with little effort to subsequently and energetically spread about, proselytizing and converting relative heathens and infidels. You will know by now that I offer not a tight-knit explanation to provide instant understanding of Reality's function, but a process whereby you can garner an Awareness of that flow via personal commitment to an Inner Journey.

So, emphatically, I am not elaborating on the words of these teachers who have come before for the purpose of supporting my message. Most often, writers will look at vaunted works of great teachers from the misty view through their own dimmer awareness, looking for meaning from the master to grasp, reflect on and reiterate in support of their own limited view. Such is the fodder of all priesthoods and sects, to mimic spiritual-sounding phrases and rote interpretations, making trite, banal dogma out of what was once, perhaps (but not necessarily), valued perspective.

On my own and through my own specified, introspective cleansing, I came to see the flow and gist of life clearly. From a higher perspective, I am able to reflect meaningfully on great teachers of the past, able to discern distortion in the message and/or lack of original vision where it might subtly fester the underlying message.

But my perspectives **stand on their own**: the innate validity to EoR rests solely on accurately reflecting the function of Reality. The value relies on your ability to make use of my illustrations to come to perceive that function on **your own**.

Thus, I ***never*** lean on the authoritative support of any of teacher or philosophical construct that has come before to confirm the validity of my viewpoint. I offer meaningful perspectives on others' messages in the anticipation that the illustration will help you see what they meant and where they fell short. The experience allows you to set your goal at joining or surpassing the great teachers in clearer awareness, not just attempting to emulate them via rote, unwitting repetition of their words.

So, the intent here in reviewing earlier teachings is to explore where the originator (or the movement) had a grasp of How Life Works and to what extent, how that person illustrated it and how that message either hit the mark or fell short by virtue of its original shortcoming or subsequent distortion.

In the case of Jesus of Nazareth and the culturally dominating religion that grew out of his influence, it is additionally important to discern the fallacy woven into Christianity's core belief system so that you can discern, personally, what subtle but damaging effect that movement has on your wellbeing. Indeed, this secondary purpose in Angle Four is to illustrate core traditional, cultural elements that permeate the western mindset, thus exposing some of the roots of compromised awareness that the reader would do well to personally jettison from his/her mindset.

Continuing on Your Journey, you will come to see that many searchers and seekers have gone this way before, and that you are not only welcome among the greatest, but can carry man's understanding beyond what it ever was.

Religion by Definition

Points of Viewing

In the process of examining belief structures, it is ***never*** my purpose to criticize or degrade the expressions I examine here. By and large, people hold ideas that seem clear and truthful within the confines of their own vision. It is never my purpose to deride their sincere perspectives.

But there is only **one mechanism** to life, ***one way*** in which Reality functions. Theology, the rendered definition behind religion, philosophy and science all purport to depict that functionality. But if each fails to do so accurately, that invalidity needs to be exposed – and the only way to do that is to point out the fallacious elements of the description. When I do so, my perspectives necessarily bring into question the conceptual tenets undergirding that theological, philosophical or scientific paradigm. This can seem, particularly to the mindset that holds any such dogma to be the basis of truth, to be a criticism of or an attack on that notion.

Realistically, I never criticize or attack anything – indeed, there isn't anything real to even confront, in that any such paradigm consists only of ideas, of synthetic conceptualizations in the minds of believers. Pointing out shortcomings in any paradigm that constitute fallacy is therefore **not an attack**. It is, well, just pointing out shortcomings. If the paradigm, including a religion based on a particular theology, were valid, ***it would withstand any and all scrutiny!***

But religions in particular don't stand up against open-minded examination, because they, as philosophical expressions, all consist of artificial definitions resting typically on archaic notions, more or less blindly accepted by adherents who learned to view life in that defined way from early childhood.

It must be obvious that the Reality we all encounter only works one way, and it functions that way **regardless of what the experiencer believes**. Of the hundreds of religions and philosophies ever entertained by the mind of man, each considered by the convinced holder to be the only valid one, only **at the very most *one*** can be accurate. If the Christian "God" is real, for example, then other gods, like the Muslim "Allah," with different characteristics, don't, indeed ***can't*** exist. You need no unique genius to realize that from the outset: both paradigms, differing, can't be valid.

Just as obvious should be the possibility, if not likelihood, if not certainty, that ***none*** of those hundreds of religions accurately depicts How Life Works.

From a standpoint of Clear Awareness, seeing without distortion How Life Works, I can only sincerely and openly discuss previous efforts at describing reality. Pointing out inaccuracies and fallacies found in these explanations, then, is never a critique of believers or organizations, but simply an effort to discern clarity in place of murky concepts. From my angle, the only thing inherently sacred in the examination of life is clear perception of how it works. Indeed, you defile clarity by ***not*** questioning things.

EoR differs in approach from Science in that same regard. Science, while a useful tool for much modern accomplishment, fails by its very nature to grasp the core, subjective nature of life, thus reiteratively causing much of the troubles it would seek to alleviate. In its core shortcoming, Science restricts the field of examination, allowing only for certain types of evidence (reproducible, verifiable in the lab, etc.), thus limiting its scope. Then, very much like Religion, it defines anything outside its artificially limited scope to be unacceptable evidence. Thus, in its ***own*** view, Science seems to be the only valid explanation, where in actuality it only pictures a constricted – and therefore distorted – subset of Reality.

The value to EoR's Fourth Angle is gleaned by examining descriptions and definitions of a given paradigm, as stated in its theology, theory, philosophical tenets and base principles, laid out by its founder or built into its traditions – and reflecting on them in light of what is real. You will see, hidden in the messages of many teachers who have gone before, a hint of awareness of the inner-outer flow I have been illustrating since page one. But there will always be found some element of distortion, of artificiality in fallacious descriptions and definitions. Once exposed, the limitations formed in your belief structure by those concepts will begin to erode – unless, of course, you are too bound to the paradigm.

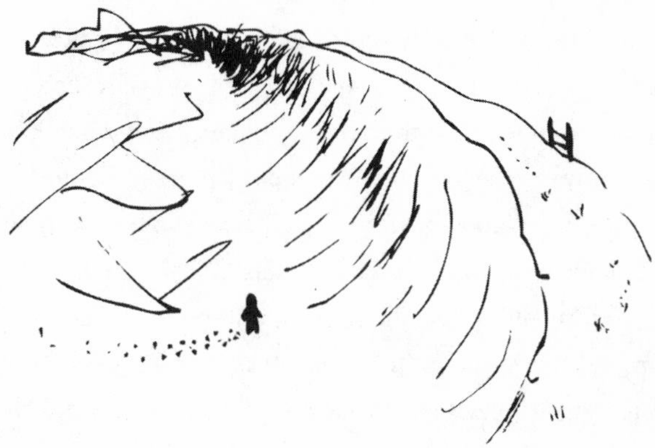

So, proceed in your examination of the Fourth Angle with the understanding that all I say here is oriented toward freeing your mind so it can attain a Clear Awareness of Reality, not to replace your old belief structure with a shiny new one. My words are never meant as an attack on the old thinking, but only to expose any invalidity ensconced within.

Indoctrination

Setting the Deck

Dominating man's world-view throughout the ages have been two rather different types of Religion. One, like Hinduism or Shamanism, consists of ancient patterns of regarding reality that evolved over a long expanse of time, spanning many generations, in which story and myth merged and emerged to embody an explanation of life. The other, generally more recent in its roots, emanates from the personal perspectives of an individual – examples being Christianity, Buddhism and Islam. Judaism is probably more of the former type than the latter. While its patriarchs lived in a pseudo-historical era (by virtue of their own writings) and its theology has been driven by charismatic individuals, principally Moses, its core beliefs stem from much more remote generations. Of course, much of Christianity is philosophically based on its roots in Judaism, but the differentiation created by the teachings of Jesus and Paul is significant, while many of its core traditional notions are actually rooted in paganism and Zoroastrianism.

Regardless of type, however, the mechanism of a religion works like this: children, from the time they can communicate, are taught to see reality in a certain way. They are indoctrinated with a pre-defined belief structure and value set. Naive, open to such teaching, given ***only*** the religious viewpoint and perhaps punished or ostracized if they don't accept it, most ultimately absorb and mimic the religion outright. (All the Mechanisms of Mind can be involved in this indoctrination process: Subtle Force, Motivation, Emulation, Suggestion, etc.) Others, even rejecting the religion, have absorbed much of the subtle cultural thinking that evolved along with the religion. In any case, fear has been instilled through an indoctrination process that keeps free thought contained and greater enlightenment out of reach.

The children then grow to adulthood and teach ***their*** children to see reality just about the same way they did, with slight evolving of doctrine as cultural notions, and thus interpretations, change over generations. That simple mechanism has been at work for millennia. Every religion carries on in that fashion, with each generation picking up fallacy camouflaged as fact with an innate blindness to its invalidity.

The only way to break this mechanism of generational indoctrination is for individuals (like you), those with inner fortitude and curiosity, to come to see more clearly – for **cultural awareness exists** ***as a collective***, resting on the status of each of its individual members.

Exactly that venture is the basis of The Essence of Reality – because Religion, along with its cousin philosophies, invariably distorts and thus destroys personal perception of Reality, rather than, in any way, accurately depicting it.

Lao Tzu and the Tao

The Way It Is

The words of Lao Tzu – literally, the "Old Philosopher," a contemporary of Confucius some 2500 years ago – as found in the Tao Te Ching, reveal a man of extraordinary awareness. Where Confucius embraced the apparent and developed recommended action for encountered events – that is, encouraged a very rational engagement of reality – Lao Tzu's approach, voicing a perceptiveness of life rooted in times well before his, was quite the opposite.

(Scholars question whether a single person called Lao Tzu really existed. Much like the old debate as to whether Shakespeare wrote the works attributed to him, however, it is irrelevant in this consideration ***who*** wrote the Tao Te Ching; somebody did and captured in the process a valued perspective on How Life Works. His name and biographical details are of little consequence.)

Lao Tzu saw in life a process he termed the "Tao," often translated as "the Way." According to legend, upon prodding by the city guard as he left for points unknown, so frustrated he was with his unseeing contemporaries, Lao Tzu pictured this Tao in a series of short poetic pieces. Effectively he was saying that life had a flow to it, a concerted flow in which events formed the currents. The Tao carries you along in a fashion, he intimated, such that the more you try to logically manipulate events, the more you operate in opposition to the flow, and the more problems you encounter…

Here are a few passages (translated by Gia-Fu Feng and Jane English) in which the "ten thousand things" refers to the realm of objects and events, and the term Tao represents a process that cannot be explicitly defined:

> "Look, it cannot be seen – it is beyond form.
> Listen, it cannot be heard – it is beyond sound…
>
> "Stand before it and there is no beginning.
> Follow it and there is no end...
>
> "The great Tao flows everywhere, both to the left and to the right.
> The ten thousand things depend upon it; it holds nothing back.
> It fulfills its purpose silently and makes no claim…
>
> "Being the stream of the universe,
> Ever true and unswerving,
> Become as a little child once more…
>
> "The Tao is forever undefined.
> Small though it is in the unformed state, it cannot be grasped…
>
> "Once the whole is divided, the parts need names.
> There are already enough names.
> One must know when to stop."

His pieces illustrate in many glimpses from various angles How Life Works. Few have ever been as perceptive – the Tao illustrations stand as one of the most profoundly clear explanations of life of ancient times.

But Lao Tzu's teaching suffers from the major problem endemic to such visionaries. In the intervening two and a half millennia, his words have been misinterpreted and distorted by generations of adherents until his message is riddled with meaningless ritual and dogma. Taoism contracted the conceptual plague: it became a religion.

Where Lao Tzu spoke of not "doing" things in opposition to the flow – i.e., taking rational action in order to manipulate the real world – his supposed followers sit in abject meditation, unwilling to engage in any "action." They follow, not the crystal point of meaning that Lao Tzu wished to communicate, but a literal distortion that a clueless priesthood through centuries of blind interpretation attached to his ancient words.

Life is indeed a Singularity of effect, in which each individual finds a pure reflection of his/her own nature in the events and relationships encountered in everyday life. Planning and manipulating these events, that is, rationally concocting and carrying out a preconceived ***action***, is the embodiment of struggle and conflict – values that lead to the continued creation of a personal reality that, in turn, ***needs*** to be manipulated. For sure Lao Tzu was intimately aware of this fundamental essence. That his message is lost on generations of followers who can hear only dogmatized distortions of a profound expression is equally certain.

Taoists fail to realize that when you recognize the flow and come to perceive that you are part of it, you already begin to meld into that flow. As you clear away manipulative tendencies based on learned mechanisms, you become the Tao! Any spontaneous, intuitive action taken is a natural part of that flow.

To avoid all action is like trying to nullify existence. In fact, the Taoist gesture to sit and "do" nothing is ***itself*** a rationally contrived gesture, made not as a spontaneous rivulet in the flow of the Tao, but derived via conclusion in attempting to further Taoist religious dogma. Taoist adherents go awry in following grandiose phrases without understanding, in following small-minded priests instead of their own hearts.

While the Tao Te Ching is of great value in its life perspectives, you will see Lao Tzu's wisdom stated therein at its clearest when **you yourself** come to see life clearly.

And you will notice the single shortcoming in his illustration: The Tao flows, not in sync to some pattern determined by gods or fate, but in response to and always consistent with **your nature**. Lao Tzu clearly perceived the Tao, but didn't recognize the ***initiator*** of the quality flow – and thus ultimate determiner – as the experiencing Self.

Cultural Roots – a Look at Judaism

Hoe the Weeds

It's generally quite easy, philosophically and emotionally, to accept that there are distortions in a distant and unrelated belief set, as in the case of Taoism. With no baggage on that train, you (typical reader with western cultural roots) can usually see how Lao Tzu's ancient Chinese teachings, while intimately perceptive and of great value, were distorted by a narrow-minded priesthood, evolving cultural norms, translation, etc., through time and thus no longer reflect his original meaning.

But regarding your own cultural values – meaningful, emotional strands interwoven into your mindset – the exploration takes on a different nature. As we move into the Judeo-Christian realm and regard its roots, validity and its ultimate impact on western culture and your personal life, the target is placed in much closer proximity to your emotional responsiveness.

It doesn't matter how religious you are in a traditional western vein. Many Christian notions, however invalid, however nonsensical they may prove to be when examined closely, permeate Western thinking and are thus loaded into the baggage you carry on ***this*** train, the one you ride in a cultural sense. As I address "truths" with which you associate or on which your mindset depends for its even-keeled perceptiveness, you may find it uncomfortable when I show them to be fallacious. **If you find yourself defensive or annoyed as I expose the invalidity of your favorite notions –** ***whatever they are*** **– take that as a key indicator of their inherent artificiality.** If your notion of How Life Works were valid and operative, ***nothing I could say*** would offend your sensibilities.

* * *

The ideological roots of Christianity and thus the conceptual/philosophical/theological trunk of western culture, grasp tenaciously in the hardened, arid soil of its mother religion, Judaism. Western culture ***itself*** grew out of

aggressive attitudes of agriculture-based groups of the Indo-European peoples, who expanded into Europe and elsewhere some 6000 years ago. However, the cosmological base of the culture's original gods – the Greek Zeus, Roman Jupiter, Germanic Wodan/Odin and their related variations along with accompanying pantheons – gave way in Roman times to an adaptation of Middle Eastern beliefs, which themselves stem back into antiquity.

Prior to adopting an imported religion, western notions of How Life Works were rooted in those archaic pantheons and, to a much more constricted degree, Greek philosophical explanations – the latter replete with concepts of a soul, but based on rational regard for the life experience and not nearly so widely accepted. In the process of absorbing Christianity, the new paradigm of a single, creative god was superimposed on the common, pagan, myth-based mindset ***without eliminating*** aspects internally inconsistent or at odds with the original. Added to that, somewhat later, was yet another layer: the scientific paradigm, a latter day belief structure.

The end effect is that you inherited via our modern western culture various notions overlaid on each other, frequently internally conflictual. Yet you hold these concepts as true and valid explanations for How Life Works.

(Interesting note: The original Indo-Europeans, emanating from a homeland around the Black Sea, whose expansion and differentiation led to the Celtic, Greek, Slavic, Germanic, Roman and many other European peoples, also became the Farsi-speaking and Hindi groups in their eastern expansion. Thus, ancient Hindu with its Veda tales is more closely aligned with core western cultural attitudes than any Semitic religious notion adopted later. Angle Four will consider western philosophical bases and eastern views shortly. For now, the focus is on the Judaist roots of Christianity and the internal fallacies they hold.)

The purpose, remember, in examining these conceptual roots is not to produce a scholarly treatise for academic consumption or debate. The sole intent is to view these religious notions from a perspective of Clear Awareness – comparing **what they espouse** to ***How Life actually Works***. As fallacy becomes exposed here, you, personally, can work toward jettisoning archaic, inaccurate definitions – along with the self-defeating mechanisms you began to uncover in Angle Two.

Clearly, when western cultures absorbed Christianity, they got an all-inclusive package: ancient Hebrew rituals and myths steeped in lost purpose, scantily recorded and broadly misinterpreted teachings of Jesus, revisions and distortions by Paul, twisted cosmology and superstitions supplied by priesthoods and bureaucratic/political distortions innate to man's traditional endeavors. While Jesus' teachings reveal some fascinating perspectives, it is imperative to lead into his appearance with a look at the religion he inherited and the setting in which he emerged.

But First…

It is difficult to speak of Judaism as a religion in the same way that one considers other religions. The early family group which originated the Hebraic belief system spread its ideas, not primarily through conversion of others outside the group thereby expanding their numbers by absorption, but rather by remaining cohesively group-oriented and reproducing: the expansion of the Jewish faith has come via the expansion, movement and further expansion of the Jewish population. Judaism has never constituted more than a small fraction of human population, but its holders have traditionally had a knack for capturing attention.

Thus the concept of Judaism covers not only religious connotations, but also culture, tradition and ethnic identity. I am **not** considering here all those aspects. Culling the cultural/traditional and ethnic from the religious, I wish to address ***only*** the religious in some depth. But it ***is*** important to first touch on the other two:

- **Culture and Tradition:**
  - ✓ The Jewish peoples have contributed greatly to western, indeed world, culture through their unique expression of tradition via music, humor, literature, art – and in many other ways. As I proceed to consider fallacious elements in religious belief enshrined in the Law and the Prophets, there should be no connection made to cultural and traditional aspects of the people who hold those notions.
  - ✓ I value the richness that **every culture and tradition** brings to the human experience. Pointing out negative elements inherent in a particular belief structure or theology, ***never implies criticism in any way*** of the group that holds those notions.

- **Ethnicity:**
  - ✓ Since the demise of our Neanderthal cousins 25 or 30 millennia ago, we are all members of the same group here. Lines drawn through humanity's populace for the purpose of subdividing mankind into groups are always artificial and invariably lead to illusory conclusions – often negative assessments of groups other than the ones doing the assessing. Never in EoR will any reference to a religious identification carry any ethnic connotations whatsoever.
  - ✓ While there may be negative traits – in terms of health tendencies, conflict, fears, struggle, group favoritism, etc. – associated with ethnic groups, those characteristics are shared only via common belief structures, not ethnic commonality or genetic similarity. Thus,

no reference by me, here or elsewhere, should ever be construed as critical or demeaning of any ethnic subset of mankind.

So, this entire Fourth Angle consideration of previous teachings intends **no criticism** ***of any group on any grounds*** **– ethnic, cultural or traditional**.

However, in regards to the theological aspects of **each** religion, tradition or philosophy, the same exacting standard must be set as measurement: does it clearly and accurately depict the functionality of Reality? That is, does the cosmology precisely describe how Reality works? If not, then the religion is invalid.

And note that it would lack validity based on its ***own inherent fallacy***, not via my personal judgment. I do not capriciously "judge" the validity of a religion, but rather observe whether Reality functions consistent with its precepts.

How It Is

Judaism and its offshoot, Christianity, proudly look back into the chronicles of Hebrew "history" recorded in the old testament and make claim that it shows a long trail of monotheism and a growing awareness of the nature of God. (That is "god" spelled with a capital "G," in that it is actually the English name for this supposed entity, just as Ra, the "Great Spirit," and Apollo were names given to other conceptualized gods.) In reality both of those cornerstone claims are false; they lead to illusory deductions of validity to the whole cosmology, to the paradigm they would imply.

For the older scriptures, the basic fallacy stems from ancient times via source writings. Much of the old testament was first recorded in writing along about 800 BCE, already having been passed by oral tradition for centuries after the events concerning Abraham (c. 1900 BCE), Isaac (shortly thereafter), on down through Moses (c. 1300 BCE). It is utterly absurd to believe that these stories were carried over many generations of retelling without ***major*** distortion to their content (and thus, veracity), then were written without yet more alteration.

Picture the mechanism: scribes – an elite, educated group (most people were illiterate) who functioned as recorders of information then (historians in effect, as there was little notion of anything resembling objective history during those centuries) – would interpret the past based on current values and demands of their clients, the priesthood. The initial scribes of old-testament tales certainly bent the interpretation of events and situations of all prior times to fit the current concepts of the priesthood at first writing. And a process of revision went on at each stage of rewriting: in these intervening 2800 years, a hundred and more generations, stories and accounts have ***always*** been undergoing further reinterpretation – and manipulation – based on current ideas.

Core to this distortion is the fundamental concept of monotheism.

In the world of Abraham, four millennia ago, there was no concept of a single, overall god who created everything – none whatsoever, not among any priesthood anywhere on Earth, not among the common man. (That notion was only ever concocted in ancient times by Akhenaton, an oddball Pharaoh in Egypt who lived about 1350 BCE – six hundred years later. His Sun God, conceptually a single, creative source, lasted precisely as briefly as his reign, then was swept away rapidly and energetically immediately following his death – because the notion was foreign to anything conceived of in those times in any locale of the Middle East.)

No, in the lifetime of Abraham, people, **highly superstitious** in their regard to causality, believed in many gods whose powers were regional and specialized. Abraham's god was named "El," the high god (or Elohim, a plural term for "the gods," or El Shaddai, "the god of the mountain"). But El was not uncommon at the time – contemporaries recognized El and his wife Asherah among other gods for specific purposes – fertility, for example, or for help during war. When people of that time journeyed to other regions, they would certainly have given sacrifice – offering of slaughtered animals was their means to elicit favorable events from the gods – to the deities most highly regarded in ***that area***, whether El or some competing god like Ba'al, Ahura Mazda, Marduk or Enlil, in order to gain favor and elicit good fortune.

In the many generations intervening between Abraham and Moses, the nature of this imagined god changed, evolving from a personal god intertwined with immediate events to more of a jealous, rather bloodthirsty war god. It was not that "God" himself changed, of course – never did El or El Shaddai exist **in Reality**, any more than Moses' later god, Yahweh or Ba'al or Isis. It was that the ***conceptualization*** – the notion along with attributed characteristics – of the god changed, based on the evolving mindset of the Hebrew clan, who were slowly converting to agriculture and a more settled lifestyle, thus slowly evolving into a more cultured state.

As that happened, even after Moses established a set of laws supposedly attained directly from Yahweh (not unlike Mohammed receiving dictates from his god, Allah, via Gabriel two millennia later), prophets came along who, based on their verve and zealous attitude, viewed their conceptualized god differently as time went on. And they explained their vision with great alacrity, energy and charisma, adding to voluminous customs and traditions – in the form of codified Law governing behavior – all along the way.

The common people, of course, as was usual for any time and place, followed along with such concepts. They had always been handed such religious notions as prophets and seers had decreed (as shamans had done in even earlier times), but had absorbed it through the same old process: via cultural immersion, through current priesthood assuredness and parental indoctrination.

This controlling group, the priesthood – **as all such priesthoods have done through time** – zealously and conservatively guarded the status quo with themselves in control of "truth," while only slowly absorbing evolving ideas from prophets' influence in revising the details of that defined truth.

(Indeed, all priests, shamans, gurus, scientists, clerics and the like have vigorously guarded their roles as experts in life functionality. They have always benefited as an elevated class by playing the role of intermediaries with their imagined gods and/or sacred rules, receiving grain, research grants, virgins, tithes and offerings, even taxes, along with status from common people who lack adequate understanding to see through their synthetic truths and theological propaganda.)

But all along the way, through those founding, old-testament time periods, the Hebrew people acknowledged other gods as well.

Consider for example, from the Ten Commandments saga, one dictate ostensibly given by Yahweh to Moses on a fiery mountain: the entreaty to "have no other gods before me!" That directive itself indicates there ***were*** other gods to be had. In Moses' contemporaries' superstitious minds, there likely were – but Moses conceived Yahweh as being jealous and put those words into his mouth while wanting his humans to divest any loyalty to other gods and aver ***his*** preferred deity.

The evolving conceptualization in the minds of the primitive people who imagined Yahweh's existence is all there. It flows through often brutal, inhumane ancient Biblical accounts: the course from a mildly interactive god of Abraham to a god of retribution, Moses' Yahweh and beyond – a major revision of qualities, characteristics and properties. Yet modern priesthoods, philosophically cloned from archaic theologies, lump El and Yahweh together into their ***modern*** conceptualization (Christians throw in Jesus' loving "Heavenly Father", yet another god with different traits), named "God" with a capital G, claim that it makes sense, retrofit it onto old stories as monotheism and pass off this absurd theology to millions of naïve, sheep-like believers. Given the diversity of stories in the whole Bible, it's easy to cherry-pick attributes, whether punishment or forgiveness, to fit the needs of your latest sermon.

Note then, these points to be drawn from the Judaist tradition:

- Christian/Jewish sacred texts do not record an increasing awareness of the nature of a real, functional god, an entity capable of creating the real world and events in it.
    - ✓ They rather reveal an **evolving mind image** of a conceptualized god.
    - ✓ This deity appears to exist only because people have passed the notion on through many generations by indoctrinating their offspring to believe in the notion.

- Judaism evolved into a basic monotheistic theology only **long after** those early old testament times.
  - ✓ Early notions pictured the Hebrew god not as exclusive, but as the strongest god around and favorable to his "chosen" people.
  - ✓ That idea was then retrofit onto past notions as monotheism became fashionable.
- It doesn't matter if you believe in a pantheon of gods, a batch of idols, big statues in temples or a single god. None of them exist as creative sources.
- And the **main point**: regardless of its nature and applied name, invariably a conceptualized god is ***imagined to wield creative power***, while the individual mortal, by virtue of his/her self image, is reduced to effective powerlessness, able only to pray for good fortune and offer sacrifices to appease the perceived needs of the deity.

And the end effect of all that, of thousands of years of belief in one god of whatever nature or many gods – the effect it has on ***you*** – is the traditional, deeply embedded cultural notion that creative power, pure causality, exists **out there** somewhere, centered in some ethereal entity, greater and much more powerful than you.

El and Yahweh don't exist and never existed, save as an image in the primitive mindset of an exclusive tribe of rather stand-offish Middle Eastern-rooted peoples. But by believing that such is the functionality of this reality, that some external entity makes things happen for reasons other than your best interest, you turn your innate creative power against your own interests. And even if you ***don't*** believe in such a god, the rigid concept of personal powerlessness is built into default cultural expectations, projecting determinative causality out to some imagined source.

Things were evolving, though, in the ever-energetic Middle East. At a highly contentious point of history in the region, along came an individual who single-handedly took on some traditional notions and added some new twists to the mindset that ultimately became your heritage.

New Ideas from a Visionary

Shifting Gears – Without the Clutch

The Middle East, with a location juxtaposed to North Africa, Asia Minor and the Indian sub-continent, with abundant flora and fauna that prompted evolving Mankind to develop agriculture and animal husbandry, has always seen great competition for use of its real estate. Civilization emerged there as agriculture took hold along the banks of the major rivers – the Nile and Tigris-Euphrates – and populations grew as a consequence.

The descendents of Abraham, never all too large a group, ended up occupying a buffer zone between major emerging cultures – the Egyptian to the West, Babylonian, Assyrian and Hittite (depending on the period) to the East, Canaanites (Phoenicians) and others to the North – when they weren't spending time as captives of one of their neighbors.

One can easily see how the nature of the gods of those times reflected the conditions of various peoples who, over time, concocted them. The Egyptian gods – sky god Horus and his mother/wife Isis, etc. – reflected the regularity and dependability with which the Nile would rise, flood the banks, thus fertilizing the soil, then recede to promote a timeless fertility and dependable support of human well-being. The gods of Mesopotamia – storm and rain god Hadad, sun god Marduk, Enlil, etc. – reflected the much more erratic flooding of the Tigris and Euphrates by differing in character and myth: seeming capricious and uncaring, sometimes threatening in comparison.

Similarly, the god that emerged to dominate among the Hebrews, whose greatest danger was the imposing threat of warlike neighbors, was – not surprisingly – a ruthless war god.

Into the first millennium BCE, it was common for tribes or, on a smaller scale, family groups, to form mutually convenient "covenants" – that is, agreements, but more emotionally bound than simple contracts – with neighbors concerning, e.g., mutual protection or non-aggression. The weaker of the two would benefit by not being attacked and would have been happy to pay tribute to avoid a worse fate. The stronger would be happy to receive valued gifts as tribute and have a buffer of a neighbor through which any more remote enemy would have to first venture.

So the concept of a covenant was a common practice already at that time.

It was this arrangement that early Hebrew prophets had set up with their conceived god, Yahweh. That deity was to protect his favored people in exchange for their undivided praise and attention. As recorded in the testaments of those times, however, neither was very good at keeping the bargain: Hebrews were repeatedly diverting their praise and sacrifices to competing gods when they needed other favors (like fertility for crops and children). And, when needed during attack, Yahweh proved pretty inept at divine protection (due mostly to the minor shortcoming of not really existing).

Historically, enemies emerged with regularity to take on the Hebrews – primarily because conflict with neighbors, a consequence of population growth due to agriculture and resultant competition for territory, had become a way of life (and remains so today) in that region. You might read in depth of the emergence of the united monarchies of David (c. 1000 BCE) and Solomon, the split into two kingdoms, Israel and Judah to the south, around 920 BCE, the fall and destruction of Israel in 722 BCE to the Assyrians, the fall of Judah c. 590 BCE to Nebuchadnezzar and the Babylonians, Hebrew exile and subsequent return to Judah over fifty years later when Cyrus II of Persia ended Babylonian rule. You would get a feel, given the caveat for questionable historical accuracy, for the displacement of El, traditionally worshipped in the north, by YHWH (Yahweh – it's easier with the vowels) when the northern kingdom fell. And you might, too, grasp the eternal conflict and strife that has always dominated that region.

Alexander passed through about 330 BCE, leaving an influence, but fading in turn. But by the end of the first millennium BCE, the leading bully in the region had become the Roman Empire. By 63 BCE, the Romans ran the show in the region, fending off the Parthian Empire to the east. They put down almost constant rebellion among the hot-blooded Judeans. In those centuries, without doubt, the nature of Yahweh evolved as ever more rituals and requirements were added to the repertory by generation after generation of prophet and priest.

It was in that setting, though, by about 25 CE, with a brutal, iron-fisted Imperial Rome in control of the region, propping up a corrupt local king, that a new visionary appeared with a substantially different message than his predecessors.

The Jews had been long looking for a Messiah, a revolutionary leader who would rally them to throw off external powers and establish Yahweh's idealized kingdom in their homeland. For sure, there emerged several such would-be leaders, all of whom would face crushing Roman wrath and devastating military might in the ensuing couple centuries.

But, as Augustus Caesar was staking a signpost to start the count of our calendar, Jesus of Nazareth emerged on the scene with a wholly different kind of rebellion in mind.

* * *

For as much as comes down to modern times in lore, myth and interpolation, the only recorded information that tells of Jesus are four treatments written between 70 CE (Mark) to 110 CE (John), i.e., 40 to 70 years after Jesus died, by people who had never met him or known him. Jesus had left behind no writings and his followers were expecting him back any day, so early writings weren't formally accumulated – not that publishing was a common venture at that point in any case, nor were his followers likely even literate (a capability reserved by the scribes).

But the synoptic gospels (offering a "synopsis" of his life) – and John's tome to a lesser degree – provide some perspectives, if third- or fourth-hand, on a rare teacher whose message of peace and forgiveness has gone on to widespread influence. Picturing the brutality of Roman times and the values commonly held for family and tribal retribution, for force applied without mercy, it is indeed a revolutionary paradigm shift that Jesus presented to his primitive, back-water towns and villages of the Galilee region.

I will regard the picture presented within Jesus' words and actions in those gospels, but you will not fully grasp the message until you have at least begun the journey to see for yourself How Life Works. Trying to achieve that Awareness by virtue of studying Jesus' attributed words alone will be as fruitless as any external path – there is simply too much distortion built in. But once your Inner Journey has clarified life's process, from a vantage point above and beyond Jesus' perspective, you will see what he was getting at.

* * *

Aramaic, Jesus' native language, did not provide nearly precise enough expression to describe Reality's flow as does modern English – not that **this perspective** would have resonated among Galilean farmers and fishermen. Jesus' contemporaries were not schooled at all, owing their only exposure to pseudo-education to an entrenched priesthood with its time-honored adherence to the Law and the Prophets (and eternal self-serving preservation of their status within the culture). People then didn't know the Earth was a sphere orbiting the sun, how agriculture had influenced the emergence of historical culture, higher math, complex literature, objective reporting of world events, technology, civil obedience, weather prediction, democratic principles or much anything else that we take for granted as background knowledge. They were basically as intelligent as we are (and have been for 20 or 30 thousand years), but they were schooled only in superstition and simple, though rigid, ***rules***: illness, physical and mental, was "caused" by evil spirits inhabiting the body; Yahweh could punish through his judgment; if you hurt me or my family, we'll get you back; you must prepare your food in a certain fashion, etc.

But Jesus came to see a different mechanism in play. And he tried to picture it for his peers in explanatory parables, cultural images that they might grasp.

Now, I need to cover several things as I present you with perspectives on Jesus' teaching…

Distortion – Subtle and Overt

First and most important, as indicated earlier, is this: any perceptive view of How Life Works, first uttered by an individual who sees that clearly, can ***never*** be enhanced by someone with lesser vision rephrasing or translating the original! The best that can happen is word-for-word repetition of what the visionary said originally. Any attempt to characterize or emphasize will only distort it towards the fallacious notions held by the interpreter/translator.

Of course, accounts of Jesus' life and teaching have been revised, translated, doctored, reinterpreted – altered in effect for two millennia even beyond the original distortions of the gospel writers. Any comments surviving that literary ordeal, but which still reflect fairly accurately the function of emerging Reality, ***must*** relate back to an original speaker who had significantly Clear Awareness.

Second, I emphasize that Jesus' teaching was first written down long after he spoke. While traditionally the gospels are attributed to the disciples, scholars generally agree that Jesus' apostles, simple peasants, speakers of Aramaic, did not write the Greek documents. In any case, whatever path Jesus' life took, the account of that life by the writer of Luke was slanted for Greek readers, by whoever wrote Matthew for Jewish readers (both drawing on the more concise Mark or all three on a common document), by the author of John to present a later, more metaphysical view, etc. None of them had likely ever met or heard Jesus and were ***certainly*** not reporting for the purpose of accurately, objectively communicating what happened, but rather with a vested interest of convincing the reader of a point of view.

Third, traditional Christian thinking has layered quotations of Jesus with highly distorted meaning, mostly based on Paul's subsequent interpretation that raised Jesus into a near god-like status. Ignoring that, I will consider here quotes from the gospels, with focus on apparent original intent.

Reminder: my purpose here is neither an academic nor critical examination of meaning in order to draw truths out of the New Testament for display purposes. I point out specific illustrations of how Jesus attempted to illustrate to his contemporaries a considerably clearer awareness for the nature of Reality than they had encountered – and how that awareness is easily seen in his words ***when you already know what to look for***.

* * *

I have shown how, in phrases illustrating the Tao, Lao-Tzu pictured the flow of Reality, that I earlier, in Angle One, depicted myself as an inner-outer emergence, a flow of events and relationships that reflect one's nature. Jesus' perspectives were similarly unique to his era.

He had certainly been exposed to traditional Jewish thinking, wherein elaborate customs and rituals were followed to satisfy cultural-religious definitions. But his teaching transcended that, moving away from strict, traditional interpretation of and means to appease the demanding nature of Yahweh, of rigid observance of the Law, to an image of a more personal, loving, forgiving reality.

Was Jesus influenced by eastern ideas carried by traders? Did he travel during his youth to gain exposure to mysticism and other philosophies? Was he simply astute enough to see through the fallacy in traditional Hebrew notions?

I can't tell you whether Jesus personally believed in a remote, aloof consciousness as prime creator, one with more peaceful, civilized characteristics than pictured in his time, and thus wanted to explain how to deal with that conceptualized entity – or whether he fully realized the inner-outer flow and simply had to put his explanation into a deity-based framework that his contemporaries could grasp. Drawing only on quotes placed into Jesus' mouth by the gospel writers, it is impossible to pinpoint just how aware Jesus was of the pure function of Reality: on one end of the scale are some highly cognizant statements indicating a very Clear Awareness and, at the other end, some oddly structured statements that make no sense in any regard. But ***exactly that*** is what one would expect from third and fourth party repetitions of original, visionary words – some would get passed on by rote repetition, others would get garbled by original misunderstanding, rephrasing, dimming memory, insensitive translation and a long, distorting tradition.

Had Jesus been regarded by his contemporaries and following generations as a wise and perceptive teacher, people might have greatly benefited by his teachings. But, following his death, the movement to spread his case as being ***the*** Messiah (Christ, in Greek, but by that time signifying not a political revolutionary leader but a direct connect to god), initiated by Paul, primarily, changed him into a mythological character: son of the conceptualized god, like the offspring of a Greek god and a human.

(In fact, the virgin birth and other miraculous elements were undoubtedly retrofit into the gospel accounts later to add a convincing argument for spreading Christianity among superstitious pagan peoples. Paul, in his writing, which predates the gospels chronologically, never referenced a virgin birth origin, where one would judge this to be a significant point if it were known at the time and not invented later. Also, the writer of the Gospel of Matthew makes a great effort to connect Jesus to the line of David through his father Joseph, when, had Jesus been born of a virgin, Joseph would have had no role in the lineage!)

The point here is that Jesus was without doubt a man with vision well beyond his peers, trying to illustrate to a primitive people a better grasp for How Life Works. Significant points of his teachings reveal that. But his message was lost on most of his listeners, and the committed followers, along with the late-arriving Paul, carried on a fallacious notion that mythologized the man and trivialized the message: you only had to believe in his status as son of their god and everything would be fine regardless of how you lived.

And that absurd, ideological notion became the root of Christianity as Paul spread his own vision while establishing and influencing the early church. So people in the name of Christianity can – and often enough do – launch wars, kill people, foment prejudice, punish, abuse and torture, whatever they choose, but somehow justify their actions as supportive of their idealistic god-notion. And they don't see the inconsistency, even when Jesus spoke of forgiveness and loving of enemies and friends alike.

We'll get back to Paul shortly, though. For now, the focus is on Jesus and…

What the Man Meant

The Aramaic language spoken by Jesus of Nazareth was widespread in the Middle East at that time. His version, from a hilly, remote district north of Judah called Galilee, would have been an unpolished, rural dialect, offering little richness in direct, explicit expression.

With a greater perspective to present to his unsophisticated listeners, Jesus had to picture concepts, not in explicit descriptions as I lay out here, but in short, picturesque stories – likening his better understanding to various situations within grasp of his listeners. His reference to a "*malkutha*" in phrases traditionally translated as "Kingdom" (either "of Heaven" or "of God"), served, like his parables, **metaphorically** for an **anticipated psychological or spiritual state**. That differs fundamentally from a real YHWH-controlled political state in a physical location, as in the more explicit traditional use of that phrase referencing the hoped-for state of Jewish legal law rid of Roman rule.

Significantly, in Luke, Jesus is quoted as saying, when pressed as to ***when*** this Kingdom of Heaven would come, "The Kingdom of God does not arrive visibly, nor will they say, 'Here it is,' or 'There it is', for the Kingdom of God is ***within you***." Consistent with his explanations that this *malkutha* is "at hand," Jesus' described, not some far off, ideological, eschatological landscape with Yahweh, a Zeus-like deity, wielding a scepter in control of his pet humans, but rather a state of mind attainable by each individual **in short order *by delving within.***

(Sound familiar? With the recourse of flexible, modern English, presented to a much more sophisticated, educated and enlightened listener, I can be much more explicit in my illustration of this mindset. I needn't resort to parables and disjointed references, as Jesus had to. And I'm writing this myself, not awaiting others' blurred accounts with dim memories of what I might have said in one of my talks.)

In Matthew Jesus is quoted thusly: "But I tell you the truth, there are some standing here who will not taste death before they see the Kingdom of God." Unlike mainline Christian theology, looking for a grand and glorious realm of special effects in a forever future time (i.e., it never seems to get here) or a post-death heavenly state following judgment (a notion out of Zoroastrianism), Jesus' key message specifically points out a state of mind **attainable in the present**, during life, for those individuals attuned to perceiving it.

Indeed, in teaching and implication, as well as through healing, Jesus repeatedly illustrated this state of mind, this Kingdom of Heaven within, likening it to situations his listeners could relate to. Here are a few examples, followed by a clarification and my comments extracting the real gist:

From the Sermon on the Mount:

- "Blessed are the meek, for they shall inherit the earth."
    - Inconsistent with any western notion of Darwinian Natural Selection, where the strong survive to dominate any given species and, counter to previous Hebrew traditions, where Yahweh was beseeched to overcome enemies, Jesus' famous words here presage EoR: in that your experience stems from your inner state, not from external forces and conceptualized sources, when you are at peace inwardly, your life will work well.
    - ✓ The meekness he refers to is a non-aggressive characteristic nature that comes naturally when you quit blaming your problems on others outside yourself and subsequently, having cleared negation from your mindset, stop having to engage them in conflict.
    - ✓ Indeed, as stated here, individuals with Clear Awareness will slowly displace those who rely on rational override and its innate conflict and struggle, just as modern man displaced the lesser Neanderthal.
- "Blessed are those who hunger and thirst after righteousness, for they will be filled."
    - If, open-minded and sincere, you seek to understand How Life

Works, you will come to see it.

- "Blessed are the pure in heart, for they shall see God."
  - As you come to disengage your complex set of beliefs and definitions, lay aside your fears and aggressions, your prejudices and pre-judgment, you will see what's happening here.
  - ✓ Yahweh, the god in Jesus' time was not to be looked upon, so powerful and fearful was he conceived to be. This could not be a realistic reference to visually perceiving a deity.
  - ✓ Only the "pure in heart" – those who had cleared away synthetic notions and distorting beliefs – would see that what was heretofore considered to be a remote, capricious, judgmental and activist god, was indeed, ***all of Reality itself***, manifesting out of the inner directives of the Self.

Love your enemies, your neighbors:

- In Matthew and Luke, Jesus implores listeners: "Love your enemies, do good to those who hate you."
  - This valuable insight indicates that negative feelings, held with a focus toward others, will always prove self-defeating – basically recycling the negative emotion into subsequent events featuring future enemies.
  - ✓ The entreaty reveals an understanding by Jesus that perceived enemies are not the ***cause*** of one's problems and shouldn't be blamed for negative effects. Clearly, he realized that one draws into experience events and relationships consistent with one's own inner nature, and that problems need to be addressed ***within one's own mindset***, not as a calculated reaction to threatening agents.
  - ✓ This perspective is largely lost on followers of Christianity, who are likely to nod their heads in agreement at the idea, then go out and do harm in retribution to perceived enemies – often harkening back on old-testament thinking to justify it.
- And, "Love your neighbor as yourself."
  - ✓ To love somebody just because Jesus said to is impossible. Real love

is a sincere feeling, not a sham put on for the purpose of satisfying some edict or fooling a god into thinking you are really a wonderful person.

- ✓ As you come to see life clearly, unbridled love – the basis of your nature in the first place – becomes the **default** feeling about all others, uncompromised by jealously, suspicion, fear and other negative feelings.

- Both gospels relate the concept of turning the other cheek when struck on one, giving up even more if somebody would take from you, etc.
  - Again, the perpetrator of negative action, while real and obvious in the living event, is only replicating in your life inner elements of conflict that your mindset itself entails.
  - ✓ To change the nature of such conflictual encounters – so they don't happen again – the vital focus must be on eliminating the conflict and struggle as they persist in your own mindset, not retaliation.
  - ✓ I don't concur with turning the other cheek, so much as disengaging the immediate situation, then delving within to understand your own nature and then change it. Jesus did not have at hand adequate tools for delving inward to affect change, as prayer in his terms would not have been too effective – even counter-productive in many ways.

Healing:

- The primitive belief set of Jesus' time attributed the cause of illness, physical and mental, to possession by evil spirits. Much of Jesus' healing was accomplished by his dismissing those evil spirits (consistent with the belief set of the sufferer), whereby the person seemed to be made whole via his power.
  - However, he often took care to state something to the effect that, "your beliefs have made you whole." Clearly, there ***were no*** such possessing spirits. But by dealing authoritatively with people within the framework of their imagined causal forces, he was perceived as more powerful than the spirits and was able to affect a healing of psychological-based illness. Healing thus fit into in the

context of ***their*** accepted paradigm of how things worked.

- ✓ What isn't recorded, of course, is what happened to those people when they went home and proceeded with their lives. If they didn't outgrow the negative inner elements, they would have simply channeled the pain and conflict into some other illness. The gospels, trying to push a particular slant, don't do any follow-up studies.
- ✓ And there was, undoubtedly, significant exaggeration of the "miracles" as these stories were told and retold prior to the accounts in the gospels.

- Modern day believers, accepting Paul's Christ-as-son-of-god notion, picture Jesus as a source of mystical power that could heal illnesses as a causal, effective force on real events.
  - However, as referenced in Mark, when Jesus returned to Nazareth, where people still saw him as the local carpenter, he was unable to bring about any healing. In Luke, his references to his own status bring the townsfolk to nearly chuck him over the cliff.
  - ✓ Had he had the power pictured by Christians, it would have been **an absolute**, not dependent on the beliefs of the recipient. In reality, his ability to heal outside his hometown relied on the beliefs of the rather superstitious population, his growing reputation and his own confidence by virtue of his self-image that events would work out for him as he traveled through the region.

Through parables, Jesus likened the Kingdom of Heaven to:

- A mustard seed, the smallest of seeds that would grow to a large tree and…
- Yeast, which, when mixed with flour, grows to permeate it completely.
  - With the mustard seed and yeast metaphors, he illustrates a state of mind that, as a small and insignificant thing, would, like a seed, grow to dominate one's mindset or like yeast, come to permeate all aspects. (Reference Lao Tzu's "Small though it is…" description.)
  - ✓ This image applies just like Clear Awareness and the process of clearing out old, restrictive programming – as you come to see life

clearly, the perspective and its resultant inner peace grow to dominate your life.

- A narrow gate through which few will pass, while most take the wide gate to destruction.
  - ○ Most people in Jesus' or my time seem content with standard, traditional ways of looking at things: the wide gate, as a metaphorical passage, guarantees conflict and trouble.
  - ✓ The journey inward is the narrow gate, indeed, and it leads to creativity, peace and the dispensing of concern over threats, ill health, death, etc, for those who make it.

The entreaties:

- In Matthew, Jesus is quoted, "Do not judge, or you also will be judged…"
  - ○ In judging others, you set up a value system that you, yourself will fall into. As seen in Angle Two, you are not immune to self-punishment, and your own self-image will be built into your reflected Reality.
  - ✓ The point here is to accept others and yourself, as they are and as you are. Full acceptance, which is love itself, doesn't judge based on rational, typically cultural, standards. Fully aware of what is "out there" reflecting your own nature, you will accept it as it is.
  - ✓ (This does not imply that you should not seek to change those elements of Self that lead to failure and rejection. Accepting yourself "as you are" can allow growth into a new nature that you also accept. Rejection of your own being by critically comparing your attributes to others' will only recycle negativity.)
- Then he is said to question, why try to take the speck out of your brother's eye, when you have a plank in your own? First, he suggests, remove the plank in your own eye so that you can see clearly to remove the brother's speck.
  - ○ Always, ***you*** need to arrive at Clear Awareness before you begin telling others the way. (See Angle Three, Passing Awareness to your

Children.)

- ✓ But caution: each step brings a greater degree of freedom and improvement, so that it is not unusual to speak as though you see from the top of the mountain, when you have only just reached a lower ridge, with a considerable climb yet to make.
- ✓ If everybody who doesn't really understand How Life Works would quit talking about it, pushing invalid paradigms and incomplete enlightenment, reiterating illusory belief structures, this world would be a much, much quieter place.

- Later, he adds, "Do not give dogs what is sacred; do not throw your pearls to swine."
  - Basically, don't offer higher perspectives to those who aren't open to them.
  - ✓ I have experienced this astute suggestion on several occasions while speaking to groups that included strong believers in religion or science. It is a waste of time to present greater perspectives to those who are not open to hearing them.
  - ✓ Worth emphasizing: there is always the tendency to share greater perspectives, as you achieve them, with friends and family. Often, though, these relationships do not involve people who are also on the Inner Journey. Those will make their way when their time is right, which may not be now, in this lifetime. Your Journey is yours alone; your perspectives, as you attain them, should be shared at the right time, with the right people – and that will be done, when the time ***is*** right. Encountering conflict and argument from others indicates ***your own*** inner struggle and conflict are still intact.
- And, "Ask and it will be given to you; seek and you will find…"
  - I covered this one way back in Angle One: set your course for clearly understanding life.
  - ✓ When you do, and you don't waver to accepting some lesser philosophy and its contrived paradigm, you will come to Clear Awareness.
- "Except you be converted and become as little children, you shall not

enter into the Kingdom of Heaven."

  - This is as close as Jesus could come to specifying a process of clearing out old beliefs and definitions. He tried to illustrate the open-minded naivety of a child and offered an entreaty for the listeners to regain it.
  - ✓ This quote, though, comes down in Christianity as a whole movement to declare yourself "born again" and thus somehow achieve what Jesus suggested. Unfortunately, people who energetically claim to be born again seem to reincarnate with exactly the same mindset as before, thus neutralizing the whole gesture.
  - ✓ In reality, this is not a trite gesture, as in a personal declaration, but a thorough effort to clear out the preexisting belief structure – which includes any archaic notions innate to fundamentalist Christianity.
  - ✓ (Note again the similarity to Lao Tzu: "Become as a little child once more…")

I could go on with this look at Jesus' perspectives, but you will understand them yourself as you proceed toward Clear Awareness. Here, though, are elements of his teaching as put forth in the gospels that **are *not*** indicative of a thoroughly enlightened status:

- His entreaty to the disciples to approach only Jews.
  - ✓ All human cultural and ethnic subgroups will have some individuals who are open to new perspectives and many who aren't. It would be out of character for a truly Aware person to arbitrarily limit the message to one ethnic group.
- His apparent painful demise via crucifixion.
  - ✓ If this really happened, it is a clear indication he had not cleared out all inner conflict. The "why have you forsaken me?" entreaty to his god indicates a surprise at the flow of events totally out of the scope of Christian image of him as son of that god. It indicates more likely the painful, stunning realization that that god didn't exist.

- ✓ It is, however, a significant message to people that consciousness survives the end of a lifetime. Jesus seemed to be aware of that, as illustrated earlier.
- ✓ But the material return of the physical body, long a fallacious notion of Jesus' time and before (e.g., Egyptian god Horus rising from the dead Osiris), is an archaic notion. Jesus' physical return from being executed via crucifixion is certainly a fabrication, as evidenced by significantly differing accounts in the gospels.

- "Blessed are the merciful, for they will obtain mercy."
  - ✓ Not necessarily, as the two aspects are not absolutely connected: witness multitudes of nice people being treated brutally.
  - ✓ Jesus was hinting at the characteristic reflection in one's life of one's own qualities, but apparently wasn't fully cognizant of complex mechanisms by which the Oneness functions. Being compassionate doesn't necessarily translate into receiving similar treatment from others: they emerge from different mind elements, as evidenced in thousands of Christian martyrs fed to lions and otherwise abused in the early centuries.
  - ✓ Indeed, how you are treated is a reflection of your self-image, your own level of authority and many other inner elements.
- The Lord's Prayer: "Our father, which art in Heaven, hallowed be thy name…"
  - ✓ This severely damaging repetition projects your will out to this ethereal, conceptualized god, thus denuding you of your innate power to realize ***your*** will and live in happiness.
  - ✓ Repeating any such ritualistic, self-deflating statement, over and over, is extremely damaging as you jam it ever deeper into the unconscious belief set.
- "Lay up for yourself treasures in Heaven…"
  - ✓ Doing without some level of comfort and abundance in ***this*** life does not inherently build up positive credits for later lives; it only assures some current level of misery.
  - ✓ Jesus too often – and incorrectly – dissociates this life and the

quality of it from some later heavenly existence. Basically, in actuality, ***this is it*** – right here, right now! If you aren't enjoying things, successful and healthy ***now***, that in itself is the issue and needs to be dealt with so that your life is reflective of your will. The Inner Journey is not undertaken only to set up some future existence, but to improve life ***NOW***, which is your only existing status.

- "Think not that I have come to send peace on earth; I came not to send peace, but a sword."
  - ✓ This is either a later fabrication, a twist of his original meaning, or something else is mighty wrong: love and peace have nothing to do with weapons.
- Changing water to wine, walking on water.
  - ✓ Sorry, but these things, like the virgin birth, didn't happen. These were likely add-ons meant to impress potential converts.
  - ✓ The purpose in life is not to create special effects out of sync with reality, but to engender a life of real, non-miraculous events that don't need fancy tricks to make it work right. The goal is not to heal life-threatening illnesses or encounters, but rather ***to not experience them*** in the first place.

Before I move on to consider the impact on Jesus' teaching as a result of Paul, time and religious bureaucracy, I would offer you an added perspective on the Beatitudes. That well-known set of teachings by Jesus is rather inconsistent. Those who are truly "blessed" – not implying sacred, deity-initiated consecration, but indicating a clear, advantageous effect on the flow of one's life – would have these characteristics, without the poetic nuance:

- **Open minds** – for only they may see life clearly.
- **Patience** – for that trait is vital to the Inner Journey.
- **Independence of spirit** – as only they will have the fortitude to ever be free.
- **A questioning, doubting nature** – only for them will a path be opened

toward clear vision.

Christianity Emerges from Paul's Corporate Takeover

Displacing Peter and the Originals from the Board

After Jesus died, his disciples, who had followed him through his teaching time, convinced that Jesus was the long sought after Messiah, tried to spread his message among the Jews. From all indications in the Gospels, Peter, John, James and the others, who became known as Apostles (messengers), really didn't grasp what Jesus was getting at. Their attempts to dent the firmly armored belief structures of their peers didn't get too far either – and indeed never has among Jews.

But another teacher entered the scene. Saul of Tarsus had been actively involved in persecuting avowed Christians, until he had a vision wherein Jesus, in a bright light from heaven, told him to stop it.

(Note: people didn't have family names attached to their monikers back then, which makes it particularly difficult to distinguish this John from that one, e.g., the Apostle from the writer of the fourth Gospel. And their names don't seem as permanent: at one point in the narrative of the Acts, the fifth New Testament book that covers the early Christian period, Saul's name simply changes to "Paul.")

(Note also: any such subjective vision is based on the mindset of the perceiver, thoroughly rooted in that person's belief structure. The Jesus whom Saul encountered on the road to Damascus was not the real, previously incarnated person, levitating in the sky, blasting out bright celestial lights and directives, but a hallucinatory version brewed up by Saul's superstitious subconscious. Such visions are ***always*** self-generated illusory perceptions, customized for meaningful content based on an individual's propensities.)

As early Christianity became a growing body of believers, according to the Acts, it was Paul who, nudging his way into the scene, began to spread the message to other peoples in the region – principally Greeks, but also to Semitic groups. This gesture opened up something of a rift between the original disciples and Paul. But, in that the originals were encountering great resistance from Jews, as did Paul in several life-threatening episodes, the pathway through non-Jewish believers came to be the route to the establishment of Christianity as a religion.

However, the core theology ultimately built into Christianity was **not** based on teachings from Jesus of Nazareth. That message, as I've illustrated, hinted at a personal state of mind that featured peace, forgiveness and fulfillment of one's will. Paul had never met nor seen Jesus. Paul's driving motivation was his image of Jesus as this glorified figure out of heaven, the object of his Damascus vision. So the nature of the religion he spread was not about an inner Kingdom of Heaven to be found ***within*** during this lifetime, a yeast that can grow to dominate life, a non-judgmental attitude wherein enemies can be loved as friends, but rather something of a self-sacrifice to a neo-mythological, aggrandized offspring of a glorified god, which he had turned Jesus into. The "Christ" moniker is simply Greek for the Aramaic word, "Messiah," but Paul vaulted it into a supernatural status almost equal to that of the imagined god.

Paul set into motion several concepts that rolled, as snowballs, real or conceptual, are wont to, into cornerstone aspects of Christianity. These are worth exploring, in that they carry subtle reflections on life that became incorporated into western attitudes along with the adoption of this religion as it spread through the Roman Empire and thus into European culture:

- The Debate over Mosaic Law.
  - Jesus and his followers, as Jews, observed practices of food preparation and condoned action as proscribed in the Law.
  - As Paul expanded presentation of the gospel out to Gentiles, the debate brewed as to whether new converts had to be circumcised, follow rigid food cleanliness standards, etc. Eventually the version of Jewish customs that did find its way into Christian practice was watered down so as not to turn away converts. (Circumcision, for

example, was not a big selling point for the potential adult male convert.)

- ✓ Of course, all of these Jewish traditions are based on artificial definitions that accumulated over millennia. Some might have hygienic advantages for improved living, but none are inherently valid – primarily because the god who was supposed to be decreeing them, or in whose name they were affixed into cultural practice, never existed.
- ✓ While such practices form a cohesive, cultural bond among Jewish peoples, there is absolutely no innate value to following them. Indeed, the jettison of such closed-minded practices must be part of any path to personal freedom.

- **Jesus as Christ** – a semi-god-equivalent figure.
    - Paul, having never encountered Jesus, the man, had no apparent interest in his life and teaching. He was always referencing the vision of Jesus he'd encountered and rolling that mind image into a puffed-up god offshoot that the naïve believer would need to accept as the Christ, "Son of God," figure. However, that Greek term no longer meant a political revolutionary, but a savior who would deliver the believer from judgment for sins.
    - And that harkens back to the notion of a vindictive, judgmental, punishing god – basically what Yahweh had morphed into. The thought was that this god would ultimately judge each person for sinful deeds following death and mete out punishment accordingly. Acceptors of this new Christianity could avoid that potentially eternal thumbs-down by simply believing the fiction that Christ was intervening to save them.
    - (Sin itself constitutes a whole mishmash of deeds carried out against one's fellow man and/or against god's dictates: simple ones like lust and adultery and more serious ones like murder and blasphemy. In Jewish lore, sin required atonement by carrying out specific acts or would be a blotch on one's record come judgment. Jesus, as pictured

by Paul, provided an easy way out: his martyred death provided blanket atonement, saving those who believed in his status from negative judgment for any and all sins committed.)

- ✓ In the complex picture of defined sinfulness, it is difficult to sort out what is really bad, since many acts regarded as sinful by Jewish or Christian tradition – particularly those in reference to sex – are only defined as such by deviance from synthetic, myth-based standards.
- ✓ Clearly, murder, carrying out wanton harm to others, thievery, etc., is not appropriate action. But such deeds are invariably perpetrated by people who perceive the world as threatening, see themselves as powerless and isolated or who feel that opposing individuals and forces must sometimes be dealt with violently. (Those are all problems, indeed, but are psychological in basis and should be dealt with as such, not regarded as wrongs against a conceptualized god – rendering it mythological in status and providing no real solution whatsoever.)
- ✓ The real problem becomes, then, not sinfulness and punishment, but **lack of Awareness for How Life actually Works**. The solution is not a batch of convoluted laws and regulations to follow or a myth to accept as truth, but personally growing out of the limited state of self-awareness into perceiving how the encountered world reflects one's own inner nature.
- ✓ **In real effect**, this over-inflated, mythic image of Christ as deliverer is fallacious and enormously counter-productive to improvement of mankind's condition.

- **Belief vs. Acts** – what gets you saved.
  - With Jesus propped up as a near-god in Paul's paradigm, then, belief in him became the ultimate insurance policy against any future judgment. Personal acts constituting, by definition, sinful, negative actions, in Jewish tradition required special acts of repentance, animal sacrifice or other gestures as "atonement". But Christianity guaranteed sinful acts to be forgiven, with Christ the hallowed and

easy way out.

- Paul's teaching did provide a watered-down version of the Law, requiring converts to abstain from certain unclean foods and sexual immorality. And he did emphasize good deeds. But with the sacrifice of Christ being the key, it included more motivation to hypocrisy than sincere good behavior.

✓ A theology or philosophy of any sort becomes a house of cards build on a paradigmatic card table. If you bump the table, i.e., jolt the underlying paradigm, the whole house tumbles into a heap. Christians, not uncharacteristic of humanity, have always looked for eternal happiness in a post-life existence free of pain and suffering and have been willing to do whatever necessary, whether cajole, bribe, entreat or agree to exclusivity, with their perceived, causal god to warrant that heavenly bliss. But the inherent shortcoming to that venture – pardon me while I bump the table – is that the god being cajoled, bribed and entreated ***never existed***. So, the whole mechanism of salvation, of glorification of Jesus, of forgiveness of sins, of judgment day and potential resurrection is a wholly concocted myth.

✓ Consciousness is a characteristic of being, ***your*** being. If you exist now, sitting somewhere in repose, reading these words, your continued existence beyond the course of this lifetime is a given, without question, without condition. Your only judge is ***you yourself***, and the mechanism of judging is based on a value system that you will become ever more aware of as you delve inward.

✓ The mythical notions attached to Jesus by Paul are simply invalid. And the complex of rules and Law, of declarations and intimations as to Jesus and his status are purely illusory. They inherently lead you away from yourself and your own innate goodness toward a never-attainable ideal, thereby depleting your integrity, your self-esteem and your initiative.

✓ Another inherent downside to Paulian Christianity is the tendency toward martyrdom. Seeing clearly the Oneness with which Reality functions, you can jettison negating elements of your mindset and improve your life with each step. Accepting the synthetic tenets of Jesus' aggrandized status, however, leads the believer invariably toward a **worse** life, having projected all power out to imaginary sources. The tendency has been to forgo life's pleasures in lieu of conceptual glorification – even, at the extreme, to sacrifice one's life via martyrdom for these grand but hollow notions.

✓ The only thing you really need to be Saved from are these fear-laced, archaic notions of sin and external judgment by a god who never existed.

- **Original Sin** – the fall of man going back to Adam and Eve.
  - Christianity, thanks in part to Paul, carries the notion that man is inherently flawed because Eve tempted Adam to eat of the tree of good and evil – heretofore forbidden by El – thus plunging man into the depths of sin from the get-go. By this absurd notion (one of the many cards now lying in a heap on the table), each of us is sinful by simply coming into being.

✓ The Adam and Eve story of early Genesis is actually quite fascinating as a metaphor. There was undoubtedly a time when our ancestors, like the wandering herds around them, lived via their senses and intuitive emersion in Reality – finding prey, locating seeds, roots and berries without the intellectual override that we need to do almost anything. In those times, the flora and fauna presented a great offering of plenty, to be gathered or hunted, even scavenged as needed. But, like Eve handing us fruit plucked from the tree of Knowledge of Good and Evil, we bit into the apple of **rationality**. God didn't throw man out of Eden; man walked out on his own by defining things, by constructing logical actions to override his natural impulses. Thus man created a distant, objective world out there and separated himself from all conceived things in the process – not the least of which was **creative power** itself.

✓ We are not sinful by birth. But, at each of our births, if we enter still laced with struggle and conflict innate to rational control, we are once again thrust into the mix of turmoil and resistance, of compromised love and frequent rejection.

✓ Our purpose is to outgrow that struggle, conflict and separation from what's out there ***now***, during a lifetime. And the path towards that is inner and private, not via some mythological pseudo-god or a son of one.

- **Eschatology.**
  - Many religions, not just the Judeo-Christian, anticipate some great, cataclysmic event that would mark the end of man or the end of time. At that point, all souls would be judged, or some other grand and glorious event would happen.

  ✓ In the final analysis, there is no final analysis. Key issues in your life need your attention now, and key problems facing mankind on this planet need solutions. The daily experience of being a human presents an extraordinarily broad potential of accomplishment, creativity, acceptance-or-rejection scenarios, etc. That needs to hold focus, along with the inner Journey towards personal peace needed to allow successful engagement of Reality. The long-distant eschatological outcome of man's destiny at the hand of mythical gods and hypothetical judgments is an illusory, intellectual quest of no real consequence. The only timeframe of importance is the one you inhabit, that of this ***now*** moment.

- **Raising of the Dead.**
  - Inherent in that end-of-time judgment or incorporated in a shorter-term end-of-life judgment is the concept of surviving death. This was pictured in ancient times as a physical return from death, some manner of spiritual reemergence or even reincarnation in another body.
  - Paul, by furthering this notion, wove it rather unspecified into Christian doctrine.

- ✓ Again, as you come to see the functional, innate Oneness between you and the Reality you encounter, you will realize without reliance on my or anybody else's assurance that your existence is timeless and unthreatened.
- ✓ But Consciousness is such that it **always** creates a meaningful Reality to encounter, one in which it can create and engage, adventure and respond. That doesn't imply rising literally from the dead, because that notion carries fallacious temporal implications. (Your old body, or what's left of it come the end of time, would be neither practical nor inviting to reoccupy.)
- ✓ You will reincarnate as something or somebody in some timeframe in somehere (as opposed to "somewhere"), because, however far you venture into Self in this lifetime, there will be much more to explore. And, indeed, there isn't much else to do: discarnate observation of a real scenario is equivalent to watching a movie vs. living the adventure first hand. (Of course, following death, you will stick around for a while to see how things you were involved in work out. But then you'll move on.)

So Paul effectively discarded Jesus' unique message and substituted his own which, while not without merit, is not reflective of How Life Works. Paul worked tirelessly to integrate his notions into the growing local groups of converts and ultimately launched a new religion laced with his own less than perceptive definitions.

Competing with various archaic pagan belief sets (or absorbing them) and even faced with vicious and brutal resistance (people, particularly the small-minded and superstitious, don't easily give up beliefs they were indoctrinated into), Christianity grew in numbers and came to dominate the Roman Empire.

We can rejoin the growth of the early church shortly. But the fertile field of pagan understandings in which the seeds of Paul's doctrine sprouted deserves a quick look; it was that base mindset onto which Christian notions were grafted, and much remains of its primitive notions in your mindset…

Querying, Appeasing and Otherwise Creating the Gods

Edible Roots of Western Thought

As the Indo-European peoples, with a bent for agriculture (and consequently a burgeoning population) along with mastery of horses, metal-working and chariots, expanded into sparsely populated regions of Europe – as well as south- and eastwards – they took their gods with them. The Greek Zeus (Pater), Roman Jupiter and Vedic Dyaus Pitar, are all rooted in similar pantheonic mythologies.

In the timeframe from 4000 BCE through the Roman Empire, while Indo-European cultures expanded, separated and thus differentiated to become the Celts, Goths, Slavs, Hittites, Anatolians, Persians, Greeks, Hindus, etc., attitudes towards these conceptualized gods evolved as well.

Generally, though, the gods were seen by each of the Indo-European offshoots to influence, if not dictate, the flow of daily events. Gods, interwoven in man's cognition of reality, had long since become associated with the planets as they moved through the night sky. They were seen to govern the days: it is no passing coincidence that the sun and moon, along with the five visible planets, each had a day of influence corresponding to the seven-day length of a week – if Uranus were visible to the naked eye, we would assuredly have a week eight days long.

Astrology grew out of this conceptual intermingling of the movement of the heavenly bodies and real events – and the former was deemed causal over the latter. Thus the common man imagined the gods to be engaged in human affairs: to influence fertility and weather, to initiate natural disasters and to impel events, each god to its own specialty.

But those gods were not worshipped in quite the same fashion as Yahweh and the Heavenly Father came to be. In pre-Roman times, the gods were beseeched for positive events and assuaged with rituals and temples (and, of course, dealt with via dedicated priesthoods who lived well off the superstitions of the people). Fearing what the gods might deliver, people queried them for prognostication purposes by gutting animals and examining their entrails (certifying at least a dim future for those animals), casting bones or consulting with oracles. The gods, with evolving personalities and separate realms of influence woven into myth and fable, were part of the way of life. Indeed, so interwoven in daily rituals were the gods, there wasn't even a ***word*** for religion until Romans evolved one in later Latin usage.

In terms of common understanding for the flow of events in daily life, however, even the gods' influence was trumped by the Fates, who appear in various forms in European lore. For the Greeks, the Moirae preset one's destiny by their actions: Clotho spun the thread of life, while Lachesis measured and Atropos snipped the thread at a length determined by…

Determined by what? Therein lies the mystery that religious notions, astrology, myth and eventually science have attempted to clarify for ages. If you can determine the process behind the unfolding of life events, then you can influence the causal forces to make things happen favorably – good health, abundance and success instead of the opposites or lack thereof.

Our European ancestors, then, maintained a mindset that events unfolded in a meaningful fashion, but that the meaning was imposed by gods and the fates based on whimsical or taunting grounds, sometimes rewarding, sometimes punishing – but always, invariably, at the behest of some ***remote, conscious, causal force*** other than the individual him- or herself.

One other factor did mildly influence the western mindset: the rational regard of philosophers, primarily emerging in Greece during their Golden Age.

* * *

It required a certain level of civilization to even tolerate free pondering about the workings of reality. Mesopotamia and Egypt, eventually the Mediterranean and Asia Minor, had hosted advanced cultures for millennia already, wherein trade, significant building, complex government and bureaucracy (although one shutters to list bureaucracy as an indicator of civilization), coordinated farming and shipping of produce, etc., were well developed. But significant, free-form musing about what ***really*** was going on here, beyond simply adding variations to the theme of the current notion of godhood, required a certain level of tolerance and openness to ideas.

It was in the rather democratic city-states of Greece, primarily Athens, by the middle of the first millennium BCE that such an unbridled form of regard for ideas and discussion could emerge. Even then, Socrates, accused of angering the gods – Athena, the prime protector of the city, had obviously been offended enough to unleash some natural disaster – encountered the limits of his time. Unwilling to stop the free exploration of open ideas, blamed for Athena's wrath, he was forced to drink poison.

But his successors, primarily Plato, achieved a rather remarkable insight into How Life Works. Platonic realism and various metaphors picturing the function of reality are highly perceptive, framing a remarkable insight for his early time. Angle Two referenced his Allegory of the Cave, with captives interpreting shadows on the wall as reality. In that metaphor, he went on to imagine that one of the captives got loose to discover the source of the shadows and even to exit the cave. Once outside, the former captive could see the sun and real things well beyond the limited focus of his cave experience. However, should he return to his fellow captives and try to explain what he'd encountered behind them and outside of the cave, he wouldn't have words to explain it and probably wouldn't get the idea across.

(That difficulty, of course, is akin to the opening to EoR where the adventurer tries to explain the essence of the White Mountain God to his tribesmen – and precisely the problem I face in weaving into these pages a notion of what's happening here beyond the current ken of the reader's usual mindset.)

In picturing the "Demiurge" as a manifestation of infinite Monad (the Oneness, the functional interrelatedness of all things) into this finite realm, Plato was very close to seeing How Life Works. Similarly, Plato's thoughts of dualism depict each real object as an imperfect iteration of a perfect Form or Idea, which exist independent of any individual thinker. In that regard, Ideas, absolute and perfect concepts behind imperfect "real" things, do indeed constitute the principal **inner** reality.

While unspecific as to how the Demiurge actually works or how Idea becomes real, Plato, living not long after Gautama the Buddha and Lao Tzu (probably) and four centuries before Jesus, pierces much deeper into Reality's illusion than any prior western source, particularly avoiding the standard attribution of causality to some, indeed, **any** external god.

But, as much as it would be worthy to examine Plato's ideas and variations that ensued through time, Greek and subsequent philosophical expression, however astute, made little inroads into the common mindset – and thus into ***your*** core understanding as absorbed through your culture via your parents. For, however intuitive, however insightful great thinkers have been through the ages, their ideas have led mostly to philosophical debate within intellectual and academic circles, not toward greater awareness of mankind in general. (Understand, too, that each philosopher hosts subtle limitations within his/her mindset and worldview that lead to hard conclusions beyond which that person could not move without changing the core definitions underlying the limitations – definitions to which they are generally blind. Thus philosophy becomes a never-ending interplay of debate between people, who, however brilliant, are neither privy to nor capable of eliminating their own limitations.)

But, for whatever disregard of specifics and eternal debate of philosophical elements that took place, at least the inquiry initiated man's curiosity to explore and examine Reality to discern a better understanding than archaic religious notions, rooted in primitive fears, did or ever could provide. And that inquiry would lead to science as a means to examine nature – but only after a while.

The next step was taking the conceptual walls that constitute the great, overriding Western Mindset, this default notion of attributing causality to the gods and their whims, to fate and luck and slapping a new coat of paint on them.

A Simpler Paradigm

Converting Heathens and Pagans via God Reduction

So, as Paul and others went about Middle East and Mediterranean towns, speaking to groups that were coalescing around the new religion, they had to replace, generally, a pantheon of tired old gods and rituals with a new concept – a single god of all things. A single, all-powerful creative god is a bit of a step from a committee of specialized gods, but the concept is the same – like a supermarket replacing the butcher, baker and produce shops. Ah, but this new god, it was said, had just incarnated his son who could do miracles and heal people. Yes, and he was going to come back one day soon to establish a kingdom where everything would be wonderful.

Given the alternatives – trite gods and brutal secular attitudes – a lot of people bought into Christianity over time. Indeed, the growing religious order and the bureaucracy that came to control it willingly bent the tenets to appeal to the pre-formatted expectations of potential converts: Christmas, a celebration of the birth of Jesus, was conveniently placed at the year-end Roman Saturnalia festival, complete with gift giving. Easter, celebrating Jesus' reputed rebirth following crucifixion, was plugged into the handy time spot of spring fertility rites heretofore pointed at Eostre (or some variant spelling), a minor Germanic god of appropriate connection – after all, Easter bunnies and eggs are purely fertility symbols, having nothing to do with Jesus in any fashion. (Not that Santa Claus, Christmas trees, Yule logs, reindeer, kitschy decorations and unending commercialism have anything to do with Jesus' birth or message…)

Anyway, the main precepts associated with early Christianity began to differentiate during the first three centuries, based on local ideas and preferences as variations on Paul's original theme. For much of that time, Christians incurred the wrath of other religions and governments – wrenching old ideas loose equates to pulling cultural teeth. By about 300 CE, though, the upstart religion began to settle in and gain official acceptance.

Constantine had grasped control of the Roman Empire and thanked the

Christian God for one of his key victories – consistent with his superstitious Roman mindset, though, he continued to pay homage to other gods. But Constantine's Edict of Milan in 313 legalized Christianity and significantly reduced its persecution. (There is a lot more to it than that, but this isn't a history book. If you have any adherence to Christianity, you ought to explore its history and evolution in detail – the more you know about the emergence of this religion, the less likely you are to retain your psychological adherence to it.) With some degree of state acknowledgement, the religion took on a greater scope – and an added institutional responsibility. It was clear the wide disparity of doctrine, with each region holding its preferred interpretation of evolving theology – often replete with significant controversy – was in need of standardization. Constantine called together the Council of Nicaea in 325 to boil things down to a concrete doctrine.

Some 300 of the 1800 bishops and church leaders invited attended this first major conference, hosted and promoted by Constantine. They addressed numerous controversies and political schisms confronting the church, primary of which was the Arian controversy. It is worth some attention here to emphasize how the focus of organized religion had changed in centuries immediately following Jesus' death from the meaning of his message as highlighted above to mythological minutiae.

By about 200, the church had enhanced the image of a single God, Jesus' "Father," into a "Trinity," consisting of the Father, the Son and the Holy Spirit, all of which were somehow (defying reason, grammar, Jesus' teaching and common sense) One. This, of course, was the result of 150 years of clueless extrapolation of Paul's teaching along with notions from the Gospel of John elevating Jesus to a super-human status.

By 300, with this Trinity now accepted as "real," Arius, a theologian from Alexandria, argued that the Son of God (one part of the Trinity), since he was begotten (or created) by the Father had his substance from nothing and therefore, prior to that, didn't exist. Alexander of Alexandria (the real authority there) claimed that the Son and Father were of the same substance and thus co-eternal in existence.

(Of course, **neither** the Father nor Son **had any substance *whatsoever***, in that they, along with the convoluted Trinity definition, were mind images, conceptualizations vivid in the wash of piety and avid imagination of early church founders. But the extensive debate for this and other bureaucratic and political banalities during this early stage indicates how the church, already by that time, had deviated from Jesus' real message toward meaningless definition of grandiose, mythological concepts – and eternal debate within the ranks about the details. Eventually, after many a twist on the Father/Son relationship and the significance of the Holy Ghost concept, recurrent infighting about the status of the Son lead to the filioque debate – look it up, as it's too absurd to get into here – and ultimately the Great Schism, a split between the Roman church in the West, i.e., Europe and the Greek "Orthodox" organization in the East.)

Thus the Council of Nicaea was called, at the behest of Constantine, to formalize a creed and doctrine in the face of continued hypothesizing, debating and bickering. It did accomplish that, producing the Nicene Creed, but that creed continued to be enhanced and debated, argued about and fought over, for many centuries.

Basically, then, Christianity, its formal tenets being the forced output of a large committee of church functionaries prodded by a pagan emperor, came down to modern times not promoting the direct word of its Savior, but an ad hoc, agreed-upon set of old writings and definitions. And the church institution, the holiest of bureaucracies, subsequently split many times over into factions that harbor pet beliefs and favored definitions, all run by people adhering to small, archaic, mythological theologies. Each denomination that germinated from the original seems content to run its own bureaucratic organization, reap wealth from its dogmatized congregation, foment ongoing definitions as truths and heap scorn on others who would criticize it.

I have pointed out what Jesus was implying in his teachings. But the Christian faith, rather than focus on his words – which would be the most significant aspect of the whole picture, if Jesus were ***really*** God incarnate or his Son, as believed – invests its beliefs in Paul's notions, distortions of selected phrases from the gospels, carryover Old Testament Yahweh attitudes and evolving images and impressions. Here are the main points generally held by various Christian groups today, with some pertinent perspectives added:

- **Belief in a single god, named "God."**
  - As pointed out, the nature of this god has changed significantly through time, evolving as the mindset of the prophets and priesthoods convinced believers in the current, fashionable version.
  - Even though this deity has evolved through its 2000 years, it somehow maintains in its current version all old characteristics, whether conflicting or consistent: readiness to punish but ability to heal, vindictiveness yet forgiveness, utter cruelty to outside non-believers but looking for converts, etc.
  - Actually, modern Christianity, devolving from monotheism, defines three gods in the Trinity – Father, Son and Holy Ghost – but calls these three "one." This notion has long been debated, mostly because it has neither substance nor validity and thus can only appear true when accepted by an individual through a combination of belief, ignorance and gullibility. (Note: there can be no debate as to How Life Works, which is apparent when you come to see it clearly. There can only be debate about how it appears to work when your perception is distorted by fallacious notions.)
  - Indeed, Christianity holds yet another god: Satan. This counter force to the "Almighty" is an antagonistic figure out of Zoroastrian and earlier lore who can make bad things happen. Does this Devil figure, apparently able in Christian mythology to conjure up negative events, have innate power of his own? Or is he somehow tolerated by an uncaring God figure? (Actually, of course, neither of these relationships exists, because neither God nor Satan exists, save in the imagination of the fearful believer.)
  - And Roman Catholicism elevates Mary, Jesus' mother, to god-like status. Not to mention many lesser gods, called prophets, who have been deemed powers just like the old pagan gods.

- ✓ Redirecting belief from numerous gods to one god with the same powers is not really advancement, just a reduction in imaginary sources.
- ✓ Early gods were worshipped in real form as idols, hand-made creations representative of the gods. Moving to an imagined god, again, isn't much different: worship of a conceptualization still constitutes projection of real, innate personal power out to some other external power source.

- **Belief that this god is the sole source that created all things at some point in the past, and still makes things happen.**
  - ○ No effort is put at explaining where this god came from, what he (He) was doing before creating this universe, what nature or substance he consists of or in what general environment he exists. (Apparently if not defined in scriptures, it has no importance.)
  - ○ No thought is wasted on imagining a mechanism by which this god makes things happen.
  - ✓ In the distant past, our ancestors imagined the heavens, i.e., the sky, as the abode of the gods – formulating those ideas with the planets (literally, the "wanderers") symbolizing or embodying those gods. They saw the earth as the field of interaction between the gods and man, with events playing out the gods' intent. As people began to explore the heavens with telescopes and rational sense, though, those old notions faded – or should have. This real universe is a vast, unbounded realm of space, with uncountable millions of galaxies visible and each of them containing unfathomable numbers of stars like the sun, each (likely) hosting solar systems like ours. The sole god imagined by early man is nowhere to be seen or detected in the field of encountered reality. But in the realm of imagination, any god with any characteristics can be speculated into existence. Thousands of such deities have been imagined – the Christian "God" is just one of them.

- **Belief that this god created humanity.**
    - He is imagined to monitor each individual's behavior for some divine purpose.
    - He is thought to judge each person's intent, actions and conclusions for ultimate reward or punishment after death.
    - ✓ As outlined above, these archaic notions evolved over time, blending pagan god-attributes with Judaistic and Paulian tenets, totally neglecting Jesus' "Kingdom within" concept.
    - ✓ That a god would create an individual, endow that person with certain specific attributes, then judge his/her performance (resulting from those attributes) based on an arbitrary standard, meting out punishment or reward for life-responses created by that god in the first place **is simply banal**.
    - ✓ As Jesus implied, the creative force is within. As I've been illustrating, far from a remote force, wielded by a divine will, the creative impetus converts elements of mind content into real events simply and automatically. The god, sought for ages out there somewhere, imagined in a myriad of forms, endowed with a plethora of powers, is **the Self**, engendering its own nature into real events and relationships, creating a Reality for its base Consciousness to encounter.

- **Belief that this god in some fashion procreated a humanized "Son"** (Jesus, or "Christ") by impregnating a virgin, for the purpose of sacrificing him later through suffering, thus atoning for man's (or each individual's) sins.
    - In the synoptic gospels, Jesus is portrayed as human, a great teacher, healer and miracle-worker. The elevation to Christ figure and near-god status was based on Paul's vision and later writing by whoever produced the Gospel of John.
    - The virgin birth, as noted, was likely a later add-on to appeal to potential converts.
    - ✓ The elevation of Jesus to super-human status supersedes his valued

message in the minds of believers and thus nullifies it. The aggrandized image fitted on the real Jesus by Paul and others later, turned him into a pantheonic stick-figure myth that, while it has appealed to gullible, superstitious believers for millennia, has no relevance to How Life Works. It only serves to deceive those who can't pierce its archaic imagery.

- **Belief that personal acceptance of Jesus as Christ and Savior would lead to forgiveness of sins and eternal life.**
  - Judaism had held notions of "sin" as affronts to Yahweh's rule, requiring atonement during life or meriting punishment after death (not unlike Zoroastrianism, by the way).
  - Christianity picked up the Sin notion and ran with it. It added "Original Sin" as though all mankind was laced with Sin due to Adam's fall from Grace. It also reemphasized prudish sex taboos and defined deviations from its artificial tenets as sins – ***but*** it substituted for atonement the blanket forgiveness that Jesus earned by dying on the cross to save man from his otherwise certain punishment for apparently unavoidable sinful actions.
  - Original Sin **as a notion** is absurd: you, as an incarnated human, are not liable to any god for anybody's previous failures.
  - ✓ You will not be judged by any god at any point for your actions, which, indeed, are a consequence of your mindset – your beliefs, self-image and worldview.
  - ✓ However, you do ***judge yourself***, based on any accepted notions in a complex mindset – and you may well punish yourself, should you hold guilt and its ramifications within the conglomeration of values and judgment that constitute your nature.

- **Belief that rejection of Jesus' status would lead to eternal damnation.**
  - It still permeates Christianity that outsiders or heretics (people who deem themselves Christian, but choose to interpret things in any

way other than the officially sanctioned, rubber-stamped, orthodox doctrine) are doomed to eternal Hell, via an after-death judgment.

✓ This, of course, has nothing to do with what Jesus was saying. His teaching had to do, as detailed above, with a state of mind attainable now, not a mythological post-death treatment.

✓ And it has nothing to do with Reality.

- **Belief that many, many rituals, basic superstitions, converted pagan practices, prayer, entreaty, sacrifice, repeated dogmatic expressions and other gestures would somehow increase the positive attitudes of this god to elicit positive events.**

  ✓ This creator god, who is supposed to have passed out negative events (accidents, illness, death), apparently for some divine purpose, should then respond to the prayers and entreaties of the recipients and others to change these things? Could a god of such power and complexity as to be able to create a vast universe, simultaneously track the thoughts of all humans, plan out vastly complex events to inflict exactly the right amount of pain on specific people, really care about such entreaties – or burnt offerings or endlessly repeated Rosaries? No, of course not – only an archaic fantasy could feature such a being.

With religion so interwoven in our cultural attitudes for so long, ***your*** personal worldview and self-image are tainted by many exceptionally subtle notions rooted in old myths and superstitions.

While interesting to note that Jesus of Nazareth had a budding awareness for the real flow of things, his clearest perspectives are found in but a few sketchy, distorted accounts of his views. And the effect of that glance pales in comparison to the major, vocal expression of those much less aware through the centuries who have dominated the many priesthoods that accumulated and magnified the misperceptions.

Yet there has long been a recurrent – though muted and limited – voice promoting an inner direction in search of understanding, rather than rote acceptance of orthodox doctrine. To complete an exploration of the roots of western thinking, that inward focus needs to be considered…

Mysticism

Where It's At – However Well Camouflaged

Some elements of the early Christian movement, particularly during the formative period prior to Constantine catalyzing the precipitation of a theology, promoted the notion that one had to ***be like*** Jesus, a mystic, delving within for self-realization, and not just bow to his elevated status. Indeed a movement with an inner emphasis (now referred to as Gnosticism) rather competed with standard orthodoxy. But it was ultimately rejected as heresy when mainstream theology became embedded in the bureaucratic power structure of the early church. (Heresy, as alluded, originally meant to "choose" to interpret teachings in one's own way. But it evolved into meaning any opinion outside Roman Catholic dogma – and became laden with negative connotations thanks to the political power of popes and their minions.)

From Valentinus through Augustine of Hippo, on to Hildegard of Bingen, Böhme, Pascal and Meister Echkart, and into more modern times with the teaching of Teilhard de Chardin and Merton, many visionary Christians have voiced perspectives beyond the scope of mainline orthodoxy. Each, presenting some real gems of wisdom, would merit attention in detail. But – pertinent to the main point here – each promoted notions that rest on a common shortcoming.

And that innate limitation permeates the mystical movement, Kabbalah, as well. This Judaist-based esoteric practice dates back probably even farther than the Christian offshoot, and pushes the boundaries of traditional religious definitions, not unlike the Christian variations.

While the inner focus of all such mysticism looks in the right direction – **inward** into mind and consciousness – that view, though often steeped in a personal mystical experience of the noted visionary, invariably carries the taint of a backdrop of religious tenets. For without exception, the mystic of bygone days venturing toward real understanding from either background would look to gain insight on the nature of, to become at one with, to realize the grandeur of or in some other fashion connect with a god who ***isn't really there***.

A line from the play *Inherit The Wind* (by Lawrence and Lee) in which I performed years ago always stuck with me. At the collapse of his ultra-religious opponent following a trial pitting evolution against religion, the protagonist comments, "he was looking for God too high up and too far away." Indeed, humans have always done just that.

The mystic, engaging meditation in conjunction with any secret, arcane practices, will fall prey to the same illusion that lurks in the shadows of the defined myth accepted by his more conventional brethren: beliefs and definitions held as true will seem to be so. Indeed, the mystic looks and searches in the correct realm, that of mind. But the lenses of belief and definition that so distort the outer view of any believer work the same way when peering within, turning imagination into pseudo-truth. And the notion of a remote, creator god is deeply burned into western thinking.

Johannes Eckhart, around 1300, could say (as quoted by the Meister Eckhart Society), "People should not worry as much about what they do but rather about what they are. If they and their ways are good, then their deeds are radiant," and in so doing presented great insight. But innate human Consciousness becomes diminished as Eckhart continues, "Whoever possesses God in their being, has him in a divine manner, and he shines out to them in all things; for them all things taste of God and in all things it is God's image that they see." (Meister Eckhart, mystic, visionary, died as a papal bull was declaring him a heretic.)

John Yepes, 250 years later, wrote "Now this is nothing else by the supernatural light giving light to the understanding, so that the human understanding becomes divine, made one with the divine…" Rather than expanding the concept of personal awareness, allowing the Self to gain its rightful nature of authority within the life forum, Yepes' could only imagine the psyche hooked up with some greater divinity to become whole.

In the early 17th century, Jacob Böhme could state profoundly, "If you will behold your own self and the outer world, and what is taking place therein, you will find that you, with regard to your external being, are that external world." The Oneness could not be depicted more succinctly. But in the next breath, he would compromise that vision by placing the source onto the external, conceptualized god his mindset had absorbed from his cultural standards, "Not I, the I that I am, know these things: but God knows them in me."

William Blake, by the late 17th century, could astutely observe, "Man's perceptions are not bound by organs of perception; he perceives more than sense (tho' ever so acute) can discover," but would ultimately compromise that astute observation by concluding, "God becomes as we are, that we may be as he is."

By the late 19th century, Walt Whitman would illustrate the flowing Oneness centered in the Self with grand brushstrokes of poetry. From his *Leaves of Grass*:

"I bring what you much need, yet always have,
I bring not money or amours or dress or eating…but I bring as good;
And send no agent or medium…and offer no representative of value – but offer the value itself.

"There is something that comes home to one now and perpetually,
It is not what is printed or preached or discussed…it eludes discussion and print,
Is it not to be put in a book…it is not in this book.
It is for you whoever you are…it is no farther from you than your hearing and sight are from you…

"We consider the bibles and religions divine…I do not say they are not divine,
I say they have all grown out of you and may grow out of you still,
Is it not they who give the life…it is you who give the life;
Leaves are not more shed from the trees or trees from the earth than they are shed out of you.
"The sum of all known value and respect I add up in you whoever you are…

"Will the whole come back then?
Can each see the signs of the best by a look in the lookingglass? Is there nothing greater or more?
Does all sit there with you and here with me?"

Whitman goes on to illustrate (in far more poetic terms that I did in introducing Angle One) the many outer aspects of life that one's Self encompasses. Yet for his enormous grasp of the human essence, he was still disposed to lapse into projecting source creativity and power to a conceptualized deity:

"O I am sure they really came from Thee,
The urge, the ardor, the unconquerable will…

"I will cling fast to Thee O God, though the waves buffet me,
Thee, Thee at least I know."

Mystics Pierre Teilhard de Chardin and Thomas Merton, both tied to monastic roles within the Catholic regime, expressed valued perspectives during the 20th century. But the views of both were repressed by the church hierarchy as not fitting in with accepted ideas. And both oriented their mystical vistas towards the preconceived "Creator".

Teilhard recognized the realms "Within" and "Without", the inner and outer phases of intangible mindset and its tangible resultant. But, as with mystics for millennia before him, he was looking for his divine source too high up and too far away.

The creative source is indeed within, for the blueprint of all permutations of Reality's effects is found in the complex of notion, information and inter-related value that constitutes the background essence of Consciousness. But that essence, while requiring a mystical focus inward to recognize, is to be found in the first person, immediate nature of the Self – not in a conceptualized, idealized, third-person divine source. Thus, while the more esoteric messages of Christian mystics and Kabbalah adherents alike express valued ideas, they invariably need to be extracted from the attribution of the ideal to a conceptualized, remote deity.

To Summarize:

The broad conglomeration of concepts, beliefs and attributes reviewed above – subtle, age-old notions built into the culturally-shared mindset and language – directly drains your power; it makes real your fear and personal powerlessness, engendering many aspects of your life in negation and neutralization of your will. And it will continue to do so until you eliminate conceptual limitations, one by one, just as you shed your self-defeating inner mechanisms.

Mysticism, as a focus within, is the sole tradition looking in the right direction. But the mystic, too, must abandon preconceived definitions, else whatever vision results will play out as summer re-runs of already seen episodes.

* * *

Indeed, there is yet another factor built into your view of life. But before moving on to the primary modern addition to your mindset, let's take a quick look outside the boundaries.

Plotinus and Neo-Platonism

A Glimpse and a Hint

Born in Egypt, Plotinus lived from 204 to 270, much of that time in Rome teaching and establishing a new look at Plato's take on things: Neo-Platonism.

Said by Porphyry, his student and biographer, to have had four mystic experiences, Plotinus offers perspectives on a supreme, totally transcendent "One." His writings reveal an attempt to capture his moments of ecstatic union with the One – as such, the Enneads are certainly worth a look. While not light reading, an occasional glimpse of great clarity is to be gleaned there.

Plotinus' One is pictured as beyond words and exceeding definition. His problem in grasping the Essence of Reality, however, and being able to reduce the notion to a viable description relates back to common shortcomings of philosophical inquiry: a tendency to overly ascribe the flow of Reality to a defined infrastructure.

As you explore the messages of such philosophers, many brilliant, many highly perceptive, you will note – and gain by the exposure – that each runs into conceptual boundaries in his ability to clearly discern the simplicity for how meaningful events flow in response to one's mindset. Those boundaries are formed by the subtle definitions previously built into the cultural worldview the philosopher carried along.

Plotinus took ideas put forth 650 years earlier by Plato and applied perspectives derived from personal, immediately experienced vision. But the structure to his depiction, the terminology and rational basis for his stated points harkens back to an overly complex paradigm that shows its interior design to be prefixed in conceptual notions.

Philosophy does that chronically.

Neo-Platonism pushed toward the concept of Monism (Greek *monas*, meaning "One") – wherein all that is consists of one essence, substance or energy. While that simple perception reflects generally what is happening here, in the philosophical examination and urge (if not Demiurge – sorry, couldn't resist) to fully define, the notion immediately hits the rational plague: need of further refinement. So Monism breaks into Substantial, Attributive and Absolute Monism or Spiritual vs. Material Monism – or even down to other more specialized definitions, with proponents of each branch, convinced of the preference of his/her favorite variation on the theme (and each according to personal, subtly held defined base "truths.")

And that is all opposed to concepts of Dualism, Existentialism, various Theisms, Nihilism and hosts of other "isms".

I could delve into all those philosophical bodies and comment on shortcomings and strengths, as I do here for the few most influential cultural expressions, but each verbal venture only confuses the point. You, as an individual engaged in a real life cycle, should you want to orient your life flow towards the positive, accomplished and healthy as you proceed, have to see life ***without all the conflicting definitions***. None of them get you closer, since virtually any philosophical expression, well written from a given standpoint, will seem valid and believable if you buy into it.

The purpose is to see clearly How Life Works. Plotinus, as a prime example, experienced episodes where he saw from the observation deck very clearly, but when he returned to his cabin to write, his account warped back into pre-fixed notions and conceptualizations of his culture and language.

Religion is not **the answer**, though it provides a multitude of ready-made pseudo-answers, should you want to accept one of them. Neo-Platonism has such answers, too, as does Science. But as I pointed out way back in Angle One, many such explanations reside out there, ripe and ready to be picked as the Final Great Truth. And any one of them **becomes** truth, ***if you accept it***.

But what you are looking for is not "truth," not a collection of fine and polished answers emanating from grand buildings, expert acknowledgement and advanced academic degrees. What you ***are*** looking for is your Self, and what I provide here are some tools and perspectives to aid a Journey through the jungle of explanations and definitions and up a mountain of perspective to where you **can** see that Self clearly.

Science – the Modern Belief Structure

Viewing Life through Binoculars – Turned the Wrong Way

Science arose through the Middle Ages as people (some of them anyway) began to look at reality and realize you could actually explore it and figure out how it works.

Certainly science has roots in Greek philosophical inquiry. And significant advancements were made in science and mathematics in India by 500 CE, in China even earlier and in pan-Arabia following the expansion of Islam. But through that time and halfway into the second millennium, Europe and the roots of our modern mindset were mired in a murky pre-Cambrian swamp of primitive religion – ostracizing and performing inquisitions to root out anybody who differed from the archaic Paulian notions I mentioned above and otherwise rejecting any enlightened thoughts whatsoever.

But that was to change as men like Copernicus and Galileo either avoided direct church conflict or defied the Roman Catholic hierarchy to move science forward. During a period when European culture was expanding into the New World, when Luther and Calvin began to challenge the church, old notions started to crumble in the face of academic inquiry. It was through this period that science and mathematics began to coalesce into structured means of examining reality based on evidence and reliable observation.

As it evolved in that direction, Science took on several bounded rules for acceptable inquiry, i.e., for an idea to be accepted as effectively true:

- **Confirmation of Theory:** Science rests on ***theories*** – proposed descriptions or structured models of the physical mechanisms concerned.

- Given a clear explanation of a proposed theory for how some aspect of reality works, experiments can be formulated and carried out which will either confirm the theory or disprove it, leading to general acceptance or rejection, with possible restructure of the theory for subsequent experiments.
- The theory, of course, even if confirmed repeatedly, can always be disproved later.

- **Empiricism:** Science accepts only results that have been confirmed via real experiment, typically in a lab under controlled conditions.
- **Reproducible results:** Any proof of a theory must be possible for others to reproduce, getting similar experimental results using the same procedures.
- **Falsifiability:** To be scientific, a theory has to have an experimental path toward being disproved.
    - It is possible to construct theories and conduct experiments that can only succeed in proving the initial concept.
    - To be valid science, there must be room for falsification of the theory through the outcome of the experiment.
- **Publication and acceptance by other scientists:** Scientific results must be fully documented in procedure and results then be published in appropriate journals for peer review.

Compared to ad hoc declarations and reliance on beliefs and notions accepted by past generations, the emergence of the scientific method was irrevocably vital for man to progress into modernity. As a conceptual tool for understanding the workings of nature and allowing technological development, science forms the bedrock on which our modern, complex society functions. Whether regarding communications, production of food, education and distribution of information, entertainment, transportation or any other aspect of modern culture, science has been a catalyst for man's advancement.

However, science, by its very nature, forms its own inherent boundaries to man's progress. While the enormous collection of information based on critical experiment and advanced theory virtually embody man's advancement from horse-drawn carts to the beginning of the space age, science does not allow comprehension of How Life Works. Focused as it is on the world **out there**, categorizing and measuring, theorizing and concluding all things based on external evidence and proof, science misses the core of life: the consciousness doing the experiencing.

Science would reduce an innately **subjective** Reality into an **objective** description – and think things to be fully defined. The scientist would look at a sphere, measure the surface in great detail, categorize the skin qualities and components, then predict evolving surface tensions and potentials. The use of that sphere, however, along with its beauty and potential would not be of interest. Science would count the bricks of a house, but not care about living in it, thus missing the point – but thinking that, by quantifying the physical, everything had been covered.

Unlike religion (which would regard the sphere ***and*** the brick house as divinely created for mysterious purposes) science grasps much of apparent reality and lends understanding to the pieces. But it can't consider the whole, based on its focus and methodology.

I criticize the Scientist here no more than cultural aspects of Judaism; I am simply pointing out the shortcomings.

Science is a valued tool, indispensable for our cultural use and future. But it is vital to pinpoint the ***limits*** of science, because, in addition to the ancient notions of celestial influence and control by a deity, notions of fate and fortune, thoughts of luck and chance, the illusion, enhanced by science, of a remote reality separated from you in space and function strongly affects your mindset, self-image and resultant worldview.

* * *

The shortcoming of science equates to the limit of the rational mind: science looks only outward for data. The rational aspect of mind has been equally cut off from the whole capability – including intuitive elements resting on the whole of subconscious access. Science, in a way, grew out of man's excess projection of creative power outwards to a god and the gross injustices perpetrated by zealous religionists in the name of phony tenets. But it overreacted by disavowing ***any*** inner realm to the apparent, cutting the heart and soul, the experiential, **the process**, out of what is a life experience – not a meaningless haze of interacting particles and silently spiraling galaxies. Thereby the scientist gains personal satisfaction and fulfillment by proving the meaninglessness of personal satisfaction and fulfillment.

In a way, techniques I present in Angle Two fall within what might be considered scientific in terms of confirmation and reproducibility: if you delve within, using the techniques as I've laid them out, you will reproduce my results – your life will improve, your body work better, your fears dissipate, your relationships improve. But would a scientific journal publish EoR? Could a skeptic, sitting in a lab with brain wave monitors attached to critical body parts achieve significant personal change? Can such improvement be quantified or proven via double-blind experiments?

The field of psychology is knocking on the door of How Life Works; it is that close to understanding the human psyche. But the problem is that, as a science, psychology stands, not on the outside turning a handle to simply enter, but on the inside of the door peeking out through the keyhole. All that is necessary to understand the Self is readily available – just turn around and look within. But the key – open-mindedness – is disallowed by tenets that require external evidence gleaned by lab studies of subjects and statistical analysis of the data.

Consciousness and Reality are as innately tied as two poles of a magnet – one cannot exist without the other. Yet Science, by its very nature, can only regard one end, the Real. The problem is, of course, that by now, centuries into the scientific paradigm, it has become a hardened belief structure – not at all unlike religion in various ways, however different the focus:

- **Facts:**
    - Science is built on theories, i.e., models that describe portions of reality that have been demonstrated as valid and accurate by

experiment and argument.

- ✓ However, according to the scientific norm, a theory stands only as long as the current model stands up to tests that confirm it. A new model can be more accurate, or new tests can disprove currently accepted theory.
- ✓ But the realm of science tends to fossilize its theories as "facts," that is, build up within the scientific community a level of accepted veracity to its notions, making them unquestionable – just like any religion – and thus not open to phenomena that might disprove the facts.

- **Bureaucratic Control:**
  - ○ The interwoven realms of academia, research and publishing, have become the rough equivalent of the priesthood and church bureaucracy. In order to gain access to research funding and gain acceptance via publication, any young, novice scientist must break through the resistance of the establishment – regardless of the quality of the idea being proposed.
  - ✓ This effect stultifies science into a status quo, satisfactory to the community, but resistant to valued change. In effect, new generations come up with new approaches to astronomy, to archeology, etc., but have to struggle for long periods to gain any acceptance, despite valid, scientific proof of their ideas. As that generation ages and grows into more politically powerful positions, it then hardens in defense of ***its*** ideas, resisting the next up-and-coming young thinkers.

- **Priesthood:**
  - ○ The insiders of any religion become a clique of privileged men, frozen into a structured hierarchy. Invariably, they are very defensive of their position – always ready to attack any outsider who would question their exclusive status of knowing all truth and judging all interpretations. Only the ordained priesthood can accept

and train any newcomers and will do so rigidly within the strict guidelines of their theology.

✓ Likewise, any of the many fields of science hold their own rigid academic body of accepted knowledge, willing to accept only those who are steeped in the basic tenets of the field, bestowing advanced degrees by committee on theses judged consistent with prior definition.

✓ In that regard, doctorate degrees are granted for performance confined fully and unquestionably within the strict norms of the already accepted, closed paradigm of the science. While regarded by society in general as high achievement – the equivalent in esteem of theological high priests – advanced degrees are only acknowledgements of academic thinking certified to be within the currently accepted box.

- **Closed regard:**
  - Any evidence gained outside of the scientific method is, by definition, **not scientific** and thus not acceptable in the field.

✓ Consequently, vital, meaningful experience and observation that might shed light on how this Reality works, if not quantifiable, testable, reproducible, etc., cannot be regarded. If, for example, a psychic predicts an event that indeed takes place, or a patient, revived from a near-death-experience, describes explicitly the resuscitation procedure as observed from above the scene, science shrugs its collective shoulders. It simply ignores the obvious disproving of an innate, particle-based, meaningless universe – because a precognitive or "out-of-body" event cannot be scientifically examined and proven.

✓ In effect, science draws boundaries in its regard for valid effects within reality. Then it proceeds, rather subtly, to define results occurring within the interior of those boundaries as valid and true if proven consistent via accepted methodology. Any results proven invalid are thrust outside the boundary and regarded as false. But, by definition, **all other effects** not approachable by the scientific method – whether valid or not – are already placed ***outside the boundary***!

- **Big, fancy buildings that inspire awe:**
  - From ancient times religious functionaries have built enormous, awe-inspiring temples with magnificent statues of their gods to impress naïve followers and secure their support.
  - ✓ Likewise, the grand laboratories, particle generators, research facilities, museums of science, etc., subtly rely on grandeur and visual special effects to impress the populace – thus aiding in securing funding and governmental support.
  - ✓ A simple ideomotor response as noted in Angle Two can reveal anything that a multi-million dollar MRI scanner could detect and a lot more. The scientific mind would surely opt for the reliability of the machine. (Indeed, for the skeptic, the machine **would** work better, as personally held doubt would inhibit the subconscious response.)

- **Fudge Factors:**
  - From time immemorial, when reality differed from the results promised by a priesthood, e.g., when rituals and conventions failed to cajole the god to provide favorable events, church authorities could rationalize some explanation to cover the obvious conclusion that, indeed, the god didn't actually exist. To the gullible, such banalities as "god works in strange ways," could and would cover all contingencies. Science inherited that cop-out technique.
  - ✓ Scientists, however rigid and demanding they might be on a theoretical scale, have always been prone, facing funding crises wherein their financial support depends on the results of various tests, to find ways to retrofit, i.e., fudge, their data to support desired results.
  - ✓ A much more subtle and widespread problem, though, is the

> tendency already frequently illustrated: the distortion of one's perception based on held beliefs and accepted definitions. However thorough a double-blind test might be structured to alleviate doubt, it always incorporates the core notion and background assumptions of the whole, fundamentally objective worldview of the scientist conducting the experiment. Thus it retains its validity, judged from within its own synthetic boundaries, but doesn't necessarily reflect the function of Reality.

Science, with its plusses and minuses, becomes vital for you to regard personally, in that it has significantly contributed to your mindset. Looking at the long trail of western thinking to which you are unavoidably heir, you will find early and enduring notions of an external controller, buttressed by changing thoughts for how that ethereal entity worked, overlaid with notions of "natural" forces, to be occasionally superceded by yet another force, fate, all subject to the personal intent of authoritative people and governmental influence.

Science blankets all that traditional thinking, embodying the core notion of Overt Sequential Causality (the illusory, apparent flow of reality I depicted back in Angle One) where reality consists of **only** the physical realm and proceeds forward in time, with an action ***causing*** a subsequent event, rather than simply triggering it. Science is the embodiment of that objective model – disallowing any validity of the psychic realm of thought, stored values, the subconscious, experience and meaning, let alone initial causality.

The Scoop

I would sum up the western mindset to which most readers of this tome owe their worldview and self-image: it has always looked outward for causality, finding sources and forces in imaginary deities, invented mechanisms and illusory processes. Even as key visionaries looked inward to discern valid aspects of the psyche, they wove prefabricated definitions into their expressed vision.

Your singular need in this existence is to shed those notions, whether rooted in ancient superstition, archaic gods, rudimentary philosophical tenets, traditional hypothetical notions or ironclad scientific proofs. As you do so, you will find yourself in a life, with **you** at the center, carving a creative and peaceful venture out of what used to be a painful and conflictual struggle.

* * *

Other traditions have yielded other viewpoints with valuable perspectives, some of which reveal the deeper roots of western thinking, others finding recent exposure to those in the west who, seeking a more meaningful understanding of life, have looked to eastern traditions. So let's move on to where mysticism doesn't have to compete with mainline thinking, because ***it is*** the main line…

Hinduism and Buddhism

A Guided Tour of the Inner Sanctum

Not unlike Jesus taking the longstanding Jewish mindset he inherited and veering it off in another direction, Siddharta Gautama had done similar maneuvers a half millennium before to Hindu thinking (or perhaps more accurately: attempts to not think).

Hinduism, or rather "Sanatana Dharma," meaning "eternal law," stems from ancient notions originally brought to the region by Indo-European groups that migrated into northern India some 3500 years ago. Indeed, the Rig Veda, "songs of knowledge," though first written down only by 800 BCE, record myth and thought of the original Indo-Europeans echoing back well before that.

As alluded above, other closely related Indo-European groups migrating westward at that time, came to dominate Europe. Thus, these oldest of ideas underlie western thinking as much as Eastern thought. However,

Vedic notions, encountering and absorbing local influences, continued to evolve with much more of a focus inward than the ultimate pagan regard of god-causality and entreaty of their westward-moving cousins.

Once again, I would cover here main points concerning Dharma-based notions pertinent to How Life Works, rather than launch into great detail as to how these eastern practices relate, breaking off into sects historically, culturally, structurally, etc. All have evolved from base notions, and all look at life with a similar attitude, if not consistent ritual, gesture or practice.

* * *

Sanatana Dharma, via a long and slowly evolving tradition, looks at the basis of life – the flow, the Tao, the whole or source or essence of all that is – and calls it "Brahman." The term Dharma refers (among other things, in that Hinduism is multi-faceted and almost cryptically complex in its variations) to a **correct understanding** of that nature, i.e., of the cosmic law they deem to be in effect for determining how reality works.

What is going on here for each of us, according to the Hindu view, is a continuum of birth and rebirth in cycles (samsara) governed by the law of cause and effect, called "Karma." Therein, each action taken during a lifetime has spiritual consequences that are carried over into subsequent lifetimes, such that bad things happening to you now reflect back on bad things ***you*** did during past incarnations. Hindu traditions allow various ways to work off the negative Karma, thereby progressing towards "Moksha," or liberation from what would otherwise be an endless cycle of rebirths into lifetimes of suffering based on your own previous negativity.

Part of the path to Moksha is seeing through the illusion of Reality in what is termed Maya, the collection of all things in the real world. (Maya, the visible, apparently real stuff, is said to hide the true Brahman, the essence of all that is.)

Gautama took the version of the above that was generally held at that time and brought a new interpretation to it. Karma at that point was generally understood to require some rituals to affect the gods' dispersal of favors. Gautama changed the focus of Dharma from an objective notion of the flow of things to a personal grasp of that flow and the concept of Karma to be an absolute measure of good and bad that gets woven into one's experience intrinsically, not at the behest of gods.

For Gautama, the need became to purify not only one's actions, but also the ***intent*** behind the action – doing good deeds only for the purpose of ultimately benefiting oneself didn't count as positive Karma. Called the Buddha, "The Enlightened One," Gautama held that lofty status to indicate a simple grasping of life's basic truths – and he specified Four Noble Truths to help clarify it all:

- **Life consists of suffering**: birth, sickness, aging, death, etc., all involve suffering.
- **The source of suffering is *desire*** – the craving of sensual pleasures, possessions, etc.
- **The end of suffering** is thus achieved ***by ending desire*** – ceasing the craving and no longer relying on attainment of the next pleasure or new possession.
- **And that end is accomplished by following the Noble Eightfold Path.**

In pursuit of ending suffering, Gautama put forth these eight suggested elements or ideals, as generally translated (the word "Right" indicating a sense of ***ideal*** or appropriate):

- **Right View** or Right Understanding – understanding the path indicated in the Four Noble Truths.
- **Right Thoughts** – focus on spiritual things.
- **Right Speech** – avoiding negative, abusive or harmful talk and idle chatter.
- **Right Conduct** – assuring that deeds are caring and thoughtful of others, particularly refraining from killing, stealing, illicit sexual conduct and lying.

- **Right Livelihood** – in earning a living, avoiding occupations that involve weapons, intoxicating drinks, killing animals, prostitution, etc.
- **Right Effort** – focusing one's endeavor towards good will, positive and creative activity and the like.
- **Right Mindfulness** – keeping the mind alert to reality, to the status of the body and conditions around it and holding good thoughts, because action arises from thoughts.
- **Right Concentration** – practicing Buddha meditation, with the stilling of thought and an inner focus.

Gautama's additional teachings are extraordinarily insightful:

- **The Doctrine of Dependent Origination** – all things exist as interdependent on all other things thus having no innate, independent existence.
- **The Impermanence of Things** – everything is in a state of flux, with nothing in this entire Reality permanent and unchanging.
- **Rejecting the infallibility of scriptures** – teachings should be taken on their value, not just blindly followed based on popular or authoritative acceptance.
- **The Illusion of the "Self"** – the self which seems to occupy the fleeting moment is really only a changing, responding series of thoughts, spawning, one after the other, based on conditions and qualities, and thus not really a consequential entity that will reincarnate in a series of lifetimes and span the interceding period.
- **Revision of the notion of Karma** – rather than Hindu ideas, picturing it as a carryover of good and bad from previous lives, Karma is understood as the **inner intent** being innately causal (not past lives, a remote god or random events), with happiness and/or suffering the result.
- **Revision of the notion of Samsara** – while Hindus expect that souls of people unliberated from their negative effect will continue to reincarnate until they've worked off the negative, Buddha pictured rebirths as

a series of stages to be worked through en route to enlightenment.

- **Moksha to Nirvana** – where the Hindu Moksha indicated the release of the "atman," the indestructible individual soul, from the Samsara cycle, Gautama saw liberation, called Nirvana, in the end of desire and craving, thus ending the cycle of reincarnation by ending the unquenchable desire that drove the process.

Once again, I cannot illustrate the above in as great a detail as it requires for you to comprehend the full scope of the original teachings. Indeed, both Hinduism and Buddhism incorporate such a range of esoteric terms with no direct translation that sorting through their overall gist, referencing each aspect and the variations placed on it by differing sects, is scarcely possible, let alone pertinent to this regard.

* * *

But to conduct an overview from my perspective: Hinduism, Sanatana Dharma, from extraordinarily ancient times, entertained the apt awareness that Consciousness innately spans lifetimes. The word Brahman, however, rooted in the ancient name of a god and meant to regard the whole of all things, falls prey to the fallacy of naming anything: it becomes no longer the whole, but a ***concept*** incorporating some portion of Reality.

Having been named, as with the word "God" or "Allah," it forms conceptual boundaries and takes on a synthetic, mind-based notion of its own. Theologians, timeless nerds of meaningless detail, can then differentiate between things like Nir-guna Brahman (without qualities) and Sa-guna Brahman (with qualities) and go on about regarding the ***idea***, not the undivided whole, the real.

As I've related and provided means for you to experience directly, the Oneness that exists is **not bounded or set apart from anything**. No word can be applied to the whole, nor to the inner-outer flow. Tao, Dharma – whatever you call it or ***try*** to call it will take on a subtly subdivided nature of its own. My singular purpose in EoR is to promote your becoming aware of that flow, not relying on verbal conceptualizations. Wonders, once named, always lead to illusory truths.

In terms of Karma, you actually bring negative elements into this life only as **current characteristics** of your Self, not as carryover consequence or judgment from "previous" incarnations. In this regard, Gautama made a significant leap forward in awareness. But even the Buddha couldn't break into details of how one's core characteristics could be discerned and revised – his Noble Eightfold Path, while highly desirable as ultimate goals, would require a subtle, rational overlay to attain them. Those eight gestures do not clear out inner, problematic and conflictual aspects of one's mindset; rather they install yet additional rational controls over all the others currently in place.

The Noble Path, for example, would have you strictly limit your verbal expression to Right Speech by rationally filtering the vent of your natural frustration to stifle cursing. If you clear out the negating and neutralizing inner elements, though, as per Angle Two techniques, you won't have the urge to swear and spew invectives because real affronts to your will ***won't be taking place***! There is a major difference. Personally, I have the same propensity to anger as I always had and the same vocabulary of four-letter English invectives to verbalize any frustration – but with my life flowing nicely, the negative events **don't ever occur** that would trigger that old anger.

Stated otherwise, it isn't the Right Thoughts and Right Speech in repression of anger that leads to significant enlightenment, but rather the elimination of inner elements that bring about negation of your will and frustration over it. Trying to hold positive thoughts is just as much a gesture as praying to a god or manipulating a parent.

Hinduism, not atypical of religions, keeps you mired in ancient notions of ***what is***. Beyond nurturing concepts of a bunch of non-existent gods, which I didn't go into above, this ancient belief structure entails two vital shortcomings beyond conceptualizing Brahman and Dharma:

- **Hinduism places Karma out of your reach**, rooting your problems in remote incarnations to which you have no access nor any means to alter

✓ Indeed, as referenced all along, you have access to all elements of your mindset. That these aspects of your Self are rooted in past lives becomes practically unimportant: to improve your life for now and ongoing, you need to change them.

- **The desire to end the cycle of incarnations is flawed.**
  ✓ In that Consciousness always creates a Reality to encounter, you will never find your conscious Self hovering in a non-existent state. You will always, during a life, during sleep in the dream state and after death, find your conscious Self peering out into a Reality.

* * *

The Buddha's shortcoming in updating those flawed notions rests on his Four Noble Truths. The deficiency is simple and obvious: however noble, ***they aren't truths.***

Life is not saturated with suffering. From the best to the worst of individual lives, experience contains an admixture of good events and relationships – and bad. And each element across the spectrum of desirability is rooted in the inner mindset of the experiencer. Suffering, then, stems not from **desiring** various pleasures, but from encountering a Reality that ***negates or neutralizes*** the desire rather than satiating it.

Gautama was right insofar as an unmitigated pursuit of sensual or physical pleasures, shallow at best in satisfying temporal needs, leads only to further craving in an endless cycle. But Consciousness inherently seeks new experience, finding in creative change the only respite from boredom. In this greater view, desire is part of the natural cycle that drives all existence – certainly all of nature. Seeking to end the cycle of incarnating, of physical engagement of values, of personal, vivid encounter with meaningful elements made real could only equate to cessation of being.

Life can and, for most, **does** contain suffering. But one core purpose of life is coming to see the inner source of that suffering and grow to eliminate it, thus garnering a personal sway over life, indeed ***existence***, itself. Of course, that Angle Two venture out of Kansas, which might as well be a journey out of Calcutta, is optional: you can ignore it and continue along mired in suffering, content to fight your neighbor, your spouse and your body, should you remain enamored with man's traditional, self-aware mindset.

So Moksha and/or Nirvana are only partially accurate in picturing the goal here. The purpose is not to disengage from the process of rebirths, but to **revise the nature of incarnating**. Rather than spend one's incarnations – and they are cheap, by the way, in fact, free – engaged in conflict and struggle, one can opt for boundless creativity. Desire will not be squelched, but rather satisfied.

Imagine in that regard, just how fruitful mankind would be, even in the current setting, if all the effort of all people were spent, not on weaponry and warfare, not on legal wrangling and litigation, not on medications trying to force the body into health against inner elements yielding ill health, not on imposing one's beliefs and mores on neighboring groups, not on drugs and prostitution meant to satisfy craving with artificial reward, but on food creation, construction, nature preservation, resource conservation and creative endeavors like art and music. By resort to the reasoning, rational mind, imposing its synthetic conclusions as overlays on natural impulses, man has managed to engineer a Hell out of what can, should and will be (for those who seek it) a Heaven.

Considering Gautama's other points:

- **Dependent Origination.**
  - ✓ It was a leap of awareness to note that all things exist as interdependent on all other things. That major step forward, though, still fails to accurately depict How Life Works. The next step is to see clearly that all things, insofar as they impact the Self perceiving them, depend on the **nature of that perceiver**.
  - ✓ All things indeed **interrelate** with all other things. But in terms of causality, they ***depend***, for the meaning they are playing out, on the value set of the Conscious entity (you, in the case of your life) for

their impetus for being. There are multitudinous triggers in Reality, but all ***cause*** reverts back to the mindset of the individual experiencing events and relationships.

- **Impermanence of Things.**
  - ✓ Yup, everything is changing – but always consistently, in repeated patterns of meaning as experienced by any individual.
- **Fallibility of Scriptures.**
  - ✓ Gautama hit dead bulls-eye with this one. Old writings are of use only insofar as they impel you to see clearly.
- **Illusion of "Self."**
  - ✓ Gautama misses the mark in his perspective on this traditional debate. By culling out "aggregates" of one's nature – form, sensory engagement, perception, the will and consciousness – the Buddha misses ***the whole***.
  - ✓ The individual Self is not a collection of fleeting impressions, of thoughts and conclusions coming and going, but the **Self is** the ***WHOLE***, experiencing its own values by direct encounter.
  - ✓ The Self is not the illusion. Indeed, the changing, flowing Self is the only Real thing. The illusion is formed in perceptiveness by any ***other*** notion – including Gautama's conclusion that the Self doesn't exist.
- **Karma.**
  - ✓ The Buddha's view of Karma was very perceptive. He just didn't quite quantify the mechanisms by which it, i.e., one's nature, manifests itself into being.
- **Samsara and Moksha/Nirvana**
  - ✓ You don't want to end the cycle of rebirths – just significantly revise the quality of the incarnations. Living creative lives is fun if things go your way – and eternity is a long time to hang around with nothing to do.

Sikhism and Jainism

Variations on a Theme

The Eastern religious ventures noted above are broken into many varied sects and exclusive practices. Before moving on, I would consider two major groups with different points of view that have diverged far enough away from root Hinduism to gain their own separate status.

The Sikhs follow ten primary gurus dating from the 16th and 17th centuries and their teachings. Sikhism entails far fewer adherents than the other Dharma religions mentioned so far, with much less impact on world thinking – but it is worthy of focus to emphasize three important concepts.

When a religion draws away from the mainstream of life – economic ventures, cultural mating habits, household activities, marriage conventions, education of children, etc. – into its own little realm, there is something askew in its premise. Time and time again throughout history charismatic leaders, with or without some degree of vision, have gone off with their followers to form new offshoots of society based on their innate verve. Most die out when the leader exits this reality; some go on, spurred by his and subsequently accumulated teaching.

It should be obvious to anybody with reasonable cognizance – but almost invariably isn't, as the mind, indoctrinated, can be thoroughly fooled by beliefs – that any god so vastly powerful as to be able to create this huge realm of uncountable galaxies, billions of star systems and billions upon billions of planets would not create this single planet Earth, also incomprehensibly complex with a plethora of life forms and interactive ecological systems, including now billions of humans, etc., then only reveal His True Nature to a select subset of those people. Yet, religion after religion holds **itself to be the only one** perceptive enough to see ***THE TRUTH***, the real nature of the Vaunted Creator.

Sikhs follow the teachings of their master, Nanak and those who succeeded him. Some of this body of wisdom is of value, but the principal notions of devotion to God, growing towards God, repetition of the name of God (whatever name one chooses) – all these are worthless in that such an entity, whether named God, Allah, Rahim, Unified Field Theory or Wealth, does not exist. (OK, Wealth might exist, but don't expect that entity, when devoted to, to bring happiness or enlightenment any more than the others.)

I've probably riddled the illusory notion of an eternal, independently existent, all-powerful, judgmental, remote, third person deity thoroughly enough by this time that I needn't elaborate.

But I would add another note about **dress-up spirituality**. The Pope of the Catholic Church, dressing up in his regal, white robe, hefting a symbolic scepter (or whatever it is – it's not worth looking up), the yogi in his white outfit surrounded by burning incense, the shaman with his bone necklace and ochre face paint, the protestant preacher in his conservative, dark robe – these are all people dressed up in outfits deemed highly spiritual by their cultures, carrying a message to those sucker enough to fall for it, that they are blessed, holy and more powerful than their peon followers. The Sikhs wear a turban for the same synthetic reason.

If you have to dress up in special costume to show off your status of wonderment, you really don't have a clue How Life Works.

* * *

As for Jainism, adherents emphasize asceticism as a means of purifying the soul and define Karma in considerable detail, recommending precisely what to do about it. They strictly avoid meat and disavow even root edibles, in that that sort of food destroys plants.

As above, their definitions and recommendations are all artificial and invalid as innate truths. But that last point is worthy of attention. Vegetarianism per se is an artificial gesture of little or no value. Jains avoid meat, noting the inhumane treatment of animals in many modern food production settings. **That** concern is well taken…

In our culture, early 21st century western-style, the industrialization of animal husbandry has become sub-human in its brutality and uncaring for sentient creatures that, indeed, supply mankind with its very sustenance. Beef cattle and pigs, even milk cows, can be kept in filthy, horrid conditions, packed together, confined so they can't move, stuffed with growth hormones and antibiotics to keep them alive long enough to slaughter (or milk). Now, (based, one must imagine, on production quotas and efficiency) they are even being cloned. Chickens and turkeys can be held in miniscule containers, with their beaks having been cut off so they can't peck each other – force-fed if needed to fatten them up. All are then sent to slaughter facilities that bespeak middle age inquisition brutality for their technique: cows held dangling by a rear leg clamped to a conveyor hook, painfully swung along until they can be bled to death, pigs with their heads bashed in, chickens with their heads pulled off mechanically.

Sorry to disturb you, but that's what a society comes to when rationality prevails – animals looked upon, not as feeling creatures symbiotically affixed to mankind, to be handled with care and dignity, but as resources in a production line, as unfeeling objects of profit in a society whose only meaning is attainment of wealth.

The farm animal, though, properly cared for, has life much better – somewhat better than its wild cousin. The wild buffalo of Africa, if it survives lion and hyena attacks as a calf, can spend its day fending off flies by the thousand, searching for waterholes free of crocodiles and looking forward to a future appointment with those same lions when it ages. A domestic cow, however, in the herd of a sincere, hard-working farmer lives in a clean stable and has open fields to graze in. Free-ranging chickens will produce eggs with rich, orange yolks and solid shells. They can enjoy their life of pecking (and satisfying the local rooster) until they are one day humanely slaughtered – an exit from here even preferable to the typical end of the farmer himself.

My point is that mistreatment of domestic animals is a problem unto itself reflective of a limited awareness on the part of small-minded industrialists – and consumers who pay no attention to such cruelty as takes place to feed them. But to avoid meat on that basis is superficial and unwise.

If confused about what is "right," you need only look at nature. Many animals eat meat – indeed, the carnivores of nature keep the herbivores healthy. (I have to laugh at the Jehovah's Witnesses who look for an idealistic future when lions will share space with lambs – eating, I suppose, soy substitute?) Humans, including you, Jainist or not, are omnivores. As such, meat tastes good, provides needed sustenance, and there is no good reason not to eat it.

There may, of course, be **reasons**, but they are artificial justifications and without substance in Reality. If the consideration is for the animal's sake, it is false: if everybody quit eating beef, cows would go extinct, as they are no longer viable in a wild setting. I doubt collective bovines would concur with that eventuality being of value.

So Jainism goes overboard with its rules – not unlike any religion, where **somebody deemed wise sets up standards and interpretations** to follow, regardless of innate nonsensicality, and ***people blindly follow them***. And that notion leads us right to…

Islam

Another House of Cards – This One Built on Sand

Have you ever seen an angel? I remember asking my parents why we didn't see angels like people used to in the Old Testament. They told me something to the effect that God didn't work like that anymore – that things had changed along the way. That explanation sounded a bit hokey even then.

You never saw an angel, because they don't exist – at least not in this Reality. They ***do*** exist in the **realm of imagination** – but then, just about anything can be conjured up there in a mind steeped in myth and lore.

Islam – meaning submission or surrender to Allah (literally, "The God") – is built on dictation ostensibly brought from that god by the angel Gabriel and given to Mohammed over a number of years, beginning in 610 CE, in Mecca and Medina of the Arabian peninsula. That "revelation" became written into the Koran (meaning the "recitation") in subsequent years. It forms, along with other writings related to Mohammed, interpretation, etc., called the Hadith, the backbone scripture of Islam.

Mohammed had considerable trouble convincing many of his peers that his dictates were valid; it took years and lots of conflict to establish the Koran as an accepted expression of a new, valid religion in the face of the old one – pushing lesser gods off the brink to establish Allah as the only one.

One always has to wonder anew how anyone could imagine a god, who, so overwhelmingly intelligent and powerful as to have been able to create this enormously complex world and the vast universe it floats around in, would populate it with a bunch of humans whose primary purpose consisted of bowing subserviently in worship. What a vain and shallow entity would this Allah, pictured in the Koran, be – if he actually existed! Even beyond this absurd picture, that creator god must have also inadvertently conjured up the great majority of humans who not only don't and didn't ever recognize his existence, but even need to be convinced by grandiose claims, rote slogans and armed conflict that he actually exists! And would that great, powerful god, once lots of his pet humans became convinced of his existence, want to hear repeated – ad infinitum – recitations of how wonderful he, himself, is for having done the job?

Welcome to Islam.

Above, in discussing the perceptive notions of Jesus, remarkable concepts of Plato or the highly introspective lessons of Gautama and Lao Tzu, it took considerable discussion to explore the meaning and relate it to How Life Works. Islam presents no such deep pool of thought to pierce.

Adherence to Islam rests on "Five Pillars." Here they are and some perspectives relevant to how life indeed functions:

- **Profession of acceptance that Allah is the only god and Mohammed was his prophet.**
  - ✓ Remember the "Conceptual Chamber" back in Angle Three? Islam is the classic trap – a chastity belt of spirituality. Allah is simply **defined** as **the god**. If you were taught that definition since birth and repeated it a million times or given the option of accepting it or be

killed, it's very likely to appear valid.

- ✓ Mohammed was not unlike many, many charismatic teachers over the ages. He fell for his own visions as self-evident truths. The more he added to them, the more valuable they seemed.
- ✓ Allah, not unlike other gods of wonderment, is pictured as beyond understanding, as permeating the whole universe. That sort of all-encompassing deity seems to appeal to a certain level of self-aware human, particularly those so indoctrinated since early life. Allah, as worshipped and pictured not only doesn't exist, but ***couldn't*** – a deity so advanced as to be able to create this Reality wouldn't set up such archaic, primitive rules and endorse such banal, conflictual activities.

- **Ritual prayer five times a day, bowing in a prescribed fashion towards Mecca.**
  - ✓ No part of this Reality is any more hallowed or sacred, intrinsically, than any other part, but are only made to appear so by the synthetic value system of the believer accepting that definition.
  - ✓ Reciting ***anything*** over and over only reinforces its apparent authenticity regardless of its inherent invalidity.
- **Helping the poor.**
  - ✓ Not a bad idea. Of course, people who really understand their own innate creative power don't need help – not from others, certainly not from a conceptualized god. Projecting your power out to Allah leaves you powerless, a great path toward poverty.
- **Fasting throughout daylight hours during Ramadan.**
  - ✓ Fasting makes little sense. If you are hungry, it is a sensual signal to eat.
  - ✓ Is one trying to impress a god with one's devotion? Or impress one's fellow man? Or just going along with the crowd because it's the "right" thing to do?
- **Making the pilgrimage to Mecca at least once during life.**
  - ✓ Joining the herd of fellow believers as they walk around the Ka'ba – an ancient, black, cubical monument in Mecca supposedly built by

Abraham (remember the effect of fancy buildings on the easily impressed?) – likely intensifies the Conceptual Trap.

✓ It would be easy to overlook that many hundreds of millions of humans have lived full, creative lives without ever having seen or heard of the Ka'ba, Islam or Allah.

I hate to sound overly harsh about Islam. I hold the same respect for the Arab peoples, Asians and many others who accept this superficial notion as true, as I stated for Judaism earlier. But this religion is a pure, unadulterated example of the basic essence with which I started this book: **whatever beliefs and definitions you hold will seem to be valid**.

For deep adherents, the Koran would seem to echo great truths given directly to a vaunted and hallowed prophet by a deity of overwhelming power and grandeur. If you don't hold any such archaic notions, however, the words attributed to Allah come across as harshly self-defensive, crude in reemphasizing old cultural standards, shaky in trying to establish new standards, brutal in places, mostly repetitious and monotonous – and thoroughly unbelievable. When you have outgrown all such unfounded religious notions, the Koran doesn't offer much by way of piercing perspective.

Adherents point out that, in its original, classical Arabic language, the phrasing is beautiful and enrapturing, forming a great cultural bond with its poetic expression – an effect generally lost when translated. And that, of course, emphasizes my point: there is no inherent validity – or even value – to the Koran's claims and statements, just an emotional appeal that has mesmerized and captivated generation after generation of gullible, thoroughly dogmatized people.

Indeed, of the major religions, Islam offers no discernable sliver of valid notion for How Life Works. It's value to the culture in which it sprouted was more logistical, providing slightly more civilized rules to go by and proving highly significant in its cohesive effect of bringing together diverse groups. As it spread – often enough by force – through decaying empires and backward, sparsely settled and nomadic regions, it coalesced large regions into a civilized, rather centralized culture. This spurred advancement: as Europe was sleep-walking through the dark ages, the Islamic cultures of North Africa and the Middle East translated and preserved ancient philosophy, developed mathematics and promoted learning.

That creative time waned, however. As subsequent generations sank deeper and deeper into rudimentary, rote repetition of the Koran's brainwashing notions, they not only didn't advance, but regressed into premedieval, ritualistic intolerance. Particularly with civil law tied irrevocably into repressive, archaic notions, Islamic countries of this age wallow in conflict and inhibit their own liberal advancement into modernity. With Islamic tenets pounded into the mindset of each generation of children, there is little opportunity to break out. (At least Christianity, separated from secular law and customs, is weak enough that the occasional open-minded individual, even indoctrinated at an early age, can break away without risking his life!)

As far as the Koran goes, much of its gist is based on declarative statements of its own validity and against anybody, any unbeliever, who would dare to doubt it. It proclaims and repeatedly glorifies its own self-defined god-source, Allah, in the grandest fashion, emphasized even more by that classical beauty of expression in Arabic – indeed, the existence of the Koran has kept the language rooted in the past: no other language spoken in the year 600 is still understood today. To the detriment of the widespread culture addicted to Islam, not only is the language preserved over 14 centuries, but the mindset it recycles throughout the generations is frozen in its primitive state as well.

There just isn't anything more to relate about Islam without sounding even more critical. (I am not criticizing, just observing.) The religion, on a personal basis, simply projects creative power out to a conceptualized god that, though attributed 99 names (certainly memorized by many), doesn't exist and never did. But it takes that projection to extremes of grandeur by endless repetition and appeal to simple, repetitive, addictive slogans and phrases. Even its mystical branch, Sufism, not unlike Christian mystics and Kabbalah adherents, finds the same anchor weight attached as it tries to progress inwardly – dragging along heavy concepts and archaic definitions to where only unfettered Clear Awareness can garner real understanding.

Hearing the meaningful phrases of Jesus noted above, the delving inquiry of Gautama, the illustrations of Plato or Plotinus or the piercing notations of Lao Tzu, one might move more toward a clearer perception of How Life Works simply through the experience. Holding any shred of Mohammed's dictates as valid can only inhibit that growth. Indeed, Islam stands, not on five pillars, but on five cards built as a house on shifting desert sand.

Many Others

Like Stars in the Night Sky – Before Air Pollution

Should I continue here to regard the teachings of the many real visionaries who recorded their perspectives through the ages, often in conflict with the going religious notions of their time, often expressing ideas way over the heads of their contemporaries, my words would spill like disappearing ink well past the back cover of the book you are holding in your hands.

I could point out the piercing perceptiveness of the sonnets and plays of Shakespeare, the perspectives of Dante, the poems of Thoreau, Emerson and many other visionary poets, the vision of Las Casas, Spinoza and Balzac or latter day teachers like Krishnamurti, Watts, Baba, Castaneda. And I can reflect as well on their shortcomings – how the life function they depict differs from How Life does indeed Work.

And I shall do that – but not here and not just yet…

Beyond the Angles – You and I

The Wish

As a child, growing up in a small, but comfy and unpretentious town amid the hills and trees of Western Pennsylvania, I played daily with a group of friends – being cowboys or soldiers, swinging on swings, playing ball in the alley or digging (nearly to China once) in a backyard until we got chased.

One folklore story that echoed through our gang was catching a “santa claus” – a fluffy seed that floated around in summer – and making a wish. If you let the seed go, didn’t tell anybody your wish and nobody else made a wish on **that** santa claus, the wish was guaranteed to come true.

Rather than wish for something concrete, my wish was almost always – and I reveal it here for the very first time – that **everybody could be happy**. Given the 55 years that have passed since then, I’m thinking the wish won’t be overly jinxed by this revelation, since it clearly hasn’t happened yet.

But if you have followed my points throughout EoR and engage in Your Journey, come to see clearly the Oneness and clean out elements that block your joy and fulfillment – you can indeed find happiness via fulfillment well beyond your current level. As more individuals join you, though it may take decades beyond my time here, centuries perhaps, a mankind endowed with Clear Awareness **will find happiness**, and that simple santa claus wish will come true.

What Now?

The focus of these four Angles has run the gamut of looking at How Life Works, Your Journey to see it clearly, Your Path taken to get there and the Teachings of others – what they had to say, how that was off target or distorted and how it impacted your personal world view.

One certainty: you will have changed in the process of reading – and even more so, should you have begun to delve inward. When you read EoR again, soon or in two years or five, you will find that it will seem to have changed. These words won’t, of course, but you will have.

Writings in The Essence of Reality represent my personal view of life. These perspectives should never be associated with a movement, an organization (save for some entity dedicated to preserving and presenting EoR intact well beyond my lifetime), a religion or any group dedicated to the study of my teachings. It must be clear by now what distortion such a gesture invariably introduces to a message.

EoR is **a personal statement to you**, the reader, for your personal use – no other individual should ever be accepted as an "expert" on my perspectives, nor should any practitioners or guru-types ever be acknowledged as promoters of my illustrations as tenets of some philosophical discipline.

You, the reader, would best ponder what I say and look within. Making **use** of EoR is that simple.

* * *

Crime, drugs, prostitution, inequity, corruption, abuse and cruelty, warfare, injustice, global climate change, pollution – all of mankind's wide range of debilitating, damaging traits are founded on one fundamental shortcoming: people not recognizing the nature of their own Consciousness and the innately conjoined Reality they encounter.

Change for the better by mankind can only take place as one person, then another, grows to Clear Awareness of his/her nature as driving impetus in the Reality he/she calls life.

So have at it!

* * *

You will find other writings of mine and many answered questions, on The Essence of Reality Website at www.nehrer.net – it's been there since the last millennium (and may well make the next). You may pose questions there, and I will endeavor to comment on them so long as I'm around.

Should you encounter this book beyond my lifetime, though, you're on your own – I won't be hanging around a Ouija board divining cryptic notations to fill in any blanks I might have left. I'll have other things to do – and I'll be having fun doing them.

All my best…

SELECT BIBLIOGRAPHY

Leslie M. LeCron, *Self-Hypnotism: The Technique and Its Use in Daily Living*, Signet, 1970

__________, *Eerdmans' Handbook to The World's Religions*, Lion Publishing, 1982

S. E. Frost, Jr. Ph.D., *Basic Teachings of the Great Philosophers*, Doubleday, 1962

Novak, *The World's Wisdom*, HarperCollins, 1994

Vermes, *The Changing Faces of Jesus*, Penguin Press, 2000

Michael Jordan, *Encyclopedia of Gods*, R. R. Donnelley & Sons, 1993

__________, *The Holy Bible*, New York International Bible Society, 1973-1978

John Renard, Ph. D., *The Handy Religion Answer Book*, Barnes & Noble, 2002

Karen Armstrong, *A History of God*, First Ballantine, 1994

Richard Maurice Bucke, *Cosmic Consciousness*, E. P. Dutton & Co., 1969, (Innes & Sons, 1901)

Peter Butter, *William Blake* (selected poetry), J. M. Dent 1996

Eckhart Society website, www.eckhartsociety.org

Walt Whitman, *Leaves of Grass*, The First (1855) Edition, Barnes and Noble Books 1997

Translated by Gia-fu Feng and Jane English, *Lao-tzu – Tao te Ching*, Vantage Books 1997

Original Images by Abraham M. Nehrer

BOOKS

O books

O is a symbol of the world, of oneness and unity. In different cultures it also means the "eye", symbolizing knowledge and insight, and in Old English it means "place of love or home". O books explores the many paths of understanding which different traditions have developed down the ages, particularly those today that express respect for the planet and all of life.

For more information on the full list of over 300 titles please visit our website
www.O-books.net

SOME RECENT O BOOKS

Back to the Truth

5000 years of Advaita

Dennis Waite

This is an extraordinary book. The scope represents a real tour de force in marshalling and laying out an encyclopaedic amount of material in way that will appeal both to the seasoned and to the introductory reader. This book will surely be the definitive work of reference for many years to come. **Network Review**

A profoundly astute and masterful guide to the field of Self-discovery. An authoritative scholar, Dennis writes with supreme clarity as he skilfully expounds, logically analyzes and insightfully integrates the wisdom of classical and contemporary teachers with the principles of Advaita. **Katie Davis**, Teacher and author of *Awake Living Joy: The Essence of Spiritual Enlightenment*

Dennis Waite is the West's pre-eminent explicator of Advaita Vedanta. In driving home his point that our nature is Awareness, Dennis brings to light many of Advaita's "hidden" teachings, which have never been circulated outside of specialist schools. He also does something I've never seen anywhere in print. He opens a critical dialogue between the ancient and the modern paths, whose exponents don't always agree. Fascinating! **Dr. Gregory Goode**, PhD (Philosophy), Philosophical Counselor and non-dual teacher

This is the most comprehensive, academic book on the so called "tradition" of non-duality we have seen. **Brian Lake** and **Naama Livni**, Teachers

1905047614 **£24.95 $49.95**

Bhagavad Gita

Alan Jacobs

The Bhagavad Gita is a sacred scripture of epic dimensions and is the key sacred text of Hinduism. It means the "Song of God" and is often called the "Song Celestial". Alan Jacobs has succeeded in revitalising the ancient text into a form that reveals the full majesty of this magnificent scripture as well as its practical message for today's men and women. The outdated English of previous translations has been transformed and given clear meaning.

Alan Jacobs uses contemporary free verse based on innovative metaphors to provide a clear meaning for today's readers. It is mandala poetry-each verse is a mandala for meditation. "It is like a great symphony. Each chapter relates to the last but leads on to the coda." His incisive philosophic commentary dusts off the archaism of 1500 years and restores the text as a transforming instrument pointing the way to self-realisation.

Despite the fact that there are now 279 English translations of the 'Bhagavad Gita' in existence, Alan Jacob's own recently pubished edition is one of the most beautiful. A transcreation rather than a translation, the author has endeavoured to preserve the essence of the nondualist teachings (also known as Advaita Vedanta) interwoven in Hinduism's best known spiritual text as well as introduce his own poetic touch. Literally meaning the 'Song of God', the 'Bhagavad Gita' recounts a key moment in the ancient Indian epic, the 'Mahabharata'. Set on the battlefield of Kurashetra between two rival royal households, Arjuna, leader of the Pandavas, is rendered impotent in the face of impending bloodshed. Krishna, Avatar and Arjuna's charioteer, thus takes the opportunity to deliver the Dharma or moral code. Indeed, the battle can be interpreted as an allegory of the inner warfare between dharma (harmony) and adharma (discord) within in all of us in the face of life's challenges and troubles. Together with his 'Principal Upanishads', the profundity of this particular edition of the 'Bhagavad Gita' is owing to the author's accessible and yet exquisite poetry. **Paula Marvelly**

1903816513 **£12.99 $19.95**

The Book of One

Dennis Waite

Advaita is the philosophy underlying most religions, including Christianity, though it is more usually associated with Hinduism. Its essence is summed up in its Sanskrit name, which essentially means 'there are not two things.' The full title of the philosophy is 'Advaita Vedanta.' Vedanta, derived from the scriptures that form the last part of the Vedas, itself means "the end of knowledge," in the sense of being the highest knowledge one can attain. It is not in itself a religion however: there are no churches or priests, but it is at the root of all wisdom.

Advaita Vedanta quite simply provides the answers to the questions of 'life, the universe and everything'. It is very practical, yet offers explanations satisfying to the intellect. It provides a simple and elegant framework within which all of the problems of life and death may be understood and resolved. The answers are ultimately surprising, and a great relief.

A masterful and profoundly insightful survey of the Advaita teaching and the contemporary scene. This book will greatly contribute to a deeper understanding of this important movement, sweeping the West, and which eventually leads to Self Realisation.

Alan Jacobs, Chair, Ramana Maharshi Foundation UK.

There are many places to find Advaita teachings-in ancient texts, modern books, in satsang, and on the Internet. Dennis Waite has found them all. He writes as a friendly tour guide, presenting the teachings with simplicity, humour and deep understanding. The appendices alone are worth the price of admission, and contain a wealth of material available nowhere else.

Greg Goode, PhD. Self-realised teacher of Advaita

A magisterial survey that belongs on the shelves of any serious student.

Scientific and Medical Network Review

1903816416 **£9.99 $17.95**

Ordinary Women, Extraordinary Wisdom

The Feminine Face of Awakening

Rita Marie Robinson

"The Extraordinary Wisdom of Ordinary Women" is a collection of intimate, heartfelt conversations with women spiritual teachers who live and look like ordinary people. They have kids, husbands, jobs, and bills to pay. What makes them extraordinary is that each woman has awakened to her true nature. And while that sounds like enlightenment, it doesn't look like the old stereotype of transcendence, detachment, and bliss. Quite the contrary. This is the feminine half of the spiritual journey—bringing it down to earth and embracing all of what it means to be human.

In the past 30 years women have emerged into the forefront of the spiritual life in the West, and the interviews in this book reflect a new generation of clear-eyed women teachers and sages.
Stephan Bodian, author of the best-selling *Meditation for Dummies*, former editor of *Yoga Journal*

This will become a milestone in female spirituality. Not only does it recount the fascinating and intimate stories of twelve 'ordinary' women in their search for peace and self knowledge, the author engages the reader with her own quest through her integrity, vulnerability and courage. Beautifully written with captivating honesty, this unique book will become an inspiration for both men and women alike, also looking for the essence of who they truly are.
Paula Marvelly, author of *Teachers of One*

"Ordinary Women, Extraordinary Wisdom" is one of those books to savor, underline like crazy, and then age with gracefully until its dog-eared pages no longer need to remind you that you're already Home.
Raphael Cushnir, author of *How Now: 100 Ways to Celebrate the Present Moment*

9781846940682 **£11.99 $24.95**

Passage to Freedom

A Path to Enlightenment

Dawn Mellowship

Thousands are seeking enlightenment but few achieve this ultimate spiritual goal. "Passage To Freedom, A Path To Enlightenment" is an inspirational book with practical techniques to help the reader attain true happiness through spiritual growth. Dawn Mellowship's book provides meditations and healing techniques that work on a physical, emotional and spiritual level, to provide the perfect remedy for finding happiness and spiritual fulfilment. They combine visualisation, intention, affirmations, controlled breathing, universal energy and healing to assist you to manage your anger, release guilt and worry, let go of the past, boost your self-esteem and love yourself and others unconditionally. Learn how to connect to your intuition to make better and healthier choices in life, and ultimately to find inner peace and balance.

In a world that moves faster by the day it is refreshing to be shown a path that slows down the pace of life and encourages reflection. Dawn writes directly, powerfully and eloquently on the fundamental issues of spiritual enlightenment and finding your 'inner-truth'.

Adam Smith, Chief Executive, Adili.com

Dawn's inspirational book gives practical, step-by-step instruction in spiritual growth to all those who feel the call and want to know how best to answer.

Rosemary Pharo, Reiki Healers and Teachers Society

There are many books out there, the secret is to read the right ones. Dawn has written one of the right ones.May her wisdoms remind you of who you truly are. This book is your precious pearl of wisdom.

Andrea Foulkes, celebrity Past Life Regression Expert on UK TV and founder of Soul Freedom Therapy

9781846940781 **£9.99 $22.95**

Suicide Dictionary

The History of Rainbow Abbey

Paul Lonely

In 1453 ce an island was discovered in the North Atlantic called Ambrojjio and donated to the Catholic Church. Pope Nicholas V (the first humanist Pope) used the land to erect a secret monastery for an artist colony of monk-poets he employed to formulate what he called a "prophetic" or "inspired" document to be published in the year 2050. This artist colony (now called the Order of Quantum Catholics) has survived to the present day and still employs monk-poets who remain hard at work on this document, now titled Quantum Psalter.

Here is the first volume describing their heroic work. Maybe you have read the Upanishads, a few Buddhist sutras, or possibly even Rumi or Blake. But those describe the spiritual experience of yesterday. Suicide Dictionary is the poetic expression of spirituality in our time. We now live in an age where to be Integral is to be on the leading edge of human consciousness. Suicide Dictionary is the product of applying these higher levels of consciousness to the art of creative writing. It offers a "Contemporary Upanishads" that captures the beauty of both western intellectuality and eastern (or mystical) spirituality in a single literary framework.

Genius. Paul Lonely has gifted the world with a genuinely unique work. "Suicide Dictionary" is a miraculous kaleidoscope of perspectives bound to stretch the mind, body and spirit of its lucky readership.

Stuart Davis, author of *Sex, God and Rock & Roll*

Ken Wilber is apparently fond of telling Paul that his readers haven't been born yet. (Henry Miller says loneliness is a prerequisite for great art - how appropriate.) I have to disagree with Ken – breathlessly, having to stop in awe after nearly every passage, I read "Suicide Dictionary", and I loved it.

Michael Garfield

9781846940613 **£7.99 $16.95**

Take Me To Truth

Undoing the Ego

Nouk Sanchez and Tomas Vieira

"Take Me to Truth" is the first book to boldly address the fundamental problem that all spiritual seekers face on the journey to awakening; the ego. As Gary Renard says in the Foreword... "despite the thousands of things we may appear to have to choose from in this world, there are really only two things, and only one of them is real." The ego is not. Most books today are still teaching how to find liberation within the dream. Take Me to Truth wakes us out of the dream. It stands alone, as an unprecedented approach to ego-relinquishment. It courageously unravels and demystifies the ego-release process and provides direct guidance on undoing the cause of all human suffering; our distorted belief system.

"Take Me To Truth" is not just a book - it's a revelation. Nouk Sanchez is a gifted spiritual teacher who knows what she is talking about and has a good idea of how to communicate her knowledge. The writing of Nouk and Tomas is uncompromising, exciting and strikingly consistent.
From the Foreword by **Gary R Renard**, author of *The Disappearance of the Universe*

This insightful and provocative blend of A Course in Miracles, the Enneagram, and non-dual wisdom clearly reflects the author's deep personal investigation into the nature of Truth. **Stephan Bodian**, author of *Meditation for Dummies; Buddhism for Dummies; Living Yoga.*

"Take Me to Truth" is the perfect book for our time. Nouk and Tomas show us how to return to truth in a remarkable way that is both fascinating and easy to understand. They distill the core truths found in "A Course in Miracles" and bring us insightful ways to heal our feelings of frustration, limitation and unhappiness that come with the ego thought system. We highly recommend this book to any serious seeker of the truth. **Robert** and **Mary Stoelting**, Co-Founders of Pathways of Light

978-1-84694-0 **£9.99 $19.95**

From the Bottom of the Pond

The forgotten art of experiencing God in the depths of the present moment

Simon Small

This is a book about knowing God. It is for those for whom just believing (or not believing) is no longer enough. Through personal experience, anecdote and story, a priest shares an ancient, but neglected aspect of Christian prayer. Contemplation takes us into the depths of the present moment, the only reality there has ever been and so the only place where God can be found. It takes us at different times into mystical oneness with the All, into profound self-knowledge and reveals love in the midst of the world.

Contemplation is the universal experience at the heart of all religions. It is the place where their differences fall away and their uniqueness is celebrated. From the Bottom of the Pond seeks simply to be helpful. It says nothing new, but says it in a new way; a way rooted in our western culture and history. It suggests that the essence of the great and wonderful enlightenment teachings of the East was always here, hidden in plain sight.

"From the Bottom of the Pond" is a profound, lucid and accessible book, full of wisdom and compassion.

Timothy Freke, author of *Lucid Living*, (with **Peter Gandy**) of *The Jesus Mysteries, The Laughing Jesus*

This is an important book. And it is coming out at the moment when it is needed. It is written in a language that we can all understand, mainly in short sentences, each of which adds something to build up a whole as we explore a mystery that is beyond words. Some good stories help us on the way. This short and profound book is a joy to read.

Rt Revd Stephen Verney, former Bishop of Repton

978-1-84694-0 **£7.99 $16.95**

Good As New

John Henson

Despite the fact that our shelves are sagging beneath the weight of all the scriptures that have appeared in the last forty years or so, we still await a version that strikes us as a genuinely contemporary version. Life and language move so quickly that it is a matter of running to stay in the same spot, and translators of the scriptures are characterised by care and caution rather than by the need to keep pace. Move on new must, however, if we believe the scriptures have abiding value for every age and culture as a unique record of humankind's adventure with God.

In reading this translation we come closer to the impact the scriptures had on the people of the time than before.

This presentation of the Christian gospel is of extraordinary power simply because it is so close to the prose and poetry of ordinary life. Instead of being taken into a specialised religious frame of reference-as happens with the most conscientious of formal modern translations-and being given a gospel addressed to specialised concerns-as happens with even the most careful of modern "devotional" books-we have here a vehicle for thinking and worshipping that is fully earthed, reconisably about our humanity. I hope that this book will help the secret to be shared, and to spread in epidemic profusion through religious and irreligious alike.
Rowan Williams, Archbishop of Canterbury

I can't rate this version of some of the Christian scriptures highly enough. It is amazingly fresh, imaginative, engaging and bold. It will startle and delight Christians and many more. Like the Bible itself, it deserves to be a bestseller.
Adrian Thatcher, Professor of Applied Theology, College of St Mark and St John, Plymouth

1905047118 **£11.99 $19.95**

The Jain Path

Ancient Wisdom for the West

Aidan Rankin

Jainism is India's oldest spiritual tradition, and one of the world's oldest religions. It is not well known in the West. But it embodies many of the ideas underlying current thinking on the interconnectedness of all living systems, the principle of non-violence and the need to live simply.

It is perhaps the most demanding, rational and radical of all religions, attaching great importance to individual responsibility. Today we are questioning our own inherited values and also rediscovering ancient traditions. We are looking for continuity and balance-a "return to the centre." Understanding of Jain principles can point us towards the elusive "paradigm shift", giving spiritual and intellectual strength to a new global ethic of compassion and interdependence.

Based around the individual's own spiritual journey and the choices he or she makes, Jainism, more than other spiritual tradition alive today, can bridge the gap between eastern and western patterns of thought.

"The Jain Path" is the best introduction to Jainism available. It is at once very topical, clear and engaging.
David Frawley (Pandit Vamdeva Shastri), Director of the American Institute of Vedic Studies

Jainism is one of the forgotten jewels of the world's faiths. Aidan Rankin introduces us to the essence of this spirituality in a book that is full of wisdom and intelligence.
William Bloom, author of *Soulution* and Director of The Holism Network.

1905047215 **£11.99 $22.95**

Ocean of Wisdom

Alan Jacobs

The first major anthology of this size and scope since 1935, The Ocean of Wisdom collects over five thousand pearls in poetry and prose, from the earliest of recorded history to modern times. Divided into 54 sections, ranging from Action to Zen, it draws on all faiths and traditions, from Zoroaster to existentialism. It covers the different ages of man, the stages of life, and is an ideal reference work and long term companion, a source of inspiration for the journey of life.

Frequently adopting a light touch it also makes a distinction between the Higher Wisdom, which consists of pointers leading to the understanding of philosophical and metaphysical truth, and practical wisdom, which consists of intelligent skills applicable to all fields of ordinary everyday life. So Germaine Greer and Hilary Rodham Clinton have their place alongside Aristotle and Sartre.

The carefully chosen quotations make this book the perfect bedside dipper, and will refresh the spirit of all who are willing to bathe in the ocean of the world's wisdom.

This book would be a valuable reference for any writer or historian, but it also makes for a good fireside or bedside book, offering bits and pieces of wisdom at whatever pace the reader wishes.

Academy of Religion and Psychical Research

190504707X **£17.99 $29.95**

Spiritual Wisdom of Marcus Aurelius

Alan Jacobs

"The Meditations of Marcus Aurelius" have been described as the best book of practical philosophy ever written. The message is simple but powerful; we have a short time on earth, we don't know what is going to happen, and it doesn't matter. External events and sensations are immaterial compared to our private quest for perfection. It gains particular authority being written by the Emperor of the most remarkable empire the world has seen, who at the same time managed to keep in perspective what is truly important.

The Stoicism of Marcus touches the frontier where reason and mysticism meet. It is the best defence available against the problems and stresses of our time. Most translations are literal and arid, but here Alan Jacobs, a distinguished poet, uses contemporary free verse and added metaphors to convey the essential emotional meaning of the text.

Most translations are literal and arid but Jacobs has paraphrased a selection of the best of Aurelius' meditations so as to give more force to the essential truths of his philosophy. The following meditation summarises Aurelius' beliefs: "Everything is interconnected, the bond is holy. All has been coordinated to combine for universal order, balance and harmony. There is one Universe made of many objects, one God who pervades all, one substance, one law, one common Reason in intelligent beings, one truth. There is also perfection in animals which are from the same Source and participate in the great drama according to their nature." Modern quantum physics could hardly eplain it better.
The Light

The author calls the book a poetic transcreation as he tries to recreate in verse form the essence of Marcus Aurelius' message. He succeeds very well. The translation is lucid and evocative, while the layout allows the reader to breathe with the text. This edition can be highly recommended. **Network Review**

1903816742 **£9.99 $14.95**

One Self

Philip Jacobs

One Self expresses the truth at the heart of the world's mystical and philosophical traditions in a simple, direct and practical way.

We can start to find meaning in our lives when we see all the varied things that happen to us, including illness and bereavement, as part of the process of letting go of lesser levels of identity. We can then find our true Being, one that is ever present and beyond change and suffering. We learn to trust the process of life's unfolding, as we are led on a journey to discover a great treasure that we all possess, yet are unaware of. In doing this we also prepare ourselves for that ultimate moment of letting go, the death of the physical body.

This is a compelling and life enhancing book for anyone having to face a long term illness, but also so wise that it can help any of us to understand our path in life even if we are not so severely challenged.

Peter Fenwick, Scientific and Medical Network

Philip Jacobs has explained the almost inexplicable idea of "Oneness" probably as clearly and accessibly as is possible here, and without religious bias. Recognising the need for a metaphorical approach to illuminate this esoteric concept, he is liberal with his use of helpful parables and anecdotes from many sources, ancient and modern. He explores topics such as consciousness, identity, suffering, happiness, love, freedom and meaning, and I particularly liked the chapter on illness. He has provided an all round summary for anyone new to, or renewing a path of spiritual growth.

Pilgrims

1905047673 **£9.99 $19.95**